D1171830

the

Mughals of India

The Peoples of Asia

General Editor: Morris Rossabi

Each volume in this series comprises a complete history, from origins to the present, of the people under consideration. Written by leading archaeologists, historians and anthropologists, the books are addressed to a wide, multi-disciplinary readership, as well as to the general reader.

Published

The Manchus
Pamela Kyle Crossley

The Mongols
David Morgan

The Mughals of India
Harbans Mukhia

The Afghans
Willem Vogelsang

In Preparation

The Persians
Gene R. Garthwaite

The Turks
Colin Heywood

The Phoenicians
James Muhly

The Japanese
Irwin Scheiner

The Chinese
Arthur Waldron

the

Mughals of India

Harbans Mukhia

Blackwell
Publishing

BLACKWELL PUBLISHING
350 Main Street, Malden, MA 02148-5020, USA
108 Cowley Road, Oxford OX4 1JF, UK
550 Swanston Street, Carlton, Victoria 3053, Australia

First published 2004 by Blackwell Publishing Ltd

Library of Congress Cataloging-in-Publication Data

Mukhia, Harbans.
   The Mughals of India / Harbans Mukhia.
      p. cm. – (Peoples of Asia)
   Includes bibliographical references and index.
   ISBN 0-631-18555-0 (alk. paper)
1. Mogul Empire–History. 2. India–History–1526-1765. I. Title. II. Series.
DS461.M87 2004
954.02'5–dc22   2003028026

A catalogue record for this title is available from the British Library.

Set in 10/12pt Sabon
by Kolam Information Services Pvt. Ltd, Pondicherry, India
Printed and bound in the United Kingdom
by MPG Books Ltd, Bodmin, Cornwall

The publisher's policy is to use permanent paper from mills that operate a sustainable
forestry policy, and which has been manufactured from pulp processed using acid-free and
elementary chlorine-free practices. Furthermore, the publisher ensures that the text paper
and cover board used have met acceptable environmental accreditation standards.

For further information on
Blackwell Publishing, visit our website:
http://www.blackwellpublishing.com

For Boni

The *Moguls* Feed high, Entertain much, and Whore not a little.
John Fryer, English traveller to India, 1672–81.

Contents

Illustrations

Acknowledgements

In writing this book I have been privileged to have accumulated an enormous wealth of the debt of gratitude from a very large number of friends, colleagues and students. It was the late Burton Stein who suggested my name to Blackwell Publishers when they were looking for an author for this volume in their 'Peoples of the World' series. In the last nearly two decades of his life, Burt had shared with me many intimate moments of joy and sorrow about virtually everything under the sun, history-writing included. My sadness at his departure is the greater for the certainty that he would have been mightily pleased to see the book in print, though he probably would not have agreed with almost anything it contains. That was Burt: forever joyful, friendly and critical, of the kind that revives one's faith in humanity.

The first chapter on legitimacy, in many ways the toughest for me to write, has been seen by several friends: Muzaffar Alam, Aijaz Ahmad, Rajat Datta, Dilbagh Singh, Monica Juneja, Urvashi Dalal. Each of them made many comments and suggestions; all of these added up to substantial help in polishing up a point here, an argument there. Some years ago I also experimented with it at a seminar which John F. Richards had chaired at the Department of History, Duke University. His observations led me to nuance several of the formulations. A couple of generations of my students at the Centre at JNU, too, read the draft, and in various ways their discussion of it, along with other writings on the theme of governance, came as very valuable feedback.

Aziz Al-Azmeh, whom I have come to know personally only lately, never allowed his other commitments to delay extending help whenever I needed it. His comments on the Introduction have been particularly suggestive and he added value to them by providing me with a manageable reading list to brush up my familiarity with the Arabic-Islamic historiographical traditions. Two of his own remarkable works, *Muslim Kingship* and *Ibn Khaldun. An Essay in Reinterpretation*, have made a lasting impact on my own understanding of Mughal history, even though he makes no reference to it. I am, however, unsure if I came up to anywhere near his expectations.

My friend Mubarak Ali, fiercely and combatively secular historian of the Mughal period, located at Lahore, was one I could always turn to whenever I needed any bit of information and guidance. If the state of relations between India and Pakistan, now mercifully somewhat on the mend, had made it impossible to exchange letters and books, fortunately the email still remained immune to government's intervention on either side. His responses to my queries were invariably prompt, full of information and insights and, of course, generous. His unpublished doctoral dissertation 'The Court of the Great Mughuls', submitted way back in 1976 to Ruhr University in Germany, and its revised Urdu version were extremely valuable, rich as these are in empirical data.

Dilbagh Singh, with the generosity that is so characteristic of him, gave me some enormously valuable information about the Rajputs and Rajasthan in the context of chapter 3 on the family mores and gender relations; his mastery over Rajasthani sources saved me from committing some grave errors of judgement.

Dr Yunus Jaffrey, who has taught Persian language to generations of scholars, gave me regular classes to explain the subtle cultural and historical meaning of words and phrases rather than merely the dictionary meaning, to which I already had access. He has contributed more than perhaps he realizes to the development of my understanding of the nuances of life and culture at the Mughal court. To all my queries, he would seek out answers for days and weeks and pass them on with the kindness of an old Ustad.

Karim Najafi Barzegar, Iranian scholar who earned his doctoral degree at JNU, was unmindful of his own preoccupations whenever I needed his help, especially to obtain any bit of data about medieval Persia. In every way he was the very embodiment of Persian culture, of which care for others and generosity are such strong elements.

Iran Culture House, part of the embassy of Iran in New Delhi, opened its doors to me at all times, and gave me access to its vast collection of books and microfilms of Persian language texts of medieval India; without this access I would have felt very diffident in writing quite a few parts of the book. Dr Khwaja Piri, in particular, treated me as an honoured guest at the collection he has built up over a quarter century of exceptional dedication.

If my friends and comrades of over four decades, Irfan Habib and Iqtidar Alam Khan, both streets ahead of me as historians of Mughal India, were ever irritated by my queries and questions, they hid it very well from me. It is not for nothing that they are both as renowned for their generosity as for their scholarship.

A pair of in-house anthropologists, my daughter Neelanjana and son-in-law Suranjan, valiantly endeavoured to bring home to me my short-comings in the evolving methodological innovations and theoretical perspectives of their discipline for a better appreciation of my data; if their success in educating me has been at best moderate, it is not for lack of trying.

My son Sudeep and daughter-in-law Sunetra, both journalists, were subjected to reading the evolving text as sort of arbitrarily identified representatives of the target audience of the book; their stern refusal to subscribe to victimology in the process is thus all the more appreciable. Sunetra's childlike laughter at the most vaguely amusing situation dis-solved a lot of the tension that is every author's destiny.

While writing the Introduction, I needed some very old articles unavailable in New Delhi. My niece Ishita Pande struggled hard to find time from her own doctoral research in history at Princeton and Oxford to send me copies: victory in the end of old filial and comradely spirit.

Dr Daljeet of the National Museum, New Delhi, went far beyond her official duty to offer assistance with the Mughal miniatures in the Museum's collection; it was wonderful to interact with someone know-ledgeable and helpful. Amina Okada, eminent historian of Mughal painting at the Musée Guimet, Paris, was prompt in sending a transpar-ency of the magnificent miniature, *Jahangir Visiting Jogi Jadrup*, from the museum's collection, and permission to reproduce it, both with compliments.

If the impress of French historical writing, especially of the *Annales* mode, on this book is quite visible, I suppose I owe it to the depth and duration of my interaction with that magnificent institution, the Maison des Sciences de l'Homme, in Paris. I have been almost a permanent fixture at the MSH each year in the summer during the tenure of the first three of its Administrateurs, Fernand Braudel, Clemens Heller and Maurice Aymard, who continues in saddle. I also received invaluable help and affection from the late Georges Duby. I revel in the fortune of having Jacques Le Goff, Guy Bois, Michel Vovelle, Etienne Balibar and above all Maurice Aymard among my closest friends, with all of whom I have spent innumerable hours discussing history, society, politics, cul-ture, indeed life in all its hues. Maurice has long treated me as virtually a member of his immediate family.

I am aware of the inadequacy of saying just 'thank you' to all of them. Language still remains such a poor means of expressing feelings; but what else does an author have to stand in for it? So I say 'thanks' to them from the depth of my being.

It is a pleasure of course to be published by Blackwell. I nevertheless harbour two regrets on this score: their reminders about the delay in completing the book were ever too gentle; and they 'persuaded' me to delete some 90 per cent of the references to the sources that I had put in in the first draft. I have had to drop virtually all references to the primary sources in the Persian language, from which I had laboriously collected data for nearly a decade and a half. I take solace in the reason given by Georges Duby for the gradually diminishing references to sources in his later works: having established his bona fides earlier on, he hoped that his readers would accept his statements as based on solid primary data even when no references had been provided. I am however aware that while in his case this reason would have been accepted as perfectly valid, with no trace of doubt, in mine it might be viewed as suspiciously evasive. I might add that the excerpts from most – though unhappily not all – Persian language medieval Indian texts given in the book have been translated afresh by me even where standard translations exist. The exceptions are *Babur Nama*, *Tuzuk-i Jahangiri* and *Shah Jahan Nama*, where I have relied exclusively on translations.

Helen Gray, freelance copy-editor, put each word of the entire text meticulously through a microscope. She also strove hard to ensure I wrote correct English; the flaws that remain are in spite of her.

Boni, like the good wife, learnt to accept her suffering in silence while I wrote this book, which she perceived as having sheer fun; she was perhaps right on both counts. To her I owe the biggest debt of all; I try to repay it in part by dedicating the book to her.

March 2004
Centre for Historical Studies
Jawaharlal Nehru University
New Delhi

Chronology of Emperors' Reigns

Zahir al-Din Babur: 1526–30
Nasir al-Din Humayun: 1530–56
  with an interregnum, 1540–55
Jalal al-Din Muhammad Akbar:
  1556–1605
Nur al-Din Jahangir: 1605–27
Shah Jahan: 1627–58
Aurangzeb Alamgir: 1658–1707
Bahadur Shah I: 1707–12
Jahandar Shah: 1712

Farrukh Siyar: 1713–19
Shah Jahan II: 1719
Rafi al-Darjat: 1719
Muhammad Shah: 1719–48
Ahmad Shah: 1748–54
Aziz al-Din Alamgir: 1754–59
Ali Gawhar Shah Alam II:
  1759–1806
Akbar II: 1806–37
Bahadur Shah Zafar: 1837–58

Introduction

This book has turned out to be an essentially experimental venture in many ways, almost independently of the author's volition. When Blackwell Publishing approached me some dozen years ago to do a volume on 'The Mughals' in their 'Peoples of the World' series, I readily agreed and gave them an outline with a commitment to hand in the script within a three-year deadline. The outline was quite simple in its essence: the Mughal conquest of India in the sixteenth century, the organization of the state, administration, economy, trade and life in urban centres, and in the countryside, and so forth. In other words, encapsulating the existing state of knowledge on the subject, not an awesome task for one who has taught this history in two major Indian universities for over four decades.

If writing the book exceeded the deadline by more than a decade, it was largely because in my enthusiasm I started reading up the primary sources over again. By and by, not only had questions that hadn't occurred to me earlier begun to arise, but the whole perspective of the project altered radically; by now virtually nothing of the original outline has remained intact.

In its place a sort of broad profile has evolved of what I, at this moment, believe are the key entry points for understanding the nature of Mughal state and society. By and large, these entry points have remained unexplored in the arena of the history-writing of Mughal India, even in the midst of innumerable studies of a whole spectrum of themes and some very innovative endeavours. This might explain the preliminary nature of my own explorations here.

Even as the title originally proposed – 'The Mughals' – could arguably be self-explanatory and self-sufficient, in that the identification of the Mughals with India is virtually given for the professional historian, the popular image – and, more importantly, the image of the Mughals constituted in India's political scenario as one of several 'foreign' Muslim dynasties ruling over India in the medieval centuries – leaves some space open for re-endorsing the identification. The Mughals themselves never had to face the problem of being 'foreigners' ruling over an 'alien' land; both these notions are of posterior, indeed of very recent origins. In an ambience where conquest constituted its own legitimation, the notions of being alien and foreign would have very doubtful provenance. This indeed was characteristic of much of the ancient and medieval world, until the arrival of nineteenth- and twentieth-centuries colonialism. Modern colonialism has altered the very meaning of conquest, with governance of land and its people, now on behalf of, and primarily for the economic benefit of a community of people inhabiting a far-off land. It stands in contrast with conquest in the medieval world when the victor either returned home taking such plunder with him as he could gather after a battle or two, or settled down in the vanquished land, submerging his and his group's identity in it to become inseparable from it. There are very few inhabited patches of land on our earth devoid of such merger between the 'conqueror' and the 'conquered' through history.

There are, besides, other branches of the same family of the Mughals, descended from Chingiz Khan and/or Timur. One had stayed 'home' in Central Asia. It was thus that a text relating to it, the *Tarikh-i Rashidi*, written in the mid-sixteenth century by Mirza Haidar Dughlat, was rendered into English by Ney Elias and Denison Ross under the title *History of the Moghuls of Central Asia*. Another branch with similar claims of descent had migrated to Iran.[1] Not quite welcome in the history of Iran, this branch was later replaced there by the Safavids. Thus *The Mughals of India* also seeks to draw some distinguishing lines among the collateral branches.

Interestingly, the term 'Mughal', now synonymous with grandeur in almost all forms in the cultural arena, might perhaps have sent a shiver of horror down the spine of the dynasty's early rulers in India. The Persian language term, pronounced 'Mughul' in Iran and 'Mughal' in India, came to acquire a generic meaning that broadly signified peoples of the Central Asian regions, speaking the Mongol languages and dialects; there were others, however, also Central Asians, seeking to draw distinct-

---

1   *The Tarikh-i Rashidi of Mirza Muhammad Haidar Dughlat. A History of the Moghuls of Central Asia*, Eng. tr. by Ney Elias and Denison Ross, Patna, 1973. Unfortunately the date of its first publication, sometime after 1895, has not been mentioned. For a competent overview of the Mughals in Iran, see Abbas Iqbal, *Tarikh-i Mughul az Hamla-i Chingiz ta Tashkeel-i Daulat-i Timur* (*History of the Mughuls from the Invasion of Chingiz to the Formation of the Timuride State*), Tehran, 1365 H./1987AD. Brief discussions of Chingiz's attacks and his descendants' rule and Timur's invasion and Timuride regime in Iran occur in David Morgan, *The Mongols*, Oxford, 1990, chapters 5 and 6, and Karim Najafi Barzegar, *Mughal Iranian Relations during the Sixteenth Century*, New Delhi, 2000, chapter 1.

ive lines from them ethnically and linguistically. They often perceived the 'Mughals', with the grand exception of Chingiz himself, as barbarians. These other groups were Turkis, Uzbegs, Uighurs, Kirghizes, Kazaks, Kipchaks, Keraits and Naimans, often with as many mixed lineages, shared culture and faiths as those whose distinction was asserted in conflict with their neighbours. Babur in his extensive and detailed memoirs in his native Turki language *Tuzuk-i Baburi* (*Babur Nama* in English translation) almost always speaks of them as if they were 'the other', and rather derisively. Comments like, '[M]ischief and devastation must always be expected from the Mughul horde' are scattered in the book. The dynasty in India proudly traced its lineage from both Chingiz and Timur, the former as ancestor of Babur's mother and the latter as the paternal progenitor, initially with greater emphasis on Chingiz, later on Timur. In Babur's home in Uzbekistan, the dynasty proclaimed its identity as Chaghtais, descended from Chaghta, son of Chingiz, 'Mughal' par excellence. A history of the dynasty in India down to the early eighteenth century was written, with the title *Tazkirat al-Salatin-i Chaghta*, 'Chronicles of the Chaghtai Sultans'. There were other histories, too, with similar titles, such as *Tarikh-i Khandan-i Timuriyya*, 'The History of the Timuride Family', although the latter title was perhaps given in the eighteenth century to a text written anonymously in the sixteenth, commissioned by Emperor Akbar. But it is hard to come across a book with the title 'A History of the Mughal State or the Mughal Dynasty' in Persian, the official court language. In all official records the family tree of the dynasty took the origin back to Timur through the paternal stem. Abul Fazl, the remarkable historian of the sixteenth century, also sought to give the family supernatural ancestry by tracing the tree to a central Asian female figure, Alanquwa, a royal widow impregnated by the rays of the Sun.[2]

This official avoidance of 'Mughal' for the imperial dynasty did not, however, come in the way of its popular nomenclature as such, even while it retained some of its ambiguity. As early as 1538, the text of conversations of a Sufi saint, Abdul Quddus Ganguhi, compiled by his son and spiritual successor, makes perhaps the first use of the term for Babur and his soldiers – a mere 12 years after the founding of the Mughal

---

2   The notion of conception without the intervention of human agency is common to several civilizations. In the Hindu epic *Mahabharat* Kunti is similarly impregnated by the Sun and gives birth to Karna from her ear. She, however, fears for her reputation as an unwed mother and, placing the infant in a wooden box, lets it float in a river. Karna grows up to be a legendary warrior waging war upon her other sons. The Japanese Emperor and the Inca ruler in Peru both claimed descent from the Sun, although the claims are not mediated through legendary birth. The whole of Christian faith is of course based upon the Immaculate Conception of Jesus Christ's mother.

rule in India – although the use is made in an Afghan milieu that was hostile to the Mughals.[3] A few other sixteenth-century texts also employ the term for some of the nobles, and at times implicitly for the regime generally, but not for the ruling dynasty.[4] There is even an inscription dated 1537–38 at a building in Hissar in the modern state of Haryana where a 'soldier martyred in Gujarat' is referred to as Mughal, responsible for the building's construction.[5] But it is the chronicle of the eighteenth century historian Khafi Khan that puts the issue in perspective. 'Although it is from the reign of the dweller in paradise Emperor Akbar that the term Mughal came into common use for the Turks and Tajiks of Ajam (non-Arab territories), indeed even for the Syeds of Iran and Turan, in reality the word is truly valid only for the tribe of Turks who had descended from Mughal Khan ... through Chingiz Khan, Hulaku, Chaghta and Amir Timur.'[6] However, the European travellers were under no obligation to be sensitive to the nuances of the term, and knew the dynasty as Mughal anyway, spelt by them variously. Ralph Fitch, one of the earliest Englishmen to travel to India between 1583 and 1591, merrily refers to the 'Great Mogor, which is the King of Agra and Delli'.[7] Edward Terry, his compatriot in India between 1616 and 1619, has a lovely bloomer on it: for him, 'Mogoll means "a circumcised man, and therefore he is called the Great Mogoll as much as to say: *the Chiefe of the Circumcision*".'[8] Sir Thomas Roe, James I's (and England's) first ambassador to India, in his *Journal* covering 1615 to 1619 forever refers to Jahangir as 'the Mogull' or 'the Great Mogull'.[9] The classic accounts of seventeenth- and early eighteenth-centuries India by the French doctor François Bernier and the Italian pretender-doctor Niccolao Manucci both

3   Rukn al-Din, *Lataif-i Quddusi*, Delhi, 1311 H./AD 1894: 64, 68. The conversations were compiled a year after the saint's death.
4   Such as Shaikh Rizq al-Allah Mushtaqi, *Waqiat-i Mushtaqi*, ed. I. A. Siddiqui, Rampur, 2002: 142, 245; Arif Qandahari, *Tarikh-i Akbari*, ed. Haji Syed Muin al-Din Nadwi et al., Rampur, 1962: 53, 185, 218.
5   *Epigraphica Indica*, II: 428. I am grateful to Professor Irfan Habib for bringing this inscription to my notice.
6   Khafi Khan, *Muntakhab al-Lubab*, ed. Maulvi Khair al-Din Ahmad and Maulvi Ghulam Qadir, Part I, Calcutta, 1869: 4. He makes some comments on Mughal and his brother Tatar's history and observes that Mughal became Khan only on ascending the throne, ibid.: 3.
7   William Foster, ed., *Early Travels in India, 1583–1619*, Delhi, 1999 (first pub. 1921): 13.
8   Ibid.: 325. The editor notes that '[T]he same statement is made by Salbank' (*Letters Received*, vol. vi, p. 184), by Roe (*Embassy*, p. 312) and by Bluteau (*Vocabulario*, 1712–21), and cautiously adds that 'there is no ground for it', ibid.
9   William Foster, ed., *The Embassy of Sir Thomas Roe to India 1615–1619*, New Delhi, 1990 (first pub. 1926): *passim*.

have Mughal in the titles, although the Persian language histories written in the court still avoided its use for the dynasty. That 'Mughal' was a term best avoided for the Indian rulers had reached Russia, too. When Peter I of Russia (r. 1682–1725) was preparing to send an embassy to Aurangzeb, he made enquiries among Indian merchants in Astrakhan regarding the appropriate mode of address for the Indian Emperor. Was it 'Mughal' or 'Shah'? He wasn't sure. The headman of the Indian traders gave him to understand that the Indian Emperor might resent 'Mughal' and that it was used wrongly by Europeans alone. He suggested Shahinshah instead.[10] By and by, however, 'Mughal' earned respect, dignity and, not least, pride, in its Indian association.

The perspective that informs this book seems to have grown along the expanding landscape of the writing of the history of medieval India, witness to radical changes in recent decades. Let me elaborate this somewhat by going back to the beginning.

The form in which the writing of history came to medieval India owes much to Arab-Islamic and Mongol-Persian traditions. With the birth of Islam, Arab historiography came to acquire a very strict adherence to the chronological sequence of events and a concept of world history.

Pre-Islamic Arabia was familiar with the tradition of genealogy and with the notion of the chronological order of events, even as uncertainty and confusion marked its practice at times. The *hijri* era firmed up the chronological base of all narratives. The boundaries between the eschatological and the historical time in Islam had been blurred too, since the birth of Islam as both a religion and a historical event could be precisely dated, as had been the case with early and medieval Christianity.

However, the complexity of time could never be reduced to simplicity. Thus we should expect to encounter several visions of time, rather than a single one. Its linearity from Creation to the Day of Judgement, inherited from Christianity, was one significant facet; the periodic appearance of prophets underlining temporal cyclicity was the other, although paradoxically this cyclicity is brought to a terminal point with the appearance of Muhammad. Indeed, on the one hand, the tradition of genealogy itself reinforces linear time, even as on the other, its extension to dynastic history implicitly replicates cyclicity again, with dynasties displacing one another in a cycle, as in the work of some landmark historians like Ibn Khaldun.

Understandably, there are several strands of the notion of eschatological time in Islam. If one strand emphasizes the eternity of cosmic time sans interruption, another views it as an infinite juxtaposition of

10   Eugenia Vanina, 'India: The Whole and Its Parts in Historical Perspective', *The Indian Historical Review*, vol. 28, 1–2, 2001: 93, n.26.

finite moments. The Quran itself envisages both eschatological and earthly time, one day of the former being equivalent to 1,000 years of the latter. This enabled historians such as Tabari to calculate the age of the universe at 14,000 earthly years, equally divided between Creation and the birth of Adam, and from Adam to the Coming of the Hour.

Even so, time had one indisputable break, i.e. before and after the rise of Islam in history and in theology. Before the birth of Islam, time was marked by *jahiliya*, ignorance or savagery, itself not one uninterrupted temporal unit, for periodic amelioration marked its flow with the descent of prophets sent by God; but the descent of the last prophet, Muhammad, makes that definitive break with the past, with *jahiliya*. Hence the one paradigmatic periodization in history centred on the *hijri* era vertically dividing the two ages.

Barring this one mega change, however, even as difference of phenomena over time is recognized by historians, it is not extended to the cognition of change. The inevitable link that post-Enlightenment European thought establishes between linearity of time and change, which is tantamount to an inner movement – progress – seems to break down here. The notion of historical periodization, underlining recognizable successive transformations, is absent from nearly all strands of Islamic historiography.

The terminal prophethood of Muhammad also gave reason for the Arab-Islamic historians to conceptualize world history. Since God's ultimate truth had been revealed through Muhammad, the truth must erase all remnants of untruth, infidelity, *kufr*, from the world before the Day of Judgement (*hashr*), and Islam must prevail wherever humanity existed. This reasoning led to the conceptualization of the world's history into a single unit by early Arab historians. Al-Yaqubi (d. *c*.897) and al-Masudi (d. 956) are the acknowledged pioneers in this endeavour and it reaches its high water mark in Ibn Khaldun in the fourteenth century.

On the other hand, this expansive scale of history also circumscribed the two basic constituents of a historiographical exercise, i.e., notions of time and space, which were now entirely drawn from the Islamic framework. The world of which most Muslim historians wrote history was the world inhabited by their co-religionists, and history began in that world a few odd years before the arrival of Islam there, as if to explain the arrival. There were very significant exceptions, of course, especially in Iran and India during the later centuries; but the predominant presence remained a reflex of the Islamic paradigm. The near universal use of the *hijri* era by them reinforced the presence.

So too in India during its medieval centuries. With the very outstanding exception of Abul Fazl, courtier and historian of Emperor Akbar (r.1556–1605), almost all other historians stuck to the *hijri* era and constituted their chronicles as the history of Muslim ruling dynasties in India. Barring Abul Fazl, they show profound ignorance and very little interest in the history of the region prior to the arrival of Islam. It is as if the prior history comprised the era of *jahiliya*, best ignored. The historians were not all uniformly orthodox practitioners of Islam; indeed, they reflected varying shades of commitment to it, from the 'liberal' Nizam al-Din Ahmad, Akbar's army's paymaster, *Bakhshi*, and Shah Jahan's historian Abdul Hamid Lahori, to Mulla Abdul Qadir Badauni, Imam of Wednesday's prayers at Akbar's court. Badauni was bitter on account of the rise of his one-time friend Abul Fazl to great heights in imperial favour, while he was stranded at near the starting point, and agonized by what he perceived as violent onslaughts by Akbar, backed by his enormous imperial power, on the most sacred tenets of Islam. He wrote his three-volume *Muntakhab al-Tawarikh* ('Elect among Histories') in secret, as a counterpoint to Abul Fazl's heretical *Akbar Nama*, composed under imperial commission and patronage. Driven by the need to seek Akbar's bounty and seething with rage at the desecration of Islam, Badauni let out his rage in the book. No such rage drove other historians. Yet, across the spectrum of historians, the paradigm of Islam remained dominant.

However, they made one extremely important departure, which implicates the segregation of history from theology. If theology perceived historical events as a patterned unfolding of divine will, medieval Indian historians did not perceive any grand pattern in history, nor did they envisage historical events as manifestations of God's will. On the contrary.

The historians of medieval India whose works we have inherited were all courtiers. As such, their horizon of what constituted historical events rarely extended beyond the court. They were primarily concerned with the accession of rulers, their battles, conquests and defeats, the administrative measures they adopted, the conduct of factions within the court, and so on. Often the historians, as courtiers, were themselves party to one or another faction, or were at the least sympathetic to one or another faction. They were thus eyewitness to, when not active participants in, the events they narrated. As such they were frequently aware of the motives that drove nobles or princes or, for that matter, denizens of the harem, to undertake an action that would enter their chronicles. For them, historical events were enacted through the medium of human volition.

Even the format of the narrative reinforces this assumption. The narrative follows the dynastic framework, derived from the Persian historiographical tradition, broken down to regnal units, with the reign of the current ruler often divided into an annual account. Within the year, events are narrated thus: 'In this year an event that took place was...'. The full account of the event is then placed on record, after which the narration of the next event is prefaced with 'another event that occurred in this year was...', and so on. Thus each event is treated as an autonomous, individual event, unrelated to the others.

This stands in contrast, for example, to medieval European historiography, composed by priests, who, owing to their distance from the scene of events, but far more importantly owing to their ideological predisposition, treated history as a branch of theology and the occurrence of all historical events as a manifestation of divine will. Since divine will encompassed all time, past, present and future, into a single, integrated whole, no event occurred by itself even if it gave human beings that impression, for each event was a piece of the grand design of God. Nothing in that design could be haphazard or autonomous. Incidentally, it is an interesting and challenging phenomenon that this theological notion of a grand, tightly knit pattern unfolding itself independently of human will has survived in Western thought, broadly in post-Enlightenment rationality and more pronouncedly in Hegelian and Marxian schema.

The very break-up of temporal units, from dynasties to single events, with no connecting thread, places history in medieval India in a different genre from theology; embedded in it is the logic of the treatment of historical causation in terms of human, rather than divine will. The sublimation of human will into human disposition and/or human nature is the furthest medieval Indian historians take us. If so-and-so behaved in such-and-such a manner, this was because such was his nature. It was thus that rulers of a weak nature remained content with the territories they had inherited and others with a stronger disposition went out for conquest. In the end, the events occurring during a reign were the manifestation of the King's nature.

The twofold perspective of dynastic history with human volition or, at best human nature, as the driving force of chiefly 'political' events narrated in a strict chronological order constituted medieval India's normative historiographical structure. Human nature as the explanatory force gave historians a double-edged framework: on one hand Islam, a major presence in the formation of almost every ruler's disposition, gave them substantial power in explaining the functioning of the state; on the other, the individuality of the nature or disposition of each ruler gave them a wide range of explanatory options.

The assumption that there was a period of Indian history coterminous with Islam, inherited from its Arab-Islamic origins, was strongly implied in these works; it also equally strongly implicated the notion of an earlier period coterminous with the regime of the Hindus. The tripartite division of Indian history into the Hindu, the Muslim and the British periods by James Mill, in his major work *The History of British India* of 1817, is not quite the sort of conspiracy of British rulers in pursuit of the policy of divide and rule that historians have often suggested.[11] Mill was treading a ground familiar enough for several centuries. However, by devising the asymmetrical 'Hindu, Muslim and British' periods, he was emphasizing the 'modern, utilitarian' nature of the British regime in India and equally the earlier obscurantist, backward-looking regimes in its history, with religion as their sole defining element, be it Hinduism or Islam. To an extent, the division also effected a paradigm shift in the structure of historical explanation. For, with religion as the exclusive defining element to explain the entirety of India's pre-British history, historical explanation became entirely monocausal. It lost that great spectrum of options, in terms of human nature and will, that medieval Indian historiography had provided for itself. From now on, it was enough that a ruler was Hindu or Muslim to explain his conduct; no other variables were required to reach a historical understanding.

With religion now as the historiographical axis, modern history-writing of medieval India developed along two empirically opposed but conceptually shared trajectories. As the medieval 'Muslim' state, all its actions were explicable in terms of the driving force of Islam. Thus much of the history of the period visualized it as one of the Muslim state's endeavours to spread Islam in India, with state power at its disposal. In reaction to it was the resistance put up by the Hindus to religious conversion. Most of the evidence for this vision was drawn from the chronicles, written by courtiers, like the ones we have mentioned above; we shall meet with several of these courtiers and get to know of their work often enough in this book. An alternative picture of the period was gradually drawn, too, in which there was indeed much give-and-take between the Muslim rulers and the Hindu subjects, especially the subjects drawn from the indigenous ruling groups into the imperial ruling class, first at the lower end of administration and gradually at the highest echelons. The first trajectory highlighted continual cultural conflict between the two religious communities; the second highlighted mutual accommodation. Each put a veil over a part of the data that defied their vision. Both focused chiefly on political and administrative history and depended upon the court histories written in the Persian language for creating their databases. One came to be characterized by the other as

---

11   For a popular but forceful statement of this conspiratorial view, see the little but influential booklet of Romila Thapar, Harbans Mukhia and Bipan Chandra, *Communalism and the Writing of Indian History*, New Delhi, 2003 (first pub. 1969).

'communal' historiography, projecting itself as its secular 'nationalist' face. The other flaunted itself as the truthful history, implying a compromise of the truth by the 'nationalist' historians on behalf of a political project.

In some very substantial ways, the two trajectories were mirror images of the political battle being fought against the British colonial regime on the ground, known as India's freedom struggle, especially in the first half of the twentieth century. The freedom struggle evolved along two paths: the 'nationalist' and the 'communalist', represented by the Indian National Congress and the Indian Muslim League respectively. Even as the two wings of the freedom struggle stood empirically as each other's negation, the difference between them appears to have been one of strategy rather than of concept. Religious community, as the conceptual tool for analysing Indian society and organizing the struggle for its liberation from colonial regime, was shared between them. The 'nationalist' mobilization was based upon the premise of the two major communities, the Hindus and the Muslims, joining hands in a drive against the British, with the identity of each community being safeguarded. The Sanskrit phrase, *sarva dharma sambhav* ('like treatment of all religions'), and the popular Hindi phrase, *Hindu-Muslim bhai-bhai* ('Hindus and Muslims are brothers'), comprised the core of nationalist ideology. It sought to preserve the community identities of the two religious groups, while merging them with their common nationalist identity.

The 'communalist' mobilization of the Muslim League also played upon the community identity of the Hindus and the Muslims and developed the 'two-nation' theory, in which each community constituted an autonomous nation with no shared premises of religion, culture or history. Both the 'nationalist' and the 'communalist' strategies mobilized history, especially medieval Indian history, to sustain their projects. Religion in general and Islam in particular remained the reference point for political mobilization and for history-writing.

A major break from the two sides of this paradigm occurred in 1956 with the publication of D. D. Kosambi's *An Introduction to the Study of Indian History*. By profession a mathematician and statistician, and an assertive Marxist, he shifted the very terms of debate in history-writing in India by replacing the category of the religious community with that of class. His work was followed by that of several others, especially Irfan Habib's magisterial *Agrarian System of Mughal India* in 1963 and R. S. Sharma's challenging conceptualization of *Indian Feudalism*, 1965. If Kosambi's book laid out principles derived straight from Marxism and provided a wide framework of analysis, Habib's was focused upon a narrower theme but based upon an extensive empirical database. It too was an avowedly Marxist endeavour. The world was changing.

Marxism exercised considerable influence upon the social sciences in general, and history-writing in particular, for about a decade and a half in India, as it did in many areas of academia elsewhere. Marxism also provided an alternative vision for shaping a human future where utopia will be. A threshold was thus crossed. India was just about catching up with developments everywhere, as it were.

By the 1980s and 1990s another threshold had emerged. Not only were the socialist regimes facing a terminal crisis on the ground, Marxism too as the theoretical apparatus of these regimes was under strain. Old certitudes of Positivism and Marxism were under severe questioning everywhere. Even as Positivism and Marxism remain extremely valuable parts of the intellectual legacy of humankind, new forms of enquiry, new problematics and new sources were constantly being uncovered, many of these way beyond the capability of the old theoretical apparatuses to cope with. Most of these were in the arena of cultural and social history, exploring 'intangible' areas such as the history of emotions, festivity, interpersonal relations, space and time.

Norbert Elias's notion of 'court society' – with all its pulls and pushes, tensions and accommodations, functioning under the model of an absolutist monarchy, seeking regulation through a highly straitjacketed mode of court etiquette, and adjusting to constantly changing equilibriums – provides a fascinating entry point into the study of any court, the Mughal included. His 'civilizing process', now somewhat under attack, also remains a useful panoramic theoretical framework, even though its counterpositioning of wealth as a modern indicator of one's standing in society and the typically medieval phenomenon of one's position in the status hierarchy has a touch of simplicity. I also found Elias's notion of cultural grandeur as a source of legitimacy for the state an extremely useful insight for studying the Mughal state.

An abiding theoretical input in the making of this book has been the Foucauldian questioning of the Positivist notion of a given, objective truth which can be apprehended through incremental knowledge. Foucault's positing of 'truths' in lieu of 'the truth' appears to me the most effective questioning of Positivism, after two centuries of its dominance. Where 'the truth' of Positivism and 'the objective reality' of Marxism were counterposed to falsehood, Foucauldian 'truths' do not posit a choice between true and false; instead each 'truth' is expressive of power relations in society. The victory of one 'truth' is not the elimination of other 'falsehoods', incrementally or suddenly; it remains the victory of the articulation of one set of power relations, constantly under threat from other articulations, other 'truths'. It is thus that the constantly competing 'truths' in society lend it dynamism in its daily passage. Barring this subscription to what I believe is a powerful and valuable postmodernist theory of 'construction', I have no more claim to being a postmodernist historian than chalk has to being cheese.

I also learnt from paintings, especially French Impressionist paintings, that fleeting moments can get frozen in time; they then cast varying light and shade on interpersonal relations that constitute a significant facet of the surge of history. Renoir was a master of capturing the fleeting moments that expressed ambiguous human relationships and rendering them immortal. With that insight it becomes fascinating to look upon our history: it has no less been shaped by transitory moments of human frailties than by impersonal forces! Must we set one off against the other and force a choice upon the historian?

I am fortunate in that during the past four and a half decades I have been witness to, and in a small measure participant in, at least three fairly distinct phases through which history-writing in India – especially of medieval India – has passed. My own evolution as a practitioner of history has to an extent conformed to this pattern in that my interests have grown from historiography during the reign of Akbar in the 1960s and early 1970s, to the heavily Marxist problematic of a comparative study of feudalism in Western Europe and India during the 1980s, and now to the themes of this book in the 1990s and after.

The first chapter seeks to understand the phenomenal durability of the legitimacy of the Mughal state in India. It dislocates the few existing explanations from their monocausal locations and tries to explore the varied landscape of this problematic. Islam of course was one significant source of the legitimacy; there were several others besides, none of them static or given.

Chapter 2 goes beyond a narration of court etiquette and seeks to understand its evolution, and more particularly its meaning, within the context of the functioning of the court as a microcosm of society. A vision of order, a vision of the world inhered in the obsessive preoccupation with the observance of the minutest detail of court etiquette and its procedures.

Chapter 3 tries to enter the world of the Mughal family. Even as there have been several studies of eminent women of the imperial family, some centred on single figures like Nur Jahan and Gul Badan, others on them as a collective, and even as there is at least one scholarly study of the Mughal harem, the problematic in this book is neither one nor the other. I do not enter the question of whether Mughal women were powerless or powerful, which appears to me a rather sterile dichotomy. Instead, the chapter seeks to explore the overarching norms in the Mughal family, the modes of their subversion, the tensions in the interpersonal relations and the relatively smooth functioning of the vast space inhabited by women of very diverse backgrounds, statuses and temperaments, at the centre of which stood a very small number of select men, the Emperor in particular. The image that emerges hardly conforms to any given model; it is the diversity of images, often mutually conflicting, that lends interest to the theme.

The last chapter looks at the problem of court culture from the bottom up, as it were. If the hegemonic assumption, that it is elite culture that has a tendency to percolate down and shape the culture at the lower rungs of the social ladder, is now not left with many takers, the relationship between the one and the other still remains unexplored in the medieval Indian context. I take folklore here as a stratum of culture prior to and below the formation of religious identities, each of which has its own spectrum of cultural forms. Folklore on the other hand has universality to it, subsisting in all human societies before religions came along. Magic, miracles and faith are crucial to folklore and through them transference is mediated as its central feature. I argue that transference is also central to the working of court culture.

The book seeks to open just a small window upon a vast arena that lies beyond it. In researching for the book, numerous other inviting themes suggested themselves almost forcibly. If I am unable to pursue them further, they have nevertheless made me aware of the minuscule scale of my endeavour. As good a lesson in humility as any.

1

For Conquest and Governance: Legitimacy, Religion and Political Culture

Ecbar Shaugh [Emperor Akbar]...never denied [his mother] any thing but this, that shee demanded of him, that our Bible might be hanged about an asses necke and beaten about the towne of Agra, for that the Portugals... tyed [the Quran] about the necke of a dogge and beat the same dogge about the towne of Ormuz. But hee denied her request, saying that, if it were ill in the Portugals to doe so to the Alcoran, being it became not a King to requite ill with ill, for that the contempt of any religion was the contempt of God.

Thomas Coryat, English traveller to India, 1612–17.

Discussion of the legitimacy of regimes has somewhat recent origins in political theory, political sociology and even more so in history. In the context of the Mughal state, even as brief and speculative statements on the theme lie scattered in historiography, the problematic has rarely been constituted. This, in the face of frequent observations that the legitimacy of the Mughal state had survived long after the state itself lay in a shambles in the first half of the eighteenth century. The centring of the great rebellion of 1857 around the last Mughal 'emperor' Bahadur Shah Zafar, physically decrepit and surrounded by a territorial and political void, symbolizes the survival of Mughal legitimacy sharply and poignantly, for it cemented bonds between the rival groups that had all chipped away at the grand imperial structure to begin with.

To the extent that historians explored the nature of the medieval state, it had a singularly monocentric location on the significance of Islam in its functioning: Did the state constitute a theocracy? Answers spawned a range from an emphatic affirmation to a nuanced denial, each itself shaded by the historian's ideological location in the story of India's colonialization and its struggle for freedom which had brought the question of history centre-stage.

More recently, Stephen Blake has suggested a hypothesis that substitutes one monolocal construction for another: following Max Weber's lead, Blake has postulated a patrimonial-bureaucratic state in Mughal India. M. Athar Ali, Douglas Streusand and John F. Richards, too, have made astute comments on the nature of the state without substantively touching upon the question of legitimacy; as indeed has the long Introduction to the volume *The State in India: 1000–1700 A.D.*, edited by Hermann Kulke, with the same result.[1] Amina Okada has on the other hand sought out traces of the state's legitimacy in Mughal paintings and Urvashi Dalal in the layout of the city of Shahjahanabad.[2] Ebba Koch too has touched upon the problem in the context of Mughal art.[3] In a regional context, Richard M. Eaton has, in his recent work, traced the outlines of the evolution of legitimacy in Bengal from its conquest by Bakhtiyar Khalji in AD 1204 to the eve of the British era; the outline evolves as the new state's assertion of its alien profile, with assimilation of the conqueror into the region's social and cultural milieu.[4]

However, in some ways the most imaginative exploration of the question of Mughal state's legitimacy was undertaken early in the twentieth century by Francis William Buckler, especially in an all-too-brief essay, 'The Oriental Despot'. Buckler looked upon Mughal sovereignty as 'corporate kingship' in which all the nobles were 'members' rather than servants – a shade of the concept of 'court society' that Norbert Elias was to develop later in the context of medieval French monarchy. The value

1 The essays by Blake and Ali were published in *Journal of Asian Studies*, 39, 1979: 77–94, and *Journal of the Royal Asiatic Society of Great Britain & Ireland*, 1978: 38–49. These have been reproduced in H. Kulke, ed., *The State in India 1000–1700*, New Delhi, 1995. Douglas Streusand, *The Formation of the Mughal Empire*, New Delhi, 1989. John F. Richards, *The Mughal Empire*, Cambridge, UK, 1993, but especially his innovative essays, 'The Formulation of Imperial Authority under Akbar and Jahangir', in J. F. Richards, ed., *Kingship and Authority in South Asia*, Madison, 1978.
2 Amina Okada, *Imperial Mughal Painters: Indian Miniatures from the Sixteenth and Seventeenth Centuries*, tr. D. Dusinberre, Paris, 1992; Urvashi Dalal, 'Shahjahanabad: An Expression of Mughal State's Legitimacy', *Islamic Culture*, 74, 4, October 2000: 1–17.
3 Ebba Koch, *Mughal Art and Imperial Ideology: Collected Essays*, New Delhi, 2001.
4 Richard M. Eaton, *The Rise of Islam and the Bengal Frontier, 1204–1760*, Berkeley and Los Angeles, 1993; New Delhi, 1997: 22–70.

of *khila't*, robe of honour, given by rulers to nobles and a few others, lay in its symbolism of ritually incorporating the recipient into the king's body, for the King would actually touch the robe with either his hand or his back before handing it out. Unfortunately, Buckler's writings did not receive the attention their original and provocative nature should have brought to them; only recently have these been put together and introduced to professional historians by M. N. Pearson.[5]

Whichever way one looks at these explorations, most have a single point location. On the other hand, it is perhaps possible to envision the Mughal state drawing sustenance from varied and varying sources of legitimacy, a legitimacy that is not given and frozen. Some of the sources could be perceived as relatively durable structures, others as somewhat more plastic, and still others as fleeting moments which yet leave a lasting impress on history.

Islam was one durable structure, for its presence at almost every level of the state's functioning was emphatic. We might explore its presence at three levels: intellectual, political and popular.

The medieval court histories understandably focused on events revolving around the ruler, his family, nobles, wars, administration, etc.; their authors were invariably courtiers. Often the titles of these chronicles themselves were suggestive: *Akbar Nama, Shah Jahan Nama, Alamgir Nama*: the story of Akbar, Shah Jahan, etc., although the story of the person was also the story of the court and indeed of the empire, for their equivalence in the perception of the courtier-historians was unambiguous.

The histories that were thus composed followed a format, with the singular exception of Abul Fazl, whom we shall encounter several times again. The book would open with a preface in praise of God, Allah, and the prophet of Islam, Muhammad. It would then endow the long sequence of the caliphs, successors of Muhammad, with encomiums, quietly taking a detour to the line of the past (Muslim) rulers of the land and terminating in the reign of the current ruler when the historian was at work. Clearly then, the history that was written was the history of the Muslim rule in India and the ruler's political descent was articulated in the exclusive lineage of Muhammad and the caliphs.

5   M. N. Pearson, ed., *Legitimacy and Symbols. The South Asian Writings of F. W. Buckler*, Michigan Papers on South and Southeast Asian Studies, The University of Michigan, no. 26, *c*.1985. More recently, Stewart Gordon has subjected the somewhat linear images sketched by Buckler to considerable and elegant nuancing. See his 'Robes of Honour: A "Transitional" Kingly Ceremony', *The Indian Economic and Social History Review*, 33, 3, 1996: 225–42; S. Gordon, ed., *Robes of Honour: Khil'at in Pre-Colonial and Colonial India*, New Delhi, 2003.

In large measure this was owing to the tradition of history-writing within which medieval Indian historians practised their craft. The perspectives of Islam determined the space and time that constituted the world and its history for them, a point touched upon in the introduction.

Abul Fazl, Akbar's courtier, historian, friend and fierce supporter, finished his massive and definitive work, the *Akbar Nama* and *Ain-i Akbari*, in the waning years of the sixteenth century; it marks a decisive and schematic departure from the predominant historiographical format, as it does in several other aspects of the construction of an alternative world view. The *Akbar Nama* opens with the praise of Allah, for sure, and then moves to Adam and traces Akbar's lineage from him as his fifty-third generation descendant. Very deliberately it dislocates historiographical axis from the groove of Islam and seeks to construct an alternative teleology of universal history – and not merely a world history – in which Akbar, his patron and idol, would not be contained within the frame of a sect of humanity, i.e. Islam; he is the heir not to Muhammad and the caliphs, but to Adam himself, the first human being, and thus the ruler of all humanity. There were other existing notions of the ruler of the universe too, for sure, such as the Shahinshah in pre-Islamic Iran and the Chakravartin in Hindu religio-political ambience, but their vision of universality coincided with territoriality; for Abul Fazl, the coincidence was with humanity instead.

But then Abul Fazl was exceptional. As indeed was Akbar. If we withdraw Abul Fazl from the scene for a while, the large number of histories that have survived to us follow the other, predominant pattern, with Islam as its frame of reference in narrating events where the court, the ruler and his nobles comprised their very core. If the intellectual and cultural ambience at the court bore the impress of Islam's considerable presence, the rulers themselves frequently invoked Islamic idiom and jargon to legitimize their actions. With some of them it might have been merely a politic manoeuvre; with others a measure of conviction, even vehemence, shaded a part of the exigency. But 'the waging of wars against *kafirs*' (infidels), 'elimination of *kufr* (infidelity) from the land' at the hands of the 'armies of Islam', etc., remained strongly expressed sentiments by most Mughal rulers, even as they revelled in life's merriment, so alien to the chilly puritanism of the zealot. Battles against non-Muslim opponents became *jihads* (holy wars) sometimes in, and at others irrespective of a context; prohibition of the construction of new temples, and, if constructed, their demolition, the demolition too of some very ancient temples and the construction of mosques in their place, the collection of *jiziya* from non-Muslims as the price of the freedom to adhere to their own religion in a Muslim state – all these, and several other acts, implemented with varying measures of coercion, marked the assertion of conquering power, perceived and projected in an accentuated Islamic profile of the state.

Babur saw himself at times as a practising Muslim; his practice of Islam was however lightened by his search for the pleasures of the senses: wines, composing of some very sensual poetry, music, flowers and gardens, women, even a young boy at one time in his youth. He was not the type of the stuff that makes proselytizing and demolishing other people's places of worship one's life's aim. Yet, even as he had gained a relatively easy victory at Panipat in 1526 against Ibrahim Lodi, a Muslim of the Afghan stock, forever the butt of ridicule in the eyes of the more refined Mughals,[6] the battle next year at Khanuwa was to be the decisive one for the opening up or the closure of space to achieve his ambitions in India. The eve of the battle had tensed up his nerves, with good reason: his opponent, Rana Sangram Singh ('the lion chief of battles') was a legendary war veteran, as yet unfamiliar with defeat, as folklore would have it; his army was terrifyingly larger than that of Babur. And then an astrologer, a Muslim at that, had forewarned the Mughal of the certainty of impending defeat if he went ahead with the battle. Astrological fore-casts were often determinant interventions in the political or personal conduct of the Mughals. Loss of hope could so demoralize a warrior.

Babur found hope in the fold of Islam. His battle cry at Khanuwa was *jihad* against the infidel Rana. In a dramatic gesture of religious piety, he renounced the drinking of liquor and broke all his drinking vessels. The words in this part of his memoirs, the *Babur Nama*, where events leading up to and immediately following this battle are recorded, wear a very uncharacteristic hue of a holy warrior battling to cleanse the earth of infidelity, *kufr*.[7] But this metamorphosis had a context.

Jahangir, on his part, was able to record only a small number of victories during his reign. Thus, every little one would appear grander to him than it did to history. One such precious victory was won at Kangra, the fortress on a hilltop in present-day Himachal Pradesh, not quite easy of access. Jahangir writes of the conquest in hyperbolic terms

---

6   Bayazid Bayat, a junior courtier of Humayun and Akbar and author of a memoir, observes of a youth: 'As he was young in years, was a fool and an Afghan...', *Tazkira-i Humayun wa Akbar*, ed. M. Hidayat Husain, Calcutta, 1941: 313.

7   Interestingly, after invoking Allah's help and grace, Babur, forever sensual, adds that 'Victory, the beautiful woman whose world adornment of waving tresses was embellished by *God will aid you with a mighty aid* [verse from the Quran], bestowed on us the good fortune that had been hidden behind a veil and made it a reality.' *Babur Nama*, English tr. A. S. Beveridge, Delhi, 1972 (first pub. 1922): 572. The sensuality of the metaphor 'beautiful woman with waving tresses' is in a manner enhanced by the invocation of God, whose 'mighty aid' undoubtedly added to her appeal. The pleasure of this sensuality thus also becomes sacred, sinless.

in his memoirs, the *Tuzuk-i Jahangiri,* and boasts of celebrating it by demolishing the temple of the Hindu goddess Durga, and constructing a mosque at the site. He also had a bull slaughtered in the fort, and carried out 'whatever was customary according to the religion of Islam'. The temple below the fort walls was, however, left untouched, though not unnoticed. Indeed, Jahangir speaks very fondly of it. Interestingly, even as Prince Khurram, later to become Emperor Shah Jahan, was the formal victor at Kangra, earlier attempts to conquer the fort had been led by Raja Bikramjit and Jauhar Mal, son of Raja Basu, among others. The fact that these high-ranking Hindu nobles were commissioned to reduce a fort, where victory was ultimately celebrated by demolishing a Hindu temple and erecting a mosque, lends a degree of irony to the enterprise, although it was far from unusual. Indeed, one strand of Muslim thought did emphasize 'a Hindu wielding the sword of Islam' as evidence of glorification of the faith.[8]

Yet Jahangir was not eager to demonstrate his devout Islamic profile, much less in opposition to *kufr.* Indeed, if there was one man in his empire for whom he had the most profound respect, it was a Hindu hermit, Yogi Jadrup, to whose hermitage he paid several visits and considered 'association with him a great privilege'. The Yogi too was effusive in his compliment to the emperor: 'In what language can I return thanks for the gift of God, that in the reign of such a just King I can be engaged in the worship of my own Deity in ease and contentment, and that from no quarter does the dust of discomposure settle on the skirt of my purpose?' Niccolao Manucci – the Italian traveller who came to India in 1656 hiding in the hold of a ship, and stayed on until his end in 1717 – observes of Jahangir that of all his subjects, he was kind to everyone except the Muslims. Indeed, this sentiment is repeated several times over in our sources. Shaikh Ahmad Sirhindi, a significant and influential theologian of Akbar's and Jahangir's time, lamented the deplorable state of Islam in India. His countrymen, he felt, set little store by the dogma of prophethood in general and that of Muhammad in particular. The law of God, which Muhammad had preached, was, in the Shaikh's view, no longer honoured in India and unbelief was openly propagated even in the Persian language. A Persian-language text composed in 1025 H./AD 1614, less than a decade after Akbar's death, records the written

---

8   Akbar's courtier and historian Abd al-Qadir Badauni cites Mulla Sheri to this effect in the context of Raja Man Singh fighting Rana Pratap of Chittor; *Muntakhab al-Tawarikh,* vol. II, ed. Captain W. N. Lees and Munshi Ahmad Ali, Calcutta, 1865: 233. Later on, Aurangzeb too referred to his great Hindu general Raja Jai Singh as the 'extender of Islam' (*mati al-Islam*). See M. A. Ansari, *Administrative Documents of Mughal India,* Delhi, 1984: 40.

instruction sent by Akbar to his son Danial, after appointing him Governor of the Deccan and Khandesh in 1601, that 'he should demolish the Jama mosque at Asir and raise a temple along the pattern of the Hindus and kafirs on its site'. The prince, though, wisely sidestepped the implementation of the order, notes the author. In a similar vein Jahangir's grandfather Humayun, too, had been accused of being anti-Muslim by a Sufi, Shaikh Abd al-Quddus Ganguhi. François Bernier, the celebrated French doctor who travelled to India in the mid-seventeenth century, announced that Jahangir 'died, as he had lived, destitute of all religion'. Manucci, also, tells the story of Jahangir's fondness for pork and wine growing more intense during the holy month of Ramazan – when devout Muslims observed strict fast from sunrise to sunset! Implored by the theologians to abstain from pork, at least, both in everyday life and more determinedly during the Ramazan, for if Christianity allowed its consumption, for Muslims it was a mortal sin, he resolved to turn to Christianity instead! He did not actually convert, but such was the casualness of his regard for Islam. He did, however, let three of his nephews, brother Danial's sons, actually turn Christian and there was a public procession through the streets of Agra to celebrate their baptism. The three were given Portuguese names: Tahmurs became Don Felipe; Baisangar, Don Carlos; and Hoshang, Don Henrique. Four years later, 'they had rejected the light and returned to their vomit', observes Maclagan in utter disgust. Sir Thomas Roe, King James I's ambassador to India during Jahangir's reign, also tells the story of two princes' conversion to Christianity only to enable Jahangir to demand a Portuguese wife for himself; on not obtaining one, 'the two Princes came to the Jesuits, and surrendered up their crosses and all other rites, professing they would be noe longer Christians'. Simple explanations do carry blissful satisfaction.

Roe, however, reinforces the emperor's image of indifference towards Islam: 'His religione is of his owne invention; for hee envyes Mahomett and wisely sees noe reason why hee should not bee as great a prophett as hee and therefore proffesseth him selfe soe . . . Finally, all sorts of religions are wellcome and free, for the King is of none.' Other European observers confirm this perception, verging on vehemence. Terry, the English traveller, mentions that when the recitation of the *azan*, the call for prayers, began in the mosques in Agra his companion Coryat would go up to the turret and substitute ' "Hazrat Eesa ibn-Allah", "Christ the son of God" for "Mohammad Rasul-Allah" '. He would further add that Mahomet was an impostor; 'which bold attempt in many other parts of Asia, where Mahomet is more zealously professed, had forfeited his life with as much torture as tyrannie could invent. But here every man hath libertie to professe his owne religion freely, and for any restriction I ever observed, to dispute against theirs with impunitie.' The King 'does not like those that change their religion; hee himselfe beeing of none but his own making and therefore suffers all religions in his kingdom,' remarks Coryat.

Yet demolition of the temple at Kangra and its replacement by a mosque came easy as assertion of conquest of a fort that had escaped the might of his predecessors, above all, his father, with whom he had a complex love–hate relationship. That was his proud moment and he

Figure 1   Rembrandt, *Shah Jahan and His Son*. Although done just two years before the Emperor's dethronement and 'imprisonment' by his third son and successor Aurangzeb, the painting shows him and his son (Dara Shukoh?) at a much younger age. The very young Prince receives affection from his father, but also wears the grim adult responsibility on his face, reinforced by the crown-like turban on his head. It was unthinkable even for a Western artist to show the Emperor without the solar halo. © Rikjsmusuem.

celebrated it by highlighting his Islamic core. Religion, state and history merged here.

The court chronicle of Shah Jahan, the *Shah Jahan Nama*, makes a point of describing his forces as the armies of Islam, and repeatedly refers to his acts as being undertaken for the glorification of Islam. Even so there are few events on record where the Emperor dramatized his Islamic identity. This was left to his third son and successor Aurangzeb, who, more than any of his ancestors, brought Islam centre-stage in state affairs. Islam moved him emotionally and he perceived its clearest manifestation in relentless antagonism with *kufr*. 'My heart burns with anger when I look at a *kafir* in prosperity,' he had exclaimed. The long historiographical tradition established on a firm footing by Sir Jadu Nath Sarkar, envisioning Aurangzeb as the indefatigable zealot whose ambition was to turn the Mughal state into an indubitably Islamic institution, still finds an echo in John F. Richards. The Emperor was, remarks Richards, 'free to fulfil his Islamic vision of the Mughal empire ... [which] was his ultimate goal'.[9] Aurangzeb could also source the justice of his imprisonment of his father and the killing of his brothers, for the capture of the throne, to his concern for Islam and their neglect of. it. The concern found expression in his general command to demolish temples of the Hindus and at times erect mosques on their debris. This included the temples at Kasi (Varanasi) and Mathura and several others.

Popular perception, too, commonly identified the state with Islam. The *Guru Granth Sahib*, scripture of the Sikhs, also revered by the Hindus in Panjab, speaks of the state as Muslim without ambiguity and without hostility, as a matter of fact. Devotional literature composed in regional languages in India's medieval centuries also refers to the state as Turk or Turkish, used as a synonym for Muslim. The Muslim Sufi saints, on their part, were content to think of the state as Islamic, for whose security and longevity they could mobilize their immense popular appeal with a clear conscience as the occasion arose.

Yet, to reconsider the old question, was the state indeed the state of Islamic theocracy? We might set two criteria to establish the characteristics of a theocracy, Islamic in this case. First, the state, ruling on behalf of a denominational god, would endeavour to use all its power for the conversion of its subjects to Islam and would eliminate all traces of

---

9   J. N. Sarkar, *History of Aurangzeb*, 5 vols, but especially vol. III, Calcutta, 1928; J. F. Richards, *The Mughal Empire*: 172. See also I. H. Qureshi, *Ulema in Politics,* Karachi, 1974, where the thrust of the argument simply is that Akbar had weakened the foundations of the Mughal empire by diluting the purity of Islam and it was Aurangzeb as ruler and the orthodox Ulema who sought to check this distasteful development. A book written for the faithful by a faithful, with no space for critical enquiry.

non-Islamic presence from its territories; it would, in other words, constantly engage in transforming the contested land, *dar al-harb* into *dar al-Islam*, land of Islam. Second, only the jurisdiction of *sharia*, Islamic law, would prevail irrespective of the religious affiliation of any of its subjects, the kind of state that came to be established in some of the Arab regions, today's Saudi Arabia, for example.

On the demolition of Hindu temples, as an act of state policy, the evidence is varied though rich. Babur visited several temples in Gwalior and even as he ordered the demolition of 'naked idols' (erotic sculptures) on one temple, he also records his 'joy' at seeing some other 'idol-houses'. Bayazid Biyat, Humayun's personal attendant, commissioned to write his memoirs by Akbar, notes that he, Bayazid, had converted a temple into a mosque and a theological school, *madrasa*, in the presence of Todar Mal, the highly respected, orthodox Hindu minister of Akbar. Akbar assigned two villages for the maintenance of the *madrasa*. During Akbar's reign, too, the zealot Hussain Khan Tukriya was out to demolish rich temples. He had set his heart on the gold idols in the Doab region between the rivers Ganga and Yamuna. 'He had all his life coveted this place and kept his eyes set upon it as a mine of gold and silver imagining in his guileless heart... visions of golden and silver idol-temples and bricks of gold and silver.' Clearly, visions of lucre were seldom far from his desire to earn religious merit. Historian Abd al-Qadir Badauni also records during Akbar's reign that in Nagarkot, near Kangra, on one occasion 200 cows were slaughtered, many Hindus killed and a temple was demolished by the Muslim soldiers while they were under the command of Raja Birbal, 'who fancied himself a saint (*pir*) among the Hindus'. A while later, Akbar seems to have made amends for it and sent a golden umbrella to cover the idol.[10] He also allowed the reconversion of a mosque to a Hindu temple, which had earlier been demolished, and a mosque had been built on its debris at Kurukshetra, the site of the legendary war of Mahabharata and thus one of the major pilgrimage sites for the Hindus. Father Monserrate's Christian heart was warmed by the Muslims' destruction of Hindu idol temples, but the Muslims did not seem to have done enough, for 'the carelessness of these same Musalmans has on the other hand allowed [Hindu ritual] sacrifices to be publicly performed, incense to be offered, oil and perfumes to be poured out, the ground to be sprinkled with flowers... either amongst the ruins of these old temples or elsewhere – any fragment of an idol is to be found'.

Jahangir made some rude remarks about 'the worthless religion of the Hindus' when he learnt of the construction at Ajmer of a temple 'of great

10   S. R. Sharma cites a local tradition to this effect, *Religious Policy of the Mughal Emperors*, New Delhi, 1972 (first pub. 1940): 37.

magnificence on which 100,000 rupees had been spent' by Rana Shankar, 'in my kingdom among the great nobles'. It was not the magnificence of the temple that the Emperor found distasteful; it was the image of a boar – sacred to the Hindus as one of Vishnu's 10 avatars and abominable to the Muslims for being filthy and a religious anathema – that was the cause of his irritation. The image was destroyed and thrown into a tank, although the temple itself seems to have been spared. However, if the Durga temple at Kangra Fort had to give way to a mosque after being defiled by the slaughter of a bull, the temple of Goddess Bhawani just below the fort was left untouched. Also left untouched was the Jwala-mukhi temple in the neighbourhood, after testing the priests' claim that the fire there was divine and eternal and could not be extinguished by water. Indeed, Jahangir allowed not only repairs to it, but also extensions. The fort episode was to signify the registering of an extremely difficult victory. S. R. Sharma, the old school historian of the Mughals' religious policy, observes that 'These exceptions apart, Jahangir usually followed the path shown by his father.' It is interesting to note that some of the Hindu shrines in Kangra and Mathura 'continued to attract a large number of Muslim pilgrims besides their Hindu votaries'.[11] The matter-of-fact statements in Jahangir's memoirs that 'Various professors of every religion and creed have taken up their abode in the city', and 'Many religions and sects flourish in India', strongly reinforce the observation of the absence of proselytising zeal as an attribute of the state's functioning.

Shah Jahan was, however, a little less tolerant of the infidels' assertion of their faith. It was reported to him that many new temples had either been constructed recently or were in the process of construction. While the *sharia* might allow the continued existence of ancient places of worship of other religions under the regime of a Muslim ruler, construction of new ones challenged the very core of the Islamic state. Shah Jahan wasn't the one to ignore this challenge. He ordered that 'whatsoever idol-temples had been recently built be razed to the ground. Accordingly... it was reported from the province of Allahabad that 70 had been demolished in Banaras alone.' In Kashmir, however, he ordered the demolition of an ancient temple at Anantnag and renamed the town Islamabad, although there was no particular provocation for either action. At Orchha in modern Madhya Pradesh, the Rajput Raja had rebelled; on arriving there the Emperor ordered the demolition of the temple built by the Raja's father 'at great expense'.

The temple at Mathura was demolished in 1670, under Aurangzeb's command. 'In a short time by the exertions of his officers, the demolition of this strong foundation of infidelity was accomplished, and on its site a

11   Ibid.: 84.

grand mosque was erected.... The name of Mathura was changed to Islamabad,' observes Saqi Mustaid Khan, chronicler of Aurangzeb's reign. A decade later, Abu Turab, who had been sent to Amber in Rajasthan to demolish temples there, returned to the court and reported that he had pulled down 66 temples. A year earlier, Khan-i Jahan Bahadur returned from Jodhpur, having demolished temples and carrying with him, in the chronicler's hyperbolic language, 'cartloads of idols', and had audience with the emperor, who praised him highly. The demolition of the Vishwanath Temple at Varanasi has on the other hand been recorded rather casually: 'It was reported that according to the emperor's command his officers had demolished the temple of Viswanath at Kashi.' Similarly casual is the report on the demolition of the temple at Malarna in Rajasthan. Following a summary narration of appointments, etc., the following occurs: 'Salih Bahadur, mace-bearer, was sent to demolish the temple at Malarna.' Elsewhere a suggestion of temple demolition as punitive action is implied. Thus, 'Darab Khan was sent with a strong force to chastise the Rajputs of Khandela and demolish the great temple there.' On yet other occasions, the zeal for keeping one's faith secure from the contaminating influence of the 'other', i.e. infidelity, but failing to do so, led to the angry reaction of demolitions. It was learnt that in Multan and Thatta in Sind, and especially at Varanasi, Brahmins attracted a large number of Muslims to their discourses. Aurangzeb, in utter disgust, ordered the governors of all these provinces 'to demolish the schools and temples of the infidels and with utmost urgency put down the teaching and the public practices of these religious misbelievers'.

Moved as Aurangzeb was by excessive religious zeal, which for him implied attempts to demolish temples of the non-believers in the land ruled by a pious and orthodox Muslim ruler, the number of temples destroyed by him probably exceeds the number desecrated by any other ruler in medieval India. Yet it was far beyond even his capacity to do what would perhaps have given him great joy: to wipe out infidelity from the land of which he was the master. The Italian traveller Manucci recorded the emperor's failure on this count with a touch of irony:

> In this realm of India, although King Aurangzeb destroyed numerous temples, there does not thereby fail to be many left at different places, both in his empire and in the territories subject to the tributary Princes. All of them are thronged with worshippers; even those that are destroyed are still venerated by the Hindus and visited for the offering of arms.

The French traveller Thevenot, too, attests to the existence of a large number of temples in Ahmedabad during the reign of Aurangzeb, even as the Emperor demolished 'the chief of these temples' and converted it into a grand congregational mosque. Indeed, even while Aurangzeb was exhibiting his religious bigotry by going on a temple demolition spree, he was also financing the maintenance of several other Hindu temples and hermitages (*maths*).[12] Religious zeal must yield to demands of the state. In the end, as recently recorded in Richard Eaton's careful tabulation, some 80 temples were demolished between 1192 and 1760 (15 in Aurangzeb's reign) and he compares this figure with the claim of 60,000 demolitions, advanced rather nonchalantly by 'Hindu nationalist' propagandists,[13] although even in that camp professional historians are slightly more moderate.

There is some inverse evidence too of the demolition of mosques by the Hindus, and conversion of these into temples. Sher Shah, the Afghan ruler who had snatched the Mughal empire from the hands of Humayun in 1540, is reported to have vowed to punish the Hindu *zamindars*,who, 'after destroying the mosques and places of worship of the Mussalmans converted them into places for idol-worship and have entered into the quarters of Dehli and Malwa'. There is an earlier story, relating to the first third of the thirteenth century, told by Muhammad Ufi. In the port-city of Cambay in Gujarat, the Parsis 'instigated the infidels to attack the Musulmans, and the minaret [atop a mosque] was destroyed, the mosque burnt and eighty Musulmans were killed'. Some of the Muslims reported the incident to the Hindu ruler, who personally went out to investigate the matter and found it true. The ruler had the mosque restored to its old state, saying it was 'his duty to see that all his subjects were afforded such protection as would enable them to live in peace'. In Akbar's time, the eminent Islamic theologian Shaikh Ahmad Sirhindi complained that:

> The infidels are demolishing mosques and are building their own places of worship in their stead. In Thanesar in the Kurukhet [Kurukshetra] tank there was a mosque and the shrine of a saint. Both these have been destroyed by the infidels and in their place they now have a big temple. Again, the infidels perform their rituals and religious practices freely while the Muslims find themselves helpless and are unable to execute ordinances of the *sharia*. On the day of *Ekadashi* [eleventh day after moonrise] when

---

12   The Bombay scholar Jnan Chandra's celebrated articles in *Pakistan Historical Society Journal,* between October 1957 and April 1959, draw historians' attention to many documents of Aurangzeb announcing or renewing the grant of land for the maintenance of several Hindu and Jain temples. K. K. Datta's *Some Firmans, Sanads and Parwanas (1578–1802),* Patna, 1962, also reproduces several such documents.

13   R. M. Eaton, 'Temple Desecration and Indo-Muslim States', in his *Essays on Islam and Indian History,* New Delhi, 2000, esp. 128–31. Eaton is legitimately suspicious of figures of temple destruction given in medieval documents, for these would often inflate the numbers to please the zealous emperors.

Hindus abstain from eating and drinking, they see to it that the Muslims also do not cook, sell or buy anything in the towns. On the contrary, in the month of Ramzan [the month of fast for Muslims], they cook and sell breads in the bazars openly.

Shah Jahan is on record, too, for having seized seven mosques 'from their unlawful proprietors' who had 'violently seized and appropriated' them for their own use in Panjab.

Auranzeb himself, in a letter, refers to one of his most eminent Rajput nobles, Jaswant Singh of Jodhpur, with whom he always had an ambivalent relationship, as 'the infidel who has destroyed mosques and built idol-temples in their stead'. The letter is dated a good two decades before the Raja's death in 1679, when the emperor's dispute with his successors began. Evidence also exists of the demolition of some churches in Agra and Lahore during Shah Jahan's reign, before as well as after his conflict with Christians at Hugli in Bengal.

If places of worship of the Hindus and Christians could not be eliminated from the medieval Indian state's domain, the conversion of Hindus to Islam under its aegis also speaks of an ambivalent endeavour. One Muslim dynasty after another had ruled over varying parts of what we know as India today, for nearly five and a half centuries, and several times a dynasty's reach extended to most of the land. The degree of centralization of administrative and economic power, beginning with the regime of the Delhi Sultanate, reached the high water mark under the Mughals, especially by the mid-seventeenth century. The key instrument that worked towards this achievement was the *mansabdari* system, formally created by Akbar, but which had evolved from the preceding *iqta* system that had served the Sultans of Delhi for over three centuries. Yet, at the end of those medieval centuries and after the lapse of another two of British rule, the Muslim population in the Indian subcontinent was below a quarter of the total.[14] If the general impression formed by Bishop Heber in 1826, confirmed by Edward Thornton's *Gazetteer* of 1854, was that the ratio of the Muslim:Hindu populace was 1:6, i.e. the Muslim population at 16 per cent, the steep climb of the ratio to 1:4, or just touching 25 per cent, seems to have occurred in the rather brief

---

14   In 1941, according to the last census before India's partition, the Muslims comprised 24.3 per cent of the total population, with Hindus accounting for 69.5 per cent. Kingsley Davis, *The Population of India and Pakistan*, New York, 1951 (1968 reprint): 196. J. N. Datta had slightly earlier estimated the ratio on the same date at 23.81 per cent in his 'Proportion of Muhammadans in India Through Centuries', *Modern Review*, vol. 78, Jan. 1948: 33. In 1901 the ratio stood at 22.14 per cent; Kingsley Davis: 179.

period from the second half of the nineteenth century and afterwards when the British regime was firmly ensconced here![15]

More striking is the pattern of demographic distribution of Muslims in the subcontinent. Their heaviest concentration occurs in two regions: in the west in the lands that now comprise Pakistan and in the east, in present-day Bangladesh, the two accounting for more than half the Indian Muslim population in 1941, located in 76 of the 435 districts in that year.[16] The next heavy density of Muslim population occurs in Kashmir Valley in the north, and on a much smaller scale towards the southern tip in the small Malappuram district of the Malabar area of the present-day Indian state of Kerala. If these comprise the geographical peripheries of the subcontinent, during medieval centuries they constituted the state's political peripheries inasmuch as the reach of the Muslim state in these regions was either constantly in dispute, or sporadic and ephemeral, or, as in Kerala, beyond its ken. Kashmir Valley, on the other hand, had turned to Islam in a long and slow social process, starting almost coterminously with the establishment of the local Muslim state there. The decisive role in Kashmir's conversion to Islam was played by the incorporation of Islam into the Rishi tradition (the Rishi *silsilah*) at the hands of a string of Muslim Rishis, the most outstanding among them being Shaikh Nuruddin Nand Rishi of Charar-i Sharif (1379–1442). The state in Kashmir was virtually sidelined in the process.[17] Indeed, Sultan Shihab al-Din (r.1354–73), when advised by his Hindu minister Udaysri to melt the brass image of the Buddha and mint coins out of the metal, was furious. 'Past generations', observed the Sultan angrily, 'have set up images to obtain fame and even merit and you propose to demolish them. Some have obtained renown by setting up images of gods, others by worshipping them; some by maintaining them and others by demolishing them. How great is the enormity of such a deed!' Clearly then, in medieval India, there is considerable divergence between regions with a high density of Muslim population, and regions with a high density of Muslim state's authority. Indeed, there seems to be an inverse relationship between the concentration of political and administrative power on the one hand and the regional density of Muslim population on the other.

---

15 K. S. Lal gives various estimates of the ratio of the Muslims to the total Indian population in the nineteenth and early twentieth centuries; see his *Indian Muslims: Who are They?*, New Delhi, 1990: 89–90.

16 Kingsley Davis, *The Population of India and Pakistan*: 196.

17 See the authoritative study by M. Ishaq Khan, *Kashmir's Transition to Islam: The Role of Muslim Rishis (Fifteenth to Eighteenth Centuries)*, New Delhi, 1994.

Figure 2 Akbar's figure looms large over the canvas as it does in history. The imperial presence is emphasized by Akbar's very being rather than any overt symbols of royalty. Seems to illustrate the Sanskrit concept of *Yug-Purush*, maker of the age, which is also the purport of Abul Fazl's *Akbar Nama* project. © The British Library (Add. Or. 1039).

The motivations that led (or did not lead) to conversions were understandably extremely varied. Akbar offered life to his first major adversary, Himu, and his 80-year-old father if they accepted Islam after defeat at the battle at Panipat in 1556. Himu was a Hindu of the trading caste who had risen high in state during the interregnum in early Mughal rule in India, when Humayun, Akbar's father and the second ruler of the dynasty in India, had suffered humiliation, defeat and exile at the hands of the Afghan upstart Sher Shah. It was in the reign of Sher Shah's second successor, Adil Shah, that Humayun was able to return and reclaim his lost empire, if only for a few months, before he tumbled down the staircase of his library and life ebbed out of him. Akbar, all of 13 years, thus ascended the throne of an 'empire', in dimensions less than a petty district. The battle at Panipat was therefore significant beyond the number of severed heads, and the victory gave his self-confidence a boost that was to characterize the rest of his time in life and on the throne.

Himu, however, spurned the offer with contempt as his father had done, with stirring words, although without hostility to Islam. Himu had, in fact, taken a vow of converting to Islam if ever he were able to defeat the Mughals. If the old father had declined conversion because he was unfamiliar with the religion, for Himu conversion under duress would be a sin, but voluntary conversion was tantamount to thanksgiving in the wake of victory. Both of them were put to the sword, the father by Pir Muhammad Khan, an important noble of Akbar's early years as ruler, and the son by Akbar himself. Decades later, the memory of the slaying of a fallen adversary troubled him, and Abul Fazl therefore portrays the slaying as entirely symbolic in that Akbar had merely touched Himu's neck with the steel. Perhaps even in that moment of victory, Akbar did not have his heart in treating it as 'the first war against *kafirs*'.

Jahangir, on ascending the throne late in 1605, issued 12 edicts; among them was an admonition to *amirs*, high nobles, especially in the border areas, against forcing Islam on any of the subjects of the empire. If anything, conversion was to be treated as an imperial prerogative. The admonition implied temptation on the *amirs'* part to let their religious zeal loose in far-off territories where quiet accretion to their power came easier. It also implied the ruler's disapproval of mass conversions by his officials: conversions were to reflect discretion rather than zeal of the state.

Jahangir himself mentions a couple of cases of conversion of Princes without giving details. One convert was a descendant of the brother of Puran Mal, once ruler of Kalinjar, whom Sher Shah had defeated in 1545, though the Afghan King himself died of a rebound of his artillery shot. Jahangir tells us that his *mansab*, rank in state's military-cum-bureaucratic hierarchy, was raised from 1000/200 to 3000/2000,[18] a very impressive rise, and a possible reason for conversion. Another, Ruh-Afzun, a Prince of the Kharagpur ruling family in Bihar and in imperial service since his youth, 'having been honoured by admission to Islam, was made Raja of the province of his father, Raja Sangram'. There is just a trace of family dispute over succession here, in which Ruh-Afzun perhaps swung the balance through conversion. On the other hand, in 1609, the fourth year of Jahangir's reign, Islam Khan, Governor of Bengal, effected a punitive transfer of an officer of his army contingent for converting the son of a defeated Hindu Raja before employing him in his service; the governor's action was applauded by 'the other officers'.

A learned Brahmin of the Deccan, however, turned to Islam entirely for reasons of intellectual conviction. He had been appointed to help Mulla Abd al-Qadir Badauni, a rather surcharged Muslim theologian of Akbar's court, to translate the *Atharva Veda* from Sanskrit into Persian. Many precepts in the ancient Hindu scripture struck the Brahmin for their proximity to Islam; this and a few other linguistic coincidences convinced him of the verity of Islam's claim to be the ultimate truth and led him into its fold, Badauni tells us and thanks God for it. Another Brahmin also converted, although we are not told why. Nizam al-Din Ahmad, Paymaster General, *Bakhshi*, of Akbar's reign and a historian, tells us of one Shaikh Abd Allah Badauni, originally a Hindu. He was reading *Gulistan*, the text of Iran's classical poet Shaikh Sa'adi, one that deals with life's foibles. When he came across the name of Muhammad, he enquired of his teacher about the Prophet. The teacher expatiated on some of the virtues of Muhammad and the young pupil 'was exalted with the honour of accepting Islam'. A ruler of Kashmir, before its conquest by Akbar in 1586, Rinjan by name, had taken to Islam 'through intimacy and association' with his Muslim minister, Shah Mir.

Bir Singh Bundela, a Rajput of eminence, had been a loyal supporter and friend of Jahangir from his tumultuous princely days. As Jahangir ascended the throne, Bir Singh was happily ensconced in his home state of Orchha in Bundelkhand at the north-western tip of Madhya Pradesh, just touching the boundaries of Uttar Pradesh. The relations between the next two generations on either side turned a little sour. Bir Singh's son Jujhar Singh rebelled and was pursued relentlessly. He was captured and killed in the end, but his sons were spared their lives on condition of accepting Islam. The wives and daughters of deceased rebels were sent to wait upon the ladies of the palace. Another young son, too, was converted, and his guardians were promised their lives on the same

18   On the *mansabdari* system, see glossary.

condition, 'but from their innate vileness they spurned the offer and met their fate', i.e. death.

In Kashmir, conversions are usually reported as results either of triumph vis-à-vis the Brahmins in religious disputation or performance of miracles by the saints. The latter is indeed a frequently cited formula in effecting conversions to other religions as well.[19] The persistence of Hindu mores, rituals and ceremonies under the upper layer of Islam has been a feature of converts in most of these regions and a good many of these still survive intact, although not surprisingly with considerable regional variations. At Rajour in Kashmir, the Hindu converts to Islam 'still have the marks of the age of ignorance', laments Jahangir. 'One of these is that just as some Hindu women burn themselves along with their husbands' bodies, so these women are put into the grave along with their (dead) husbands.' If that was bad enough, Jahangir observes further on that 'Setting aside the infidels whose custom is the worship of idols, crowds upon crowds of the people of Islam, traversing long distances, bring their offerings and pray to the black stone.'[20] On the other hand, Badauni had also noted the excessive zeal of recent Hindu converts to Islam.

The story of reverse conversion from Islam to the Hindu faith continues well into Shah Jahan's reign. At Bhimbar in Kashmir, in the seventh year of his reign, he learnt of the convenient arrangement between the Hindus and the Muslims that if the daughter of one community was married to the son of another, her death should end in the cremation or burial that accorded with the faith of her husband rather than according to her own faith. This minor concession to male superordination within the family structure flew in the face of the Islamic precept of marriage being legal only upon conversion of the non-Muslim partner to Islam. However, so widespread was the practice that upon inquiry 5,000 such marriages were discovered in one locality, Jogu, alone. Similar complaints were heard in Panjab. Shah Jahan did seek to enforce the Shariat and prohibit such intercommunity marriages and by

19   For miracle as an instrument of conversion to Christianity in the Middle Ages, Aron Gurevich, *Medieval Popular Culture: Problems of Belief and Perception*, tr. János M. Bak and Paul A. Hollingsworth, Cambridge, UK, 1988. In the Indian context, Fr. Fernão Guerreiro also narrates incidents of conversion to Christianity following performance of miracles, especially miraculous cures of chronic patients. See his *Jahangir and the Jesuits*, Eng. tr. C. H. Payne, New Delhi, 1997 (first pub. 1930): 41–2.

20   *Tuzuk-i Jahangiri*, Eng. tr. Alexander Rogers, New Delhi, 1989 (first pub. 1909–14), vol. II: 180–1 and 224. The Italian Niccolao Manucci had similarly observed the persistence of many pre-Christian rituals among the neo-Christians in Tanjore and Malabar; Manucci, *Storia do Mogor*, vol. III, Eng. tr. Willliam Irivne, New Delhi, 1981 (first pub. 1907): 294–351, and vol. IV: 358–9.

converting the Hindu members of such families to Islam, but by the tenth year he had perhaps realized that the force of social energy was greater than that of the state and seems to have resigned himself to the prevalence of the practice.

From the sixteenth century on many Europeans had settled in Hugli, near modern Kolkata, had turned their habitat into a fortress and converted local people to Christianity, also treated as *kufr* in Islam, albeit with a somewhat more muted hostility in theology than in history. Nicolas Withington speaks of 'a verye fayer church in Agra buylte them by the Kinge and a howse allsoe' built by Jahangir for the Jesuits. The Jesuits also received a handsome daily allowance from the King. 'They have licence to turne as manye to Christianitie as they can, and they have allreddy converted manye; but (alas) it is for money's sake, for the Jesuits give them 3d. a daye.' The conversions, however, involved no change of heart: When the Jesuits were unable to pay them, they announced that they were withdrawing from Christianity.

This could work the other way round too. Withington again tells us several stories of conversions and reconversions for pragmatic considerations, where the monetary allowance was a greater attraction than salvation of the soul. One Robert Johnson, passing through the 'Deccanes countrye' (Ahmednagar?) was persuaded to convert to Islam by another Englishman who had turned Muslim. Which he did and was circumcised. The King (of the Deccan) was pleased and gave him an allowance of 7s., 6d. per day. Eight days later he died. On hearing of the allowance, 'another of our companie called Robert Trullye' arrived in the Deccan and offered to convert, an offer 'kyndlye accepted by the Kinge. So Trullye was circumcized and had a new name given him and greate allowance given him by the Kinge, with whom hee continued.' Trullye had a companion, a German, who too offered to convert and have himself circumcised. But then it was discovered that he had already been through the process while in Persia and was just trying to grab the king's allowance, which was denied to him. So he returned to Agra and became Christian again.

Yet another Englishman, Robert Claxton, on hearing of the allowance that Trullye had received on conversion, arrived there and converted too. However, he seems to have set his sight higher than the king's generosity; he returned to Surat, pretending to be penitent and penniless, collected some 40 odd pounds of money, and disappeared again to the Deccan to partake of the king's allowance. 'So there is with the Kinge of Deccane fower [four] Englishmen which are turned Moores.'

Shah Jahan dispatched one Qasim Khan to deal with the troublesome Europeans around Hugli and he returned with some 400 of them as prisoners. A few of them saved themselves by taking to Islam, others were left to die or were enslaved. Later on some more Europeans, settled further to the east in Bengal, were also converted, although no further details are known. Shah Jahan appointed a superintendent for the new converts.

Of all the Mughal rulers, one could expect Aurangzeb to put energy, conviction and state power into converting vast masses of infidels in India. Significantly, there is very scant evidence to this effect, even as 'popular Hindu and Sikh tradition ascribes mass conversion to Aurangzeb's reign', remarks S.R. Sharma, and adds, 'Of course it has heightened the colours in the picture.'[21] The Italian Niccolao Manucci does observe that some Hindus and Christians became Muslim at Aurangzeb's behest to win promotion in the official hierarchy or obtain employment there, or else to earn some money on the sly, but he leaves it as an impressionistic observation without details.

Several cases of tactical and casual conversions are on record too. A Raja, Kishan Singh (of an unspecified region, perhaps in central India), wished to replace his father as the ruler of his state and, to win Aurangzeb's approval, offered to convert. The Emperor appeared pleased and transferred some imperial troops to assist him. However, his mother's help proved more economical: she got rid of his father by the simpler device of mixing poison with his food. On learning this, Kishan Singh slit the throats of all Muslim royal soldiers in the camp, and whose services had now become dispensable, and fled. The Emperor appointed Mukhtar Khan, Governor of Ujjain, to suppress the Raja but the Khan himself was killed along with his son. Also in central India, again involving a dispute between a Raja and his son Ratan Singh, the latter converted to Islam and adopted the name of Islam Khan for himself and Islampur for his state, Rampur. However, a later Rajasthani chronicler, Shyamal Das, astutely observes that he took care to behave as a Muslim in Muslim company and a Hindu Rajput while amidst Rajputs.

During the reign of Aurangzeb again one Udairaj Munshi, accountant in the employ of Rustam Khan Bahadur Zafar Jang Dakkani, on his master's death took service with Raja Jai Singh, eminent Rajput figure in Aurangzeb's court, and ultimately gained his confidence. As the Raja died politically broken-hearted and in somewhat suspicious circumstances, the Munshi feared being implicated, went over to Daud Khan, Governor of Burhanpur, and 'embraced the religion of Islam', which convinced the Rajputs of his guilt. They were keen to hold him to account for it but he managed to avoid giving them a chance.

Interestingly, the number of cases of conversion as a subterfuge for some gain or other keeps pace with the increasingly aggressive Muslim

21 S. R. Sharma, *Religious Policy*: 206

profile of the state. Yet, on all accounts, the actual material benefits that flowed into the hands of converts for reason of conversion are far from impressive.[22] Manucci notes succinctly the regret of three Rajas over the loss of their faith but the gain of scarce else. 'Three of these rajahs', he observes with a touch of the caustic, 'became Mahomedans owing to the great promises made to them by Aurangzeb. But after they had been circumcised, he seized their territories, and has given them the little [read title] of "noble" in his kingdom; but with this he leaves them very little to live upon.'

Thevenot tells us of a Christian woman's conversion for being able 'to live licentiously'; clearly his Christian heart had not taken kindly to the change of religion. However, earlier in the reign of Jahangir, Fr Guerreiro was aghast to observe that 'There were in Cambaya some Armenians who were living sinfully with some Moorish women whom they kept in their houses. The Father pointed out to them the depravity of their conduct, and remonstrated with them to such good purpose that the women became Christians and were married to the Armenians according to the law of the Church.' On the other hand, a Portuguese gentleman in Bijapur wished to turn Muslim for love of a Muslim woman, but was refused permission by Aurangzeb, who too might have looked upon it as a pretext for 'licentiousness'. Akbar had also disallowed women's conversion to marry Muslim lovers; they were to be forcibly removed from their husbands and restored to their natal families. That conviction rather than convenience should guide the change of ancestral religion was perhaps the ruling principle; if it showed a high regard for the nobility of religion, it also moderated excessive zeal for the spread of Islam.

Aurangzeb did, however, induce a Hindu scribe to turn to Islam as punishment short of execution after he had had killed his sister's paramour, a Muslim eunuch, when the affair became public. Another Hindu scribe, Chandi Das, needed no persuasion to convert. It happened that he felt haunted by a ghost (*jinn*) in the town of Aurangabad during Aurangzeb's reign. For a long year he lay in bed, all medical treatment proving ineffective. A friend visited him and advised him to engage in constant (Muslim) prayer in lieu of medicine. Chandi Das took the advice and experienced a swift recovery. The efficacy of the prayer convinced him of the verity of Islam and so he turned to it. He was given the name Muhammad Hadi (by Aurangzeb) and later on the title of Kamwar

22   S. Inayat Zaidi and Sunita Zaidi, 'Conversion to Islam and Formation of Castes in Medieval Rajasthan' in A. J. Qaisar and S. P. Verma, eds, *Art and Culture*, Jaipur, 1993: 36–7.

Khan. He is the author of *Tazkirat al-Salatin-i Chaghta,* a general history of the Mughal period down to 1724.[23]

Among Mughal measures of administrative control, one of the most important was the appointment of *waqai-navis,* news reporters, in every part of the empire. The reporters were expected to bring directly to the emperor's notice details of each and every event within their territorial jurisdiction. Contained in these reports were incidents of conversion of some Hindu women in Ajmer, in Rajasthan, in the twenty-first year of Aurangzeb's reign. This was the year when a decisive shift to a more assertive Muslim identity of the state was in the offing, with Rajasthan as the prime locale of this assertion. Two of the reports are brief and matter-of-fact: One woman, Rupli (a Hindu name), who was the mistress of a Muslim, 'received the honour of conversion to Islam with a view to getting married after a while'. Another unnamed woman also 'brought honour upon herself with conversion'. The Qazi, Hamid, suggested conversion to her husband who declined. On this ground, the Qazi took this woman into his custody so that, after the lapse of the obligatory period of three months (*iddat*), he could marry her off to a Muslim.

A third case is slightly less plain. In the twenty-first regnal year again, one Ganga Ram, resident of Ajmer, lodged a complaint that Muhammad Alam of the *pargana* Dindwana had killed his son-in-law without reason and had taken his daughter, the slain man's wife, into his own custody. The two, Alam and the lady, were brought before the (Muslim) *faujdar,* administrator, of the region and Alam was asked to explain his conduct. The man, said Alam, had died of illness and the woman sought to burn herself with her husband's corpse. He dissuaded her from committing the act of sati and suggested conversion to Islam, which had no provision for this horrendous practice. She accepted the suggestion, and, on thus freeing her from the clutches of Hinduism, he allowed her to go wherever she wished. However, no man would cast a glance at her in view of the fact that her body had eruptions of leprosy all over. This was checked and found true. Her father nevertheless persisted in pursuing his complaint. The matter was thus sent to the Emperor for adjudication.

The casual nature of the proceedings of conversion in these reports is remarkable, when one would have expected some hyperbole. Similarly casual is the report of the conversion of Mulraj, a Rajput, 'who entered into the glory of Islam and became known as Abdullah'. For sure, casual references to cases of conversion to Islam are not the only form of recording them; equally frequently there is an aura of celebration when such conversion is put on record. There is, too, constant suspicion of the

---

23   The major manuscript of the text is located at Khuda Bakhsh Library, Patna. Asia Publishing House, New Delhi, published its latter part, edited by Muzaffar Alam, in 1980.

inadequacy of neo-converts' break from their old faith and commitment to the new. Sultan Firuz Shah (r. 1351–88) had expressed these doubts, as did Babur, Jahangir and the Muslim theologian of the eighteenth century, Shah Waliullah.

Fr. Guerreiro mentions instances of the conversion of some Muslims and Hindus to the faith of Christ during Jahangir's reign. One of them, an old man, native of Basra, 'begged the Fathers to make him a Christian', and then insisted that his conversion remain a dead secret. The reason given by the Father for this paradox appears rather laboured: 'so evil-minded are the Moors [Muslims] that he would have been unable to live with those of his house, had they known that he was a Christian.' In Agra, according to the Father's testimony, 'about twenty people had been baptised'. Sir Thomas Roe, who was also located at Agra at the same time, is sceptical of any true conversions to the Christian faith. 'I cannot fynd', he says with a sense of finality, 'by good search that ther is one Christian really and orderly converted, nor makes the profession, except some few that have become baptised for mony.'

It would thus appear somewhat of an excess to argue that the Muslim state in medieval India carried the burden of eradicating infidelity from the lands it conquered and governed, that it was the exclusive agency of religious conversion, and use of force by it was the main instrument of effecting the change. Scarce as the evidence is, it is far too varied to sustain that conclusion. It would also imply that the state exercised its utmost power in areas where its presence was least impressive and neglected what, by theocratic logic, would be its primary obligation in the region that constituted the heart of its territories, for all of five centuries and a half, i.e. Delhi, UP, Bihar, where the Muslim population has never surpassed the range of 15 per cent. The map of the Muslim population's distribution in the subcontinent seriously undermines the logic of the state as the exclusive, or even the primary, agency of conversion to Islam in medieval India.

It could perhaps be argued that strong resistance to conversion by the Hindus of medieval India should explain their overwhelming survival through the travails of all those tortuous centuries. We could thus expect a considerable amount of conflict, even violence, on the issue and consequently a large body of historical and literary documentation on both sides of the religious fence, to tell each version of the long-drawn story. A small window does open once in a while to give us impressions of motivations. Akbar observes with a touch of regret that 'we by fear and force compelled many believers in the Brahmin religion to adopt the faith of our ancestors'. Abul Fazl has, towards the concluding part of the *Ain*, recorded 'The Sayings of His Majesty'. Among them is a repetition of the above confession, now tinged with a sense of shame: 'Formerly I used force upon men to conform to my faith and deemed it Islam. As my knowledge grew, I felt ashamed of my deed. Not being a Muslim myself, it was unfair to compel others to become such. What constancy might one expect from those converted under duress?'

These, however, still remain occasional glimpses and history generally is remarkably reticent on this score. Thus, even as the Muslim population in the subcontinent comprises the world's largest single concentration, the story of its conversion to Islam remains virtually unexplored, primarily for lack of even suggestive data, barring a few scattered references. The data that we do encounter at the state level relate to individuals and families converting to Islam; most of these point to conversion by those politically significant persons who had committed what in the eyes of the state constituted an act of defiance or dereliction of duty, or an entire range of offences covered in the generic term rebellion, *fitna*. S. R. Sharma assiduously collected information on conversions and is able to enumerate less than 200 converts during Aurangzeb's reign. Of these, some come from the bottom rungs of society, with a willingness to convert for petty pecuniary benefits, while others could be traced to higher social and official echelons.[24] He also notes that the emperor's proselytizing zeal became manifest only from 1666, the eighth regnal year.

Conversion to Islam at the hands of the state was projected as a punishment to those found guilty of some crime or other. The most common punishment in serious offences of this nature led the person to the gallows; occasionally, however, either in view of his creditable past services or a still notable balance of utility as the ruler saw it, he was offered pardon if he were to forsake his religion to turn to Islam. As far as the state was concerned, conversion to Islam under its aegis was in most cases a punishment of the second order for what in its perception constituted very serious crimes. Akbar's lamentful observation perhaps refers to this type of conversion. We come across extremely rare cases where loyal non-Muslim officers of state were induced to change their religion and even fewer cases of common subjects being offered lures for converting. Missionary zeal for proselytization was not an attribute of the medieval Indian state, even in the midst of varying degrees of each ruler's attachment to Islam.

Interestingly, there is also testimony to reverse conversion of Muslims to Hinduism, as well as reconversion of Muslims to their former Hindu religion, both unthinkable in a state of Islamic orthodoxy. Mahmud bin Amir Ali Balkhi, a central Asian traveller in Jahangir's reign, was horrified to see a group of 23 Muslims in Banaras (Varanasi) who had deserted

24   S. R. Sharma, *Religious Policy*: 203–13.

their religion and turned Hindu, having fallen in love with Hindu women. 'For some time I held their company and questioned them about their mistaken way. They pointed towards the sky and put their fingers at their foreheads. By this gesture I understood that they attributed it to Providence.' Zain al-Abidin, very liberal pre-Mughal ruler of Kashmir (r. 1420–70), formally permitted return to the Hindu faith by converted Muslims. Social gratitude for it was expressed in a story that gained currency that a Hindu recluse had transferred his soul into the body of the dying ruler. Akbar too, in his forty-fifth regnal year, proclaimed that a Hindu converted against his will at any age could 'return to the religion of his forefathers'. Eminent fifteenth-century saint-poet Chaitanya reconverted the Muslim governor of Orissa; he also converted a group of Pathans, men from the rugged north-western region of the subcontinent settled in the east, who were not Hindus in the first instance, even as Hinduism is not a proselytizing religion. They earned the sobriquet of 'Pathan Vaisnavas'.[25] Shah Jahan's face-off vis-à-vis theologians had been feebler than his grandfather's and he had forbidden withdrawal from the fold of Islam; even so reconversion went on apace, usually of Muslim women married to Hindu men but also of Muslim husbands of Hindu women. Another source of reconversion was the sale of Muslim slaves to Hindus, although such a transaction was held by theologians to be contrary to the *shariat*. After the tenth regnal year, the Emperor seems to have reconciled himself to the futility of state intervention in prohibiting reconversion. A Hindu saint Kalyan Bhati travelled to Iran, converted to Islam, returned home and to Hinduism. The Persian language text of the seventeenth century, *Dabistan-i Mazahib*, implies the existence of a pervasive phenomenon of reconversion at all levels and mentions, among others, two high nobles of the imperial court – Mirza Salih and Mirza Haidar – who were thus persuaded to change their religion a second time. At the mass level, Shah Jahan discovered that in the Bhimbar region of Kashmir it was common for Muslim girls to marry Hindu boys, but, instead of the boys converting to Islam, the Muslim girls were being persuaded to turn to the Hindu religion. The Sikh Guru Hargobind reconverted a large number and the *Dabistan* records this with an unusual trace of hyperbole: 'Not a Muslim was left between the hills of Kiratpur in Panjab and the frontiers of Tibet and Khotan.'

It is interesting to turn to the second criterion of an Islamic theocracy: *sharia* as the exclusive form of jurisprudence. Such was clearly not the

---

25   Krishna Das Kaviraj, *Madhya Lila: Chaitnaya-charitamrita*, Eng. tr. J. N. Sarkar, New Delhi, 1988, as *Chaitanya's Life and Teachings*: 149–50 and 169–70. The tr. was first published in Calcutta in 1913 as *Chaitanya: His Pilgrimages and Teachings*.

case; *sharia* was not the only basis of the administration of law by the state. Criminal offences invited punishment in accordance with the *sharia*, for sure. But civil law, which concerns an overwhelming part of life for all subjects of state except the infinitesimal number with a record of crime, was far from uniform and each community of subjects was governed by its own religio-legal codes. Thus marriage, family life, property, and its inheritance, among the Hindus followed the Hindu religious codes and among Zoroastrian Parsis theirs, and so too with the Christians and the Sikhs, the Jains and the Buddhists. The vast numbers of tribal groups were still outside the fold of denominational religions and their civil life was self-governing, scarcely subject to extraneous jurisdictional controls.

Nevertheless, Islam had a strong presence in the operative categories of the medieval Indian state and was a significant source of its legitimacy for the greater part of India's medieval centuries. Of course, Islam did mean different things to different people. If Shaikh Ahmad Sirhindi's and Mulla Abd al-Qadir Badauni's hearts bled at seeing the dilution of Islam's orthodoxy, the same orthodoxy also came in for popular lampooning. Ja'afar Zatalli was one of the earliest poets of the Urdu language, composing some extremely 'obscene', i.e. sexually explicit poetry in the late seventeenth and early eighteenth centuries. In one of his less 'obscene' poems, 'The Problem that a Maulavi Discussed with his Wife', orthodoxy comes in for some delightful lampooning. The poet, in a superbly fluent composition, goes on to tell the story of a young Maulavi, Islamic theologian, who had announced with conviction to the young lady that a man's sexual intercourse with his wife equalled the winning of religious merit earned from killing a *kafir*. Having said that, the matter slipped from his mind. When a few days had passed and there was no sign of the killing of a *kafir*, the restless lady decided to remind the Maulavi of the need to practise what one preached and to induce him to earn high religious merit without further delay. Thus reminded, the devout man waited for the day to pass and, as the night fell, waged a veritable *jihad* on an army of *kafirs*; the wife of course was delighted.

Aurangzeb was understandably horrified that, during his pious reign, such sacrilegious acts as gambling and drinking in the Sufi shrines should be committed – and that by Muslims under the eye of his second son Muazzam. Gambling had taken place at an unspecified shrine by a state official, and drinking at the shrine of one of the holiest figures in the history of Indian Sufism, Gesu Daraz ('the long haired').

Aurangzeb, indeed, had a lot more to worry about: the erosion of his world of orthodox values, which had no space for a drink, celebration of the arrival of spring, music and conviviality in general. His Mullas prevailed upon him to proclaim the law banning liquor-drinking by women. Since the days of Babur, the women had grown quite accustomed to the consumption of a variety of intoxicants, such as opium, *bhang* (an intoxicating herb), nutmeg and other drugs, and the earlier ban on these at the outset of Aurangzeb's reign had had little impact. Indeed, the womenfolk took delight in circumventing the ban on the cute plea that it was meant exclusively for the men.

When his sister Jahan Ara heard of the renewed affirmation of the ban, she invited wives of the *qazis* to her apartment and served them enough liquor to leave them tipsy and unconscious. She then invited Aurangzeb to see the legitimacy of the *qazis'* demand and the real state of things for himself. She also delivered a homily to her brother to see that the learned men of Islam put their own house in order before setting out to do the same to others. 'Thus was appeased the storm that had been raised against women,' observes Manucci, never one to let go of a juicy bit of gossip. Manucci also attests to the fondness for the best of wines and heavy drinking by Jahan Ara herself, her younger sister Raushan Ara, and Udaipuri Mahal, Aurangzeb's favourite wife. Aurangzeb spoke to his vizir Jafar Khan to persuade him to give up drinking; the vizir made excuses of being old and infirm, justifying his evening cup as a source of energy. 'Wine could make the poor rich, the blind to see, the fragile robust and the cripple whole,' said the vizir. The Emperor felt helpless against these powerful arguments. Edward Norris, English ambassador to the court of Aurangzeb towards the closing years of his reign, mentions that the emperor's *qazi* requested him for a bottle of English liquor on the sly and this was duly dispatched to him.

These quiet erosions apart, there was no getting away from the presence of Islam as a source of the state's legitimacy for most of its duration, barring a phase in Akbar's reign. However, if Islam was one source of its legitimacy, there were several others besides and these were constantly expansive. Although the most significant expansion was in the construction of the ideology of paternalism, a completely new and growing ensemble of sources of legitimacy began to evolve. The conceptual architecture of this legitimacy was without doubt the creation of Abul Fazl. His endeavour synthesizes elements from the vast landscape of evolving political practices, conscious and unconscious social ethos, a mosaic of religious and secular streams and their strands, positing of an alternative reconstitution of history, and the construction of 'harmony' as the encompassing ideological frame that would remain the keystone of the Mughal state's legitimacy and its posthumous legacy. Abul Fazl's five revisions of his massive work and his exceedingly painstaking choice of each word attest to the deliberation that marks his endeavour; yet several influences nuance the grand structure through silent intrusion. In his structure there is a deliberate distancing from the use of any terminology and idiom associated with the theology and history of Islam, made more emphatic through silence. Even the mention of Muhammad's name is usually avoided, except as part of a quotation. Indeed, reference to Islam itself is substituted by a phrase of Abul Fazl's own coinage: '*Ahmadi kaish*, the sect of Ahmad (Muhammad)'. Clearly, the phrase not only conceptually distances Abul Fazl from any association, or even proximity to Islam, it also carries a slightly belittling overtone set against Islam's ambition of being a universal religion. And even as Abul Fazl refers to Hindu nobles or rulers at times with strong disapproval, at others with approbation in the course of his narrative, he never uses the term *kafir* for them. Indeed, in a scintillating inversion of meaning, he propounds that the absence of belief in Islam does not comprise *kufr*; on the contrary, it rests on the belief that there is only one path of submission to God even as He manifests himself in all directions.[26]

Comparing Babur's and Abul Fazl's versions of the battle of Khanuwa between Babur and Rana Sangram Singh makes an interesting exercise. If, on the eve of the battle and afterwards, Babur turns a fanatic Muslim in his narration, Abul Fazl, even as he remains very hostile to the Rana, avoids any term suggestive of religious dogma. The only time a religious element enters his account is when he records the chronogram of victory – *fath-i badshah-i Islam*, 'victory of the ruler of Islam' – but then he was merely quoting the chronogram. This is the only piece excerpted by him from Babur's vituperatively worded *Fath Nama*, the 'Proclamation of Victory', which had been drafted by the emperor's *Sadr*, chief religious official, Shaikh Zain. Abul Fazl, on his part, even avoids a reference to Babur's oath of abstinence from liquor on the eve of the battle, with his long and highly charged denominational harangue to his men. His account of the second battle of Panipat, where Akbar faced his first major opponent Himu, is full of abuse for Himu, but nowhere is he referred to as a Hindu, much less a *kafir*.

Abul Fazl constructs the theory of sovereignty with several interrelated constituents. The tracing of Akbar's descent from Adam instead of Muhammad establishes his universal, human, in lieu of Islamic, lineage. Strongly embedded in this construction was the teleological vision in which Akbar's person and his reign appear as the fulfilment of human history – an inevitable divine destiny. In the narrative, there is a quiet welcome of the accidental death of Humayun as a sign of the approaching sublimation of human history, i.e. enthronement of his son Akbar. The divinity of Akbar's person forms the core of this notion of sover-

26 S. A. A. Rizvi, '*Munajat* (Invocation to God) of Shaykh Abu'l Fazl Allami (1551–1602)', in Iqtidar Husain Siddiqui, ed., *Medieval India: Essays in Intellectual Thought and Culture*, vol. I, New Delhi, 2003: 128.

eignty. There is frequent, if deliberately understated, suggestion of prophethood in Akbar's being, a suggestion the Emperor himself never found
displeasing.[27] Yet, even as Abul Fazl posits a dichotomy between universalist religiosity derived from all of humanity's common God, Allah, and
denominational religions – including, and above all, Islam, with its own
partisan conception of God, Allah – the quiet incorporation of the
suggestion of prophethood in Akbar's person and the implicit inevitabil-
ity of the fulfilment of divine mission are elements pointing towards
Islam as the source of this vision. The teleology of the mission, too,
implies a finality in Akbar's appearance for its fulfilment, a notion central
to Islam in the context of Muhammad's prophethood.[28] Akbar is visualized also as 'the Perfect Man' (*Insan-i Kamil*), a complex concept primarily developed by the great mystic thinker, Ibn al-Arabi, for his millenary
appearance on earth at God's command. Muhammad, for Ibn al-Arabi
was the exemplary Perfect Man;[29] Akbar was for Abul Fazl.

But contrary to the Islam vs *kufr* dichotomy, where perpetual conflict
until the eventual subjugation of infidelity to faith was implicated, Abul
Fazl's emphasis was on universality of the perspective of sovereignty with
the establishment of social harmony as its missionary goal. Akbar's own
measures had been moving his polity in the direction of 'universal peace'

27 Akbar is said to have smiled at his birth as Zoroaster had done, and even spoke some
words, as Christ had done. See Abul Fazl, *Akbar Nama* (*AN*), vol. I, Maulavi Abd al-
Rahim, ed., Calcutta, 1878: 44. For reference to Zoroaster, *Akbar Nama*, vol. I, Eng. tr.
H. Beveridge, New Delhi, 1989 (first pub. 1902): 132 n.2; Abul Fazl, *Ain-i Akbari* (*Ain*),
Eng. tr. H. Blochmann, vol. I, 172 and n. 2. Akbar was rather fond of comparison with
Jesus, *AN*, I (tr.): 33 and n.1. Mulla Sheri, Akbar's courtier, renowned for his devastating
one-liners as much as for his Islamic orthodoxy, put it succinctly: 'This year His Majesty has
laid claim to being the Prophet; next year, if God wills, he will become God himself';
Badauni, *Muntakhab*, II: 309. Rafiuddin Ibrahim Shirazi, an Iranian visitor to Akbar's
court, makes the same point: 'He nursed a grievance against the Holy Prophet on account
of his being the last of the prophets. Otherwise, he could have claimed the position of a
prophet for himself without facing opposition.' See his *Tazkirat al-Muluk*, ff. 231b-232a, in
I. A. Khan, 'The *Tazkirat ul-Muluk* by Rafiuddin Ibrahim Shirazi: As a Source on the
History of Akbar's Reign', *Studies in History*, 2, 1, 1980: 41–55.
28 Even the 'illiteracy' of Akbar is largely Abul Fazl's construction to establish the
'divinity' of his knowledge and wisdom; it remotely mimics Muhammad who too was
illiterate.
29 Abul Fazl in fact synthesizes several streams to create the idea of Akbar as the Perfect
Man. He 'blends the philosophy of Farabi with the mystic ideologies of Ibn Arabi and Jili
for the justification of his theory that Akbar was the Perfect Man', S. A. A. Rizvi, *Religious
and Intellectual History of the Muslims in Akbar's Reign*, New Delhi, 1975: 356–7. The
notion of the Perfect Man raised the Emperor above denominational identity marks of
Hindu and Muslim. Akbar had also been declared to be the *sahib-i zaman*, (Master of the
Age), 'who would eradicate all differences among the seventy-two sects of Islam and the
Hindus', and many Muslim theologians, Maulanas, brought forward proof that Akbar's
appearance as the *sahib-i zaman* had long been predicted. Badauni, *Muntakhab*, II: 286–7.

(lit. 'absolute peace', *sulh kul*). Besides the abolition of discriminatory taxes against the Hindus in his early years as ruler, by about 1579 Akbar had recomposed the higher echelons of his nobility in a manner that ensured that no single group constituted more than a quarter of the entire nobility. This was a radical transformation from the debut of his reign, when the nobles were more or less equally divided between the Turanis from his own ancestral land in central Asia, and Iranis, with a slight edge for the former.[30] Midway through his reign Akbar had ensured that no group would be in a position to dominate the others – a pragmatic step towards the realization of 'absolute peace' in the distribution of political resources. Even as the social and ethnic composition of the Mughal nobility kept mutating during subsequent reigns, this principle remained the keystone of the Mughal polity. But then much more than exigent measures were involved in the polity's evolution; a view of the world, a vision of history was involved.

Alien conquest and rule in India had been part of its remote and recent history and integral to the evolution of its culture and civilization over centuries; the Muslim conquest beginning with the last decade of the twelfth century was a link in that chain. While Islam, as a young and energetic proselytizing religion, gave a distinctive identity to the rulers, governance evolved through a sharing of power and resources between the victors and the vanquished elites – an uneasy combination of tension and harmony, but one in which change of religion was neither a condition nor a guarantee of access to power. Islam did assert itself as the enveloping presence as the all-too-important idiom of conquest and governance, but in terms of state measures its assertion was at best episodic, anecdotal. Sultan Alauddin Khalji (r.1296–1316) put it most succinctly. Concerned to establish his credentials as a good Muslim ruler, he asked a theologian and was informed that all the measures he took for maintaining the flamboyant dignity of his person and the state were contrary to the injunctions of the *sharia*, and that his primary and much neglected obligation was to convert the infidels to Islam by inflicting humiliation on those who declined conversion. He retorted that he did what he thought was in the best interests of the state without caring if his actions conformed to or defied Islam's tenets. Indeed, at one stage, slightly fatigued by his mundane kingly duties, he thought up a scheme to establish a new religion and attain immortality – clearly to rival Islam and Muhammad – on the plea that if the prophet of Islam had been able

---

30   See Iqtidar Alam Khan's classic essay, 'The Nobility under Akbar and the Development of his Religious Policy, 1560–80', *Journal of Royal Asiatic Society*, 1968, parts 1 and 2, reproduced in Richard M. Eaton, ed., *India's Economic Traditions, 1711–1750*, New Delhi, 2003: 120–32.

to do so with the help of four companions, he too was blessed with such a company! Subdued rivalry with Muhammad was to recur among some of the Mughal rulers later. Sultan Firuz Shah was the only ruler of the Sultanate of Delhi (1206–1526) who showed distinct, if moderate, inclination towards enforcing some of the *sharia's* prescriptions through the institutions of the state.

Then, Islam sat lightly on the Mughals. Their conversion to it was rather recent and it had not succeeded in eradicating pre-Islamic pagan beliefs and practices, which had quietly become intertwined with the new faith and had mellowed its puritanical stridency. Babur mentions several persons, including his father, who were as pious in their faith as they were fond of the cup of wine, without noticing any incompatibility between the two, although Islamic orthodoxy would frown upon even the smell of liquor. Sultan Ahmad Mirza, his uncle, 'was a True Believer, pure in the Faith; five times daily, without fail, he recited the Prayers.... Once settled down to drink, he would drink for 20 or 30 days at a stretch; once risen, would not drink again for another 20 or 30 days.' His own guardian and tutor, Baba Quli, 'prayed not; he kept no fasts.' Sultan Husain Mirza was, in Babur's eyes, 'a great ruler. He could not perform the Prayers on account of trouble in the joints and kept no fasts.' He could, however, find no equally compelling reason to turn away a glass of wine. 'During the forty years of his rule in Khurasan, there may not have been a single day on which he did not drink after the mid-day Prayer; earlier than that, however, he did not drink.' Nothing much seems to have changed for the next couple of generations. Bayazid Biyat narrates the story of the Qazis of Mandrawal in Afghanistan, who never failed to bring along liquor and 'its accompaniments' as gifts whenever they went to see state officials. And the eminent Maulana Matrabi ('Epicurean Theologian'!) of Samarqand, home of the Indian Mughals, reported to Jahangir with a sense of delight that 'in Samarqand...no one spends a moment without a drink of wine'. He narrated a charming story of a tug of war between the theologians seeking to ban, or at least restrict, drinking during the days of *Nauruz* (Persian New Year) celebrations and the revellers insisting on their cup, with the censors losing out in the end. This polytonal history of the Muslim ruling class in India found space in Abul Fazl's conception of sovereignty.

In imaging Akbar as the personification and symbol of divinity, Abul Fazl was treading a well-beaten path, for the conception of divine sovereign has traces in several early and medieval polities, including Islam.[31] However, in India's medieval centuries, the history of the rulers' claim to

---

31 See for a scintillating treatment of the subject Aziz al-Azmeh, *Muslim Kingship. Power and the Sacred in Muslim, Christian and Pagan Polities*, London/New York, 1997.

divinity is rather sporadic. Sultan Balban (r.1266–86) had claimed the title of *Zil Allah*, Shadow of God, if only to put a veil on his origin as a slave-boy; and Sultan Muhammad bin Tughlaq too had engraved the title on his coins, although there is little other evidence of his use of it, suggesting a lack of emphasis. It was to be revived by Akbar nearly three centuries later. However, in delineating Akbar's divinity, Abul Fazl was not merely repeating an old idiom. In focusing on the divine origin of Akbar, he was, in pursuit of the dichotomy between universal religiosity and denominational religions, seeking distance from the parameters set by Islam. The metaphor of light dominates his conceptualization of divinity, and the Sun in turn dominates the metaphor of light. Divine light permeates Akbar's very being. It is the light of the Sun. 'Nursling of divine light' (*nur parwarda-i izdi*) is his favourite phrase for Akbar, at one place yielding to 'divine light in human form'. At yet another place Akbar's and the Sun's light simultaneously 'shed lustre on the exalted house'.[32] It is hard to excel Abul Fazl's mastery in creating ambiguous and permeable verbal images as the backdrop for the emergence of one solid icon: that of Akbar's universal divinity.

For, indeed, light is celebrated in several cultural milieus. In Islam itself, God is conceived of as an immense light. Thus, when Sultan Balban claimed the status of being God's shadow he took care to place a heavy veil before his face in the court, lest even the shadow of the powerful light blind an onlooker. The term for light is *nur* in Arabic, from where it has travelled into the Persian language. In the imaging of imageless God as *nur*, the term acquires a strong association with Islam. But then Abul Fazl's emphasis on light as the manifestation of divinity incorporates but does not coincide with the Islamic hue. Hence he seeks out a pre-Islamic Persian term for it: *farr* is the preferred term. *Farr-i Izdi*, to be precise, divine light, traceable to the Sasanid imaging of the King in ancient Iran. In Iran itself *Farr-i Izdi* has a long history. The Avesta vision has space for a *Farr-i Kiyani*, in effect a *Farr-i Irani*, to assert the eminence and grandeur of Iran among civilizations; this gave way to *Farr-i Izdi*, celebrated, among other works, in Firdausi's epic, *Shah Nama*. *Zil Allah*, shadow of God, was to come with Islam.

Farr has an ambiguous space for *nur*, but it also has space for the Sun as the chief source of light, along with fire. There are innumerable references in our sources to Akbar's growing devotion to the Sun, especially in the form in which it is worshipped by the Hindus, and reciting its

---

32   *Nur-i Akbar wa nayyar-i azam ba bait al-sharf partaw-i saadat andakht*. Abul Fazl makes a pun twice over in framing this phrase: *Nur-i Akbar* is both the great light (the Sun) and the light of Akbar; *bait al-sharf* is both the sign of the zodiac and the exalted mansion, here a metaphor for Akbar's empire.

1,001 Sanskrit names. The Sun was also a 'powerful symbol in ancient Persian Zoroastrianism and its view of a polarized and dark universe; solar images were affixed to Sasanian emblems of sovereignty such as crowns, sceptres and royal daises.'[33] The Sun and fire in turn bring into *Farr-i Izdi*, divine light, links with several other religio-cultural land-scapes: Hindu, where Sun-worship is a very important feature and fire has a high ritual sanctity; pre-Islamic Egyptian culture, where the Phar-aohs are proclaimed as the children of the Sun, *Amun-Ra*; Ancient Mesopotamia, Zoroastrianism, and, not least, paganism. Then, illumin-ation of the soul through unreserved devotion to God and the *Pir*, the spiritual master, is the central moment of the Sufi doctrine: human beings, born into dark ignorance of the real significance of life, mired in the search for temporal success and therefore unmindful of the hidden real meaning of the universe, grow out of the apparent to the real through the illumined path of spiritual attainment. Abul Fazl admits the influence of the Ishraqi, Eastern, School of Philosophy in Iran, especially the Sufi doctrines of Suhrawardi Maqtul, in interpreting the meanings of illumination. He places repeated emphasis on Akbar as the spiritual guide of his subjects and the relationship between the *Pir* and his disciple, *murid*, was replicated by the Emperor in the creation of a new order of faith, the Din-i Ilahi, in which Abul Fazl was amongst the first, and few, to enrol. His preoccupation with light as the symbol of divinity and with Akbar as its manifestation is so intense that, following his elder brother the poet Faizi's suggestion, he turns sceptical of the felicity of the earlier title for the emperor, *Zil Allah*, shadow of God, for how could one so luminous be a mere shadow, even if it be of God! Akbar indeed was the emanation of God's light, not His shadow. It was Akbar's divinity which marked him out as the real and the true King from the whole chain of preceding rulers, and Abul Fazl constantly plays with the dichotomy of the true and the false, the real and the apparent, the hidden and the perceptible, all terms and dichotomies derived from Sufi discourse.

The depiction of the solar halo behind every Mughal sovereign and prince, in Mughal miniature as a distinctive mark, however, dates from Jahangir onwards. Akbar himself had turned a devotee of the Sun, beginning his day with *Surya Namaskar*, salutation to the rising sun, an important Yogic practice. Abul Fazl also constantly refers to the shine on and between Akbar's eyebrows. This too has Yogic origins where a bright light is supposed to burn constantly between the eyebrows. Sun worship had also been introduced into his harem. Akbar even had the verse in praise of the Sun by the poet Faizi inscribed on the biggest gold coin of

33   Colin Paul Mitchell, *Sir Thomas Roe and the Mughal Empire*, Karachi, 2000: 120.

Figure 3 Aurangzeb in the last year of his life, here depicted as turning his eyes away from the world and immersing himself in the holy task of reading the Quran; yet the accoutrements of royalty, the bejewelled turban, but especially the high-lighted solar halo, also form part of his presence. The common adage of saint in the form of king seems to be the motif. © The British Library (*J.2.2.*).

his reign, weighing about 1,200 grams. Jahangir had adopted Nur al-Din (Light of the Faith) as his name on accession to the throne for two reasons: that Nur had association with the Sun and that Indian sages had ages ago predicted that one Nur al-Din would succeed Akbar. The 46 magnificent illustrations of the *Padshah Nama*, in the Queen's library at Windsor Palace, open with an exquisite representation of the Sun on two pages.[34] Aurangzeb himself is said to have coined the following chronogram of his accession to the throne: *Aftab-i Alamtab*, the world-illuminating Sun, and one superb Mughal miniature depicts him in his old age, the Quran held reverentially in both hands and a very prominent solar halo bringing his profile into relief. The image of the Sun on Mughal standards had become an imperial prerogative. Aurangzeb's son, and his great-grandfather's namesake, Prince Akbar, still remembered the significance attached to *farr* and named his own son Muhammad Faridun Farr.

Akbar's divinity also manifests itself in the association of miraculous powers with his person – his breath or touch could cure ailments: 'Not a day passes but people bring cups of water to him beseeching him to breathe upon it.... A chopped off tongue was thus cured by Akbar's miraculous powers'; springs would sprout forth in the desert with a strike of his stick; long droughts would end as he offered a prayer and rain came pouring down. He could even stop the downpour. Once the Ganga was in flood due to heavy rain. Akbar plunged his elephant into it and 'impossible as it was to cross that murderous river, due to the miraculous personality of His Majesty the swelling ocean gave a passage to that mine of holiness'.[35] Even European travellers did not fail to record the association of miracles with Akbar. Jerome Xavier noted of him thus: 'He works miracles through healing of the sick by means of water in which he washes his feet. Women make vows to him for the restoration of health to their children.' Coryat, however, was a trifle less credulous and made no effort to conceal his scepticism: 'Eckbar Shaugh had learned all kinds of sorcery.' These attributes of thaumaturgy, 'the royal touch' and performance of miracles, are derivatives of folklore. They had also been assimilated into Islam, Christianity and Buddhism, even as all these religious systems expressed strong disapproval of the association of miraculous energies with any human being, other than Christ, Muhammad or the Buddha. There was much that was common between folklore and the Mughal court culture.

---

34 All these Mughal miniatures have been reproduced in Milo C. Beach and Ebba Koch, eds, *King of the World*, London, 1997.
35 Clearly reminds one of Moses. The transformation of the river into an ocean, *bahr*, reinforces the suggestion.

The divinity of sovereignty clearly defied any restraints on its power and authority. Of his several classifications of human beings in different contexts, Abul Fazl divides one of them into three groups: The noblest souls are those whose loyalty to the king, Akbar, is absolute, unquestioning and undemanding, a virtue in itself; placed below them are ones whose display of loyalty is on a par with tangible gain, 'who made a traffic of their service'. The worst never show any sign of loyalty. 'Rebellion', 'rebelliousness' and their synonyms are the most damning language of abuse in medieval court literature; defeating rebels becomes 'a cleansing operation'. For Abul Fazl, the rebellious are not merely the ones who defied imperial authority; even those like Rana Sangram Singh and Mahmud in Bihar, who refused to surrender to Mughal conquering power, were rebels; they defied the divine destiny manifest in history's teleology. Unlike the double-edged Chinese conception of the Mandate of Heaven as the source of the ruler's or dynasty's legitimacy, in which the ruler too is forever on trial before his subjects and signs of the withdrawal of the mandate are set out with considerable clarity, Abul Fazl's normative structure of the sovereign's absolute power is linear rather than rounded, devoid of a countervailing balance. Yet this absolute power is nuanced with a broad and strong vision of the king's responsibility towards his subjects.

The history of legitimation of conquest of territories in India's medieval centuries is not terribly complex. Sultan Mahmud of Ghazni had tactfully combined his love of plunder with religious zeal. Later rulers did not seek justification of conquest except in terms of conquest itself. Zia al-Din Barani, historian and theoretician of the state in the fourteenth century, envisioned both conquest and governance as an exercise of terror by the king; conquest of territories was a manifestation of the king's virility. Babur claimed to have conquered India because 'it belonged to my ancestor', a Turk. Indeed, he repeatedly asserts that he pictured the region as his for this reason and thus ordered his soldiers not to harass the people during their marches, for they were already his subjects, entitled to protection.

For Akbar, however, the reference point of conquest lay in establishing peace, justice, and relieving the subjects of a territory of the oppression of the existing ruler. 'Sympathy for and relief of the oppressed are the attributes of a true king,' observes Abul Fazl, as he narrates Akbar's resolve to conquer Malwa. His arrival there 'opens the gates of justice and benevolence'. Indeed, God sometimes deprives some territories of just rulers, as he did in Malwa, so that 'the truthful sovereigns' conquer these. He, Akbar, annexes Gujarat to throw 'the shadow of justice over the province'; he dreams of imparting repose and justice to the Bengalis; he decides on conquering Bihar and Bengal to rescue the suffering peasantry from oppressive rulers, and his conquest of Kashmir was for removing tyranny. In contrast, for Aurangzeb, the conquest of Hyderabad was legitimized in terms of Islam having been marginalized while Hinduism and Shi'ism were allowed to flourish.

Abul Fazl envisions the sovereign essentially as paterfamilias, even as power is envisaged as absolute. Everything that the ruler does, every gift or *mansab* or reward bestowed by him upon his nobles, Princes or subjects is a favour; nothing is gained by anyone as a matter of right. On the other hand, Abul Fazl binds the ruler with bestowing paternal care to his subjects. 'Subjects are a trust from God' seems to be Abul Fazl's favourite phrase for the king, as also the metaphors of 'shepherd', 'gardener', 'physician'. The 'King as father' motif is of course almost universal and has an ancient history with a vast regional and civilizational spread, from Buddhist to Greco-Roman, ancient Egyptian, Assyrian and biblical. In his portrayal of the relationship between the sovereign and his subjects as emphatically paternalistic, if Abul Fazl was not being original, he was nevertheless effecting a shift of focus in his own context.

Enumeration of the requisite qualities of a ruler have understandably been of central concern to medieval political thought. For Zia al-Din Barani, strong determination to conquer and govern nearly exhausted these qualities; for Babur, good governance implied that the town walls be solid, subjects be thriving, provisions be in store and the treasury be full. But the running thread in Abul Fazl's several discussions of kingship is the composite of 'a paternal love towards his subjects', 'the priceless jewel of justice' and fair play, and observance of 'absolute peace', *sulh kul*, without discrimination; other conditions vary with the context, at times out of step with one another. There is a grander vision to Abul Fazl's conception of sovereignty than enumerating a king's qualities: The 'true' King must understand the 'spirit of the age' (*mizaj-i zamana, mizaj-i ruzgar*).

> Kingship is a gift of God, and until many thousand grand requisites have been gathered together in an individual, the great gift does not emanate from His court. Merely one's lineage, collection of wealth and the assembling of a mob are not enough for this rare dignity.... And on coming to the exalted status if he did not establish absolute peace (*sulh kul*) for all time and did not regard all groups of humanity and all religious sects with the single eye of favour and benevolence, – and not be the mother to some and step-mother to others, – he will not become worthy of the exalted dignity.

Universalism and paternalism, then, constitute 'the spirit of the age' that manifests itself in the attributes of the true King. For him, conquest and governance are more than mundane activity; they are a form of worship of God. Abul Fazl is aware of the conceptual departure he is effecting, for in the 'normal' perception conquest of territories and divine worship are an established dichotomy; but then the 'normal' perception is indicative of the short-sightedness and superficiality of minds that are unable to see the hidden meaning of things. Abul Fazl brings us back here, as he does ever so frequently, to the Sufi counterpositioning of the apparent and the real meanings of phenomena, the real always hidden, revealed only to an elect few, and the superior of the two for its spiritual associations.

The king's absolute power then gets circumscribed by the responsibility to establish absolute peace among his subjects through the practice of non-discrimination, and to bring about tranquillity and prosperity through paternalistic care. The insistence on harmony as the ideological underpinning of the state introduces a bilateral endeavour inasmuch as it is not predicated upon unilateral submission. It also limits the King by setting out his responsibilities towards his subjects, the responsibilities of being paterfamilias. If therefore Abul Fazl demands complete submission of the subjects to the sovereign's command, he also limits the sovereign's discretion by constantly reminding him of his paternalist role. Perhaps the most frequently used pair of terms in Mughal historical literature is 'soldiers and peasantry', whose care redeems the state. Whereas in the *Babur Nama* such care gets recorded as a noble sentiment and the Emperor passes strict instructions to his soldiers to bring no harm to the fields while on the march, and while the state generally did intervene in myriad ways to alleviate climactic suffering of the peasantry, with Abul Fazl it forms the centrepiece of his grand legitimization of divine monarchy by introducing an element of reciprocity into it, an element that survived even as other elements, Islam for one, suffered fluctuating fortunes. Muhammad Baqir Najm-i Sani, a high-ranking noble of Jahangir's reign, in a text in the genre of the Mirror of Princes, titled *Mau'iza-i Jahangiri*, puts it feelingly: 'A just ruler is the refuge to the oppressed and the holder of the hands of the fallen.' If the bazaar gossip lampooned Shah Jahan's assiduously cultivated image of impeccable decorum, unimpeachable dignity and undying love for his wife Mumtaz Mahal, it nevertheless looked upon him and cherished him 'more like a father than a King'.[36] Akbar takes his normative role as the father of his

36   Such is the picture we receive of Shah Jahan from the court chronicles of his reign, such as *Padshah Nama*, *Amal-i Salih* and *Shah Jahan Nama*, besides one of perfect harmony among members of his family. When the evidence of tension nearly overwhelms the portrayal of equanimity, the balance in the picture gets disturbed, although even there the language is usually very muted and storms in interpersonal relations are portrayed as slightly unpleasant gusts of wind. European travellers like François Bernier, Jean-Baptiste

subjects almost literally. 'Had I become wise earlier,' he observes, 'I would have taken no woman from my kingdom into the seraglio, for subjects have the status of one's children.' Indeed, even the royal hunt – apparently for excursion and game – was in reality an exercise in collecting authentic information about the condition of the subjects and to give them free access to the royal ear, assures a text of Shah Jahan's court.

Aurangzeb's dream in the initial stages of his reign was to see an India where Islam held supremacy; he also wished to see a prosperous India without beggars. Upon his accession, an old teacher of his turned up at the court in expectation of rich rewards; instead, Aurangzeb lambasted him for inadequately preparing him for kingly duties. 'There can surely be but one opinion among you learned men', the newly enthroned Emperor thundered, 'as to the obligation imposed upon a sovereign, in seasons of difficulty and danger, to hazard his life, and, if necessary, to die sword in hand in defence of the people committed to his care. And yet this good and considerate man would fain persuade me that the public weal ought to cause me no solicitude; that in devising means to promote it, I should never pass a sleepless night, nor spare a single day from the pursuit of some low and sensual gratification.'

The regret that Aurangzeb ultimately carried into his grave was that he could not bestow as much care on the peasantry as would have redeemed a worthy ruler. Hours before he died, he opened his treasury to pay the soldiers their long-overdue salaries; he would have found it hard to carry this guilt along, too. Bahadur Shah Zafar, the last of the Mughal rulers and a poet of considerable merit in Urdu, the language which had risen from the marketplace to the court, gave expression to his failure as ruler thus:

> I bring no light to anyone's eye
> Nor solace to any heart

In imperial vision justice, prosperity of the subjects and the absence of fear were the objects of governance. The vision of the absence of fear finds representation in several forms: many Mughal miniatures depict

---

Tavernier and Niccolao Manucci, on the other hand, record scandalous goings-on in the court and the harem, in all of which Shah Jahan stood at the centre, stories they had picked up from the bazaar with a degree of relish, for these reinforced their image of 'the other'. Clearly, the court and the bazaar were constructing contrasting images of the Emperor, the imperial family and the high nobility. If the court was reinforcing the distance between 'us' and 'them', between the ruling elite and the subjects, the bazaar was bridging the gap by lampooning the highest in the land. Yet, the one image that touched Tavernier and John Francis Careri most was that Shah Jahan 'reigned less an Emperor over his subjects than as a father of a family over his house and children', Jean-Baptiste Tavernier, *Travels in India*, Eng. tr. V. Ball, ed. William Crooke, vol. I, New Delhi, 1977: 260, and Careri, *Indian Travels of Thevenot and Careri*, S. N. Sen, ed., New Delhi, 1949: 222.

lions and cows or lambs sitting side by side under the imperial throne.[37] There are several recorded instances of emperors going out incognito to assess for themselves the actual conditions in which their subjects lived. Ritual assurance of everyone – young or old, male or female, rich or poor – feeling secure walking around even at night, is repeatedly encountered in court literature. In the paintings, infrequently as the common folk are depicted, they carry an aura of prosperity that reflects how the Emperor would like to see them under his regime. There are innumerable references to compensation from the imperial treasury for damage caused to crops when the army was on the march.

In conceptualizing the ruler's power as absolute, but tempered with justice, paternalistic generosity and the spirit of forgiveness, Abul Fazl was in tune with the subjects' vision. For such was the conception of God, perceived by them in the image of the King with all the paraphernalia of the court, the soldiery, the accountants, even the dancers, in contemporary popular literature. God's power over human beings in this image was absolute; yet he was generous, kind and forgiving. If Abul Fazl had written in the Indian vernaculars, he would have been easily comprehensible to the villagers and townspeople who had heard their saint-poets sing in the language that was their own.

The notion of paterfamilias also finds expression in another form: governance through the metaphor of 'the family', which remains the dominant metaphor. Humayun had been witness to several misdeeds of Qurjah Khan, who, in his opinion, clearly deserved death. The emperor's supporters drew out their swords and one of them placed his sword on the Khan's neck. But the sword was withdrawn on Humayun's instruction, who remarked that the man's beard had grown grey and that he, Humayun, had once spoken of him as father, *pidr*. Akbar had in his childhood learnt to address Bairam Khan as *Baba*, father, and continued to do so even after becoming King. He also so addressed Munim Khan, the next Khan-i Khanan. Jahangir gave the high title of Khan-i Jahan to 'my son', *farzand*, Salabat Khan. Shah Jahan addressed Asaf Khan as *Ammu* (Uncle), 'making him the envied of all'. Aurangzeb too, after his accession to the throne, continued to address Mir Jumla, his indefatigable supporter, as *Baba*, as he did Raja Jai Singh on at least one occasion.

This form of address implicates an interesting nominal inversion of the normative state hierarchy: in the state the Emperor is supreme and

---

37   Ebba Koch attributes the repeated appearance of this motif in Mughal art forms to the influence of the *Royal Polyglot Bible*, published in Antwerp between 1568 and 1572 and brought by the Jesuits to the Mughal court in 1580. The engraving lithographed on the title page reproduced the motif and from then onwards, in Koch's view, it became a running theme for the Mughal Emperors in their search for the portrayal of ideal kingship. See Ebba Koch, *Mughal Art and Imperial Ideology*, New Delhi, 2001.

everyone remains subordinate to him, as his 'slave', *banda*; but in the family hierarchy, *Baba*, the father, stands above the son and it is the son who is subordinate. The most powerful of Mughal emperors engaged in this inversion, in a court where every little gesture and word wore layers of symbolic meanings. In the show of respect to their elders, a quiet recognition of the centrality of the category of the family in state functioning was embedded.

One of the most coveted honorifics in the court was that of *farzand*, son, and the conferring of it by the Emperor on any noble never failed to get into histories. Akbar, Jahangir and other emperors used this term of endearment to signify a close personal bond between them and the recipient – which also raised the latter's status in the eyes of other courtiers. *Koka*, foster-brother, was another indicator of high status in the family and the court. 'A river of milk binds me to Aziz,' Akbar had remarked movingly on his relationship with his *koka*, son of Jiji Anaga. Once a nursing woman, not necessarily from the higher echelons of the court society, had given her milk to a Prince who grew up to be emperor, she became a surrogate mother, *anaga*, for all time, and was treated like one. On two occasions Akbar as Emperor shaved off his head and moustaches as a ritual of mourning for a close relation: on the death of his favourite foster-mother Jiji Anaga, and then following the death of his own mother Mariam Makani. *Koka*, the foster-mother's son, became part of the imperial family, too, and rose high in state hierarchy. Mirza Aziz Koka, son of Jiji Anaga, had, along with Raja Man Singh, risen to the highest rank allowed to a noble in Akbar's reign, below only that of a Prince of the royal blood. He had been awarded the title of Khan-i Azam (the Great Khan) by Akbar. His daughter was married to the emperor's grandson, Salim's son Khusrau. When Khusrau rebelled against his father, Jahangir found the Mirza implicated, and he lost royal favour and his *jagir* – part of the risk of proximity to powers that be. Incidentally, Man Singh too had earned the title of *farzand* (son) from Akbar. Indeed, foster-mothers' husbands (*atakaha*) also climbed high on the ladder of his Majesty's favours, virtually as members of the royal family. Shams al-Din Ataka, Jiji Anaga's husband and Aziz Koka's father, was the empire's *vakil*, highest official, when he was murdered by another *koka* of Akbar, Adham Khan, son of Maham Anaga. Bayazid Biyat records a fascinating conversation between Akbar and his second Khan-i Khanan, Munim Khan. Anxious for reassurance on how he was faring as ruler, the young Emperor enquired of the Khan what people said of him.

May my Emperor live a hundred and twenty years [the Khan replied], people speak very highly of you for killing Adham Khan for the murder of [Shams al-Din] Ataka and Muazzam for the murder of the daughter of Bibi Fatima. They consider it justice, true and proper. His Majesty then remarked that 'he had done other things that were even better; it was strange that people did not speak of those. Or is it that you know of it but keep it to yourself for my sake?' The Khan-i Khanan replied: How was it possible that he knew of something but kept it from his Majesty? [The Emperor] said among the other things that he had mentioned was that he had brought a whole lot of Atakas from Lahore and, like the constellation of the Bear, spread them around in Hindustan allotting to each a jagir in different corners.

Even 'honorary' membership of the imperial family went a long way.

Much later, when Shah Jahan's eldest son Dara Shukoh was on the run, with his brother Aurangzeb's soldiers in hot pursuit, his favourite wife Nadira Begum sought loyalty and support from a Rajput warrior, Raja Sarup Singh, by addressing him as her son, whom she looked upon in place of Sulaiman Shukoh, her real son. 'Then she did a thing never done before in the Mogul's empire – that is to say, she offered him water to drink with which she had washed her breasts, not having milk in them, as a confirmation of her words. He drank with the greatest acceptance and swore he would ever be true and never fail in his duties of a son.' Sanctity of the mother–son relationship would make betrayal unthinkable for anyone, especially for a Rajput who would normatively fling his life away at the altar of the pledged word without a moment's demur. This Rajput, however, lost no time in betraying her in return for some money.

There are several paintings of Jahangir that depict an imaginary meeting with Iranian King Shah Abbas I, in some of which the inscribed legend describes him as *biradaram*, my brother, and he installed a portrait of the Shah in the gallery of paintings of the imperial Mughal family, along with his own, right opposite Humayun's and Akbar's. 'My brother' is the term Jahangir also keeps using for the Shah in his memoirs. After the Shah detached Qandahar from the Mughal empire in 1622, *biradaram* was ruefully dropped from any further reference to him. He was no longer a member of the family; he was just another ruler in the neighbourhood! Muhammad Baqir expresses the equation of the empire and the family in a slightly more picturesque idiom: The empire is like a beloved, beautiful and elegant, and has to be won over and nurtured like a bride, with love.

Considerations of family honour at the court, and imperial levels, also governed a large part of political activity. Indeed, the entire historiography of medieval India, of Mughal India in particular, narrates the events of the court (and therefore of the empire) with the imperial family as its axis, though with the female half slightly in the shade. The normative projection of the imperial family in the court chronicles –

extraordinary, well ordered, generous yet aloof, and of course great patron of the arts – constituted the quintessential characteristics of the state. The basic social unit thus acquired a governing presence at the highest level of the state. In writing the history of one, the historians were simultaneously writing the history of the other. The legitimacy of the state lay in the manifest working of these characteristics; its working would have made sense in every family home.

Mughal court chronicles from the *Akbar Nama* onwards seem to depict the ruler, Princes, the royal family and others in a format: The Emperor is usually spoken of in very grandiose terms, Princes just a little less so; their behaviour is generally marked by equanimity, generosity and dignity. Very rarely, and only when it turns inescapable, interpersonal tensions within the imperial family are opened to the reader's gaze. Thus fathers and sons, brothers, sisters and cousins all live in harmony in the chronicles except when harmony is shattered all too visibly. Embedded in this format is an expression of eternity; the person of the King and the Princes changes, but their conduct, mores, even disposition, are in a large measure standardized and follow the impersonal, normative eternal format of kingship, princehood and so on. The task for the chroniclers was to convey the singularities of each individual among the chief dramatis personae, within the format of the standard, the normative, the eternal.

Paradoxically, this format was laid down by Abul Fazl in the *Akbar Nama*. Paradoxical because Abul Fazl was so obsessed with the personal eminence of Akbar that his entire world view revolved around him. Perhaps for this reason Abul Fazl sought to elevate Akbar to superhuman status. Akbar was not merely a human individual for Abul Fazl, but the personified fulfilment of a divine mission. Akbar thus established a standard, a format for monarchy, to which each person, each monarch had to seek to approximate himself. The subsequent Mughal historians emulate, if never entirely, this aspect of Abul Fazl's formidable, though implicit, straitjacketing of historiography. It is only in an occasional 'informal' work of history, such as Mulla Abd al-Qadir Badauni's *Muntakhab al-Tawarikh*, that the straitjacket is abandoned, and a far more human history emerges. But then Badauni wrote the *Muntakhab* precisely as a reaction to, as a rebuttal of the *Akbar Nama*.

Then there are the travellers' accounts, gathered from the bazaars as much as from court circles, that depict court figures in all their myriad hues. If Abul Fazl created a historiographical format, clearly historians of the Delhi Sultanate could not have written their works within it. The individual figures much more emphatically in the chronicles of the Delhi Sultanate than in the *Akbar Nama* and after – the individual ruler's psyche, disposition, idiosyncrasies, strengths and failings are far more prominent in the narratives of the Sultanate. The chronicles of this period place no emphasis on the eternity of the rule of their masters either.

The diverse elements drawn from varied sources – and not always consciously – are woven by Abul Fazl into a coherent fabric of the state's legitimacy that is sustained above all by 'the intoxicating wine of harmony'. The repeated emphasis on harmony, and the absence of discrimination on the basis of religious or sectarian identities,[38] both acknowledges the history of the state's practice of discrimination and posits a visionary ideal of its eradication, a vision that Akbar during his time as Emperor sought to formulate and realize in a large measure. 'As the world's lord exercises sway over it on the principle of *sulh kul*, absolute peace,' declares Abul Fazl, 'every group of people can live in accordance with its own doctrine without apprehension, and everyone can worship God after his own fashion.' Abul Fazl's passion for harmony turns into an obsession. Harmony is not merely a good policy; it is indeed a form of worship, the best tribute he could pay to a phenomenon. In 'the hideousness of discord and the beauty of concord' Abul Fazl perceives an aesthetic quality. *Sulh kul* is 'a four-squared garden of concord' – a compliment to both the four-cornered Sufi cap that represents the world's entirety and the beauty of the square gardens the Mughals had brought to India.

In many significant ways harmony as social and cultural ethos had been an important aspect of popular religious movements among both the Hindus and the Muslims. movements, known as Bhakti, devotional, and Sufi, mystical, during the fifteenth and sixteenth centuries. If harmony as ethos amounted to a passive 'tolerance' of all religions and sects, in its travel upwards to the level of the state, it was constituted by Akbar and Abul Fazl into an active ideological paradigm. For them, *sulh kul* allowed freedom of worship; there was no space in it for abusing the form of worship of another. 'Mulla Ahmad Thattavi', records Abul Fazl with strong disapproval, 'was a firm adherent of the Imami [Shia] doctrine and had a long tongue [i.e. constantly talked of it], continually bringing forth discourse about Sunnis and Shias. Given to despicable speech, he hit the lowest depth.'

Deeply immersed in the notion of universalism and harmony is the vision of a social order. The very minutely detailed rules and regulations

---

38   The absence of discrimination as state policy is traced back to the *Yasa-i Chingizi*, the edicts of Chingiz Khan, by Alauddin Ata Juwaini. The *Yasa* required the ruler 'to consider all sects as one and not to distinguish one from another'. It was thus that Chingiz Khan 'eschewed bigotry and preference of one faith over another, placing some above others', Juwaini, *Tarikh-i Jahangusha*, vol. I,, ed. Mirza Muhammad, London, 1912: 18–19, cited in Iqtidar Alam Khan, 'Akbar's Personality traits and World Outlook – A Critical Reappraisal', in Irfan Habib, ed., *Akbar and His Age*, New Delhi, 1997: 81.

of etiquette which governed court proceedings point to an obsessive preoccupation with order, for the court was the microcosmic encapsulation of society, a theme to which we turn in the next chapter. The sovereign's primary responsibility appears to have been the prevention of upheavals in society. In Abul Fazl's formulation, 'If the majesty of royalty did not exist, how would various disturbances subside?', the intense urgency is hard to miss. Among the principles of governance enunciated at one of several places, 'having regard to the ranks of mankind and the preservation of their honour' is juxtaposed to 'the observing of absolute peace'. Indeed, so pervasive is the consciousness of hierarchy that order of precedence is established even for the imperial horses and, when a cheetah leapt a distance of 25 yards, Akbar raised his *mansab* and ordered that a drum be beaten ahead of the animal, a rare privilege even for high *mansabdars*.

But the order is not based on closure. Indeed, the repeated emphasis on merit, that is personal rather than hereditary or owing to social position, or owing for that matter to recommendation, is surprising in the medieval context, attuned as we are to looking at personal merit as entirely a modern phenomenon. 'May merit have an open market,' Abul Fazl observes. He is particularly partial to the use of the market as a metaphor in virtually every kind of context. The insistence on merit as an inherently individual quality and the metaphor of the market, where each commodity normatively establishes its value according to its innate worth, is an interesting contrast to Zia Barani, for whom merit is exclusive to high status (or the high born, as he designates them) and any sign of merit in a low-born person can only be a deception. 'His Majesty', says Abul Fazl of Akbar, 'respected merit, not recommendation', nor genealogy, for he 'encourages everything which is excellent and knows the value of talent, honours people of various classes with appointments in the ranks of the army, and raises them from the position of a common soldier to the dignity of a grandee.' Akbar himself advised his son Danial: 'Judge the nobility of any one's being and great lineage from the essence of his merit, and not from the pedigree of his ancestors or greatness of the seed.'

But a look at the network of relationship among the Mughal nobles of various ranks would forcefully point to a very high proportion originating in a limited number of families.[39] Indeed, a cherished privilege came

39 Several works comprising brief biographies of Mughal nobles were compiled in Mughal India. Shah Nawaz Khan's three-volume *Maasir al-Umra* is the most detailed among them, finished in about 1780. For a modern version, see M. Athar Ali, *The Apparatus of Empire: Awards of Ranks, Offices and Titles to the Mughal Nobility, 1574–1658*, New Delhi, 1985.

to be attached to being a *khanazad*, a 'house-born'. The social order then was structured along the principle of hierarchy, but with space and flexibility for meritorious individuals, devoid of inherited status. The history of the Mughal ruling class has numerous examples of individuals with nondescript origins making it to high ranks.

Norbert Elias has thoughtfully reminded us that awe-inspiring cultural grandeur in any medieval regime has more than an aesthetic quality to it; it is, in the absence of modern institutional structures, a source of the regime's legitimacy. A similar insight was implied in Abul Fazl's statement: 'when the veil of reverence had been torn, they became rebellious'. Awe, reverence, inspires compliance as long as it lasts. Multifarious experimentation and creativity in the sphere of culture on a grand scale was one of the most significant and durable moments of Mughal history in India, the term Mughal virtually becoming synonymous with cultural grandeur. Embedded in the awesome grandeur of scale and aesthetic quality is the assumption of eternity of the regime. 'As long as the sun and the moon last' was a standard phrase in Mughal documents alienating lands in charity that signified the assumption of the regime's durability. The assumption of eternity was also central to the vision that became manifest in the great monuments – forts, mosques and tombs. They were built, as it were, to last forever. The Mughals generally, and Akbar ever more than others, were saturated with a sense of history, for the number of histories commissioned, and the preparations made for these during the Mughal period far exceed those in any other span of political time in India's pre-colonial past. Abul Fazl, as the great master of the craft, deliberately focused on change in a way that took him to the very origin of humanity, Adam himself. Yet all history, all change, came to a dead stop as its teleological mission reached fulfilment, i.e. the reign of Akbar. After Akbar there was eternity.

This structure of legitimacy was not devoid of some space for variation of individual emphasis, temper and choice. The coincidence between state, history and the person of the Emperor was close in most medieval polities, as it was in the Mughal state. Had the Mughal rulers heard of Louis XIV's exclamation, '*l'Etat, c'est moi!*', they wouldn't have needed to search for its meaning. And so when Francis William Buckler expatiates on the notion that the person of the Mughal Emperor filled the entire space of the empire, he was drawing upon the near universality of the notion, although he seemed to project it as specific to the Mughals. Indeed, Mughals often perceived themselves as conquerors of the world, the titles they gave themselves on accession spoke of this grandiose presumption: Jahangir (capturer of the world), Shah Jahan (king of the world), Alamgir (same as Jahangir). In the traveller Careri's perception, Aurangzeb believed that he was lord of three-quarters of the world and emphasized it symbolically. 'For this reason' observes Careri acutely, 'he carry'd as his peculiar Ensign a Golden-Globe, and had it in his Seal; and always tore off one corner of the Paper he wrote on, to express that the fourth part of the World was not his.' Even a small, almost pitiable figure in the pantheon of the Mughal emperors, Shah Alam II, who had been blinded and rendered a virtual pensioner of the East India Company, would still style himself as the King of the world.

Within the empire, the ruler adopted several modes to fill the space with his presence. Travelling to many parts of his dominion accompanied by the court's accoutrements was one. Wherever the Emperor went his entire court and its layout and rituals, palace, army, treasury and clerks were replicated in exact details, as if to emphasize that he was present everywhere. The notion of a moving rather than a fixed capital is thus nearer the Mughal reality. If he sent out a *farman* to any part of the empire, the recipient was required to accord it ritual respect and obeisance as if he were receiving it at the court. The *farman* was an extension of His Majesty in person. The robe of honour, granted to several persons almost every day for one reason or another, was cherished because the Emperor had touched it with his hand or his back; the honour of receiving it rose manifold if he had actually worn it. If the *Shah Jahan Nama* observes that the emperor's personal glory 'filled the palace and the realm', Bernier noted of the same ruler that even his illness filled his dominions.

This allowed considerable space for the play of individual idiosyncrasies. A subtle movement of energy and shifts of personal predilections were forever at play: from Babur's love of things sensual and his delight at being perceived as a recluse, *qalandar*, one unattached to worldly possessions, to Akbar's experimentation with constructing a mighty empire based on absolute peace, with clearly laid-down principles and rules of governance, and his joy at being projected by Abul Fazl as an ascetic rather than a king, to Aurangzeb's Islamic puritanism that led him to ban both music and history-writing from his court.

But then legitimacy is not quite legitimate unless it is so perceived by the eyes of the subjects. Is there a way of locating the subjects' response to the elaborate construction of legitimacy? Medieval societies did not record subjects' voices as carefully as they did the rulers', and the handicap of this silence is therefore severe. We do however have some suggestive genres of evidence which enable us to faintly hear those ignored voices: popular religious literature, folktales and bazaar gossip.

In popular religious literature, the Bhakti literature, already briefly encountered above, known for its emphasis on each one's personal devotion to God, who too is personalized, kingship is socialized by visualizing God in the king's image: powerful but kind. This is also a literature of protest against social inequities such as caste, and oppression unleashed by state's officials, usually petty ones in the village. Yet their conception of state and the social order is one in which each one adheres to the normative bounds, *maryada*. The ideal King is immensely powerful and prevents the transgression of these bounds by anyone, above all by himself. It is thus that in the second half of the sixteenth century, contemporaneously with Akbar's reign, utopia was projected on to the mythical past when the legendary Ram suffered great privation in order to conform to the call of social obligations, and in the end establish his kingdom, *Ram rajya*, where each one would equally adhere to his/her status obligations. It was a conception that Abul Fazl would have found hard to quarrel with.

Of folk tales, the most widely circulated ones were Akbar-Birbal stories. Birbal was a courtier of the emperor, honoured with the high title of 'Raja', having risen from being a rank commoner; hence, easy folk identification with him. His reputation for quick wit, repartee and simple solutions to apparently tough problems is not without historical grounding; it was thus easy to transform him in these tales into the archetypal jester who outwits the king, the priest and all the high, the mighty and the intelligent in the end.[40] Birbal is always a friendly adversary of Akbar in a contest of wits; it is the fictitious Mulla-do-piaza – a 'two-onion-theologian', clearly a fantasy name – who is the foe and whom he takes particular delight in outwitting. Going by the curses and abuses historian Mulla Abd al-Qadir Badauni loads on Birbal even after his death, one might suspect that he, the Mulla, was perhaps the model for the fictitious character. The stories seek to reproduce a simplified enactment of Akbar's court ambience in which Akbar and Birbal are on one side and the orthodox Mulla on the other, even as Birbal the commoner frequently gets the better of Akbar the king, an essential component of folktales. There is an owning of Akbar as a friend, one you could make fun of.

There is owning of Akbar in other modes too. In Rajasthani literature he is celebrated as the incarnation of Ram and Krishna, Hindu mythological gods, and also referred to as Lakshmana, Ram's brother, and Arjuna, a central figure in the Hindu epic, the *Mahabharata*. Narottam, a medieval Rajasthani poet, cannot stop admiring him as an incarnation of Partha, Arjuna, and even places him in the age gone by, the *dwapar* age, that preceded the current age in the four-age cyclic rhythm of the

40   C. M. Naim has done some path-breaking research on the theme of Akbar-Birbal stories, the element of historicity in them and their significance, in 'Popular Jokes and Political History: The Case of Akbar, Birbal and Mulla Do-Piyaza', *The Economic and Political Weekly*, 17 June 1995: 1456–64.

Hindu concept of *yuga*. The poet declares that Akbar 'loves the Hindus and has a feeling of alienation towards the Turks (Muslims); he does not feel close to them'. He concludes with vehemence that 'Akbar's is a Hindu Raj. Who will call it Muslim Raj?' The Jains of Gujarat too look upon him with great courtesy and intimacy.[41]

There is also an owning of several other Mughal emperors. Manucci narrates a story that had probably been in circulation in the bazaars nearly a century and a half before he recorded it. Babur had been ruling with the sage counsel of one Rangil Das and the empire flourished. The counsellor's rise in the emperor's estimate led to jealousy in other nobles' hearts, a conspiracy and his dismissal. Devoid of good advice, Babur's rule began to flounder. Babur then realized his error, but, unaware of Rangil Das's whereabouts, he set up an impossible task, knowing that his former counsellor alone would find a solution. So it came to be; Babur located and reinstated his man and the empire began to flourish again.

Manucci swears in his account that every minute bit of information he has recorded has been thoroughly screened for its verity; presumably this story too was a veritable historical fact for him. But, besides the total absence of other evidence bearing out any part of the story, it is in any case in the classic genre of folk tales where the King himself is a knave but rules well with the help of good counsel; then there is jealousy, dismissal, loss of contact, recovery of the counsellor through the setting up of an impossible task, and so on. However, even as Babur perceives and projects himself in the *Babur Nama* as the conqueror of India, as indeed do all court chronicles and official and unofficial histories, it is precisely the image of Babur as conqueror that is absent in this tale. The fact that Rangil Das is a clearly Hindu name but no mention is made of this points to the easy acceptance of Babur's rule, and gives it indigenous roots in folk vision quietly, unobtrusively.

---

41 B. L. Bhadani, 'The Profile of Akbar in Contemporary Rajasthani Literature', *Social Scientist*, 20, 9–10, 1992: 46–53, and Shirin Mehta, 'Akbar as Reflected in Contemporary Jain Literature in Gujarat', ibid.: 54–60. Indeed, the Mughal Emperor as such often came to be equated in Rajput society with Ram. See Norman P. Ziegler's stimulating essay, 'Some Notes on Rajput Loyalties During the Mughal Period', in John F. Richards, ed., *Kingship and Authority in South Asia*, Madison, 1978: 278. Ziegler cites the impeccable authority of the seventeenth-century bard of Rajasthan, Nainsi, for this statement. Kum Kum Sangari has very sensitively dealt with the theme in 'Tracing Akbar: Hagiographies, Popular Narrative, Traditions and the Subject of Conversion', in Neera Chandoke, ed., *Mapping Histories: Essays Presented to Ravinder Kumar*, New Delhi, 2000: 61–103. See also Narottam, *Man Charit Raso*, cited in V. S. Bhatnagar, 'The Impact of Akbar's Religious Policy as reflected in the Literary and Archival Sources', Manohar Singh Ranawat, ed., *Princely Historian*, Commemoration volume of Maharajkumar Dr Raghubir Sinh, Jaipur, 1994: 468.

Tales of this and of many other sorts abounded in the villages, transmitted orally through generations, and in the town bazaars from where European travellers picked them up and recorded them, often as historical facts. Manucci's account in particular is teeming with stories, all with a clear folk tale flavour, about nearly all great Mughals except Aurangzeb. In most of the tales, the ruler turns out to be either a knave or a Solomon-like dispenser of justice. Often, his personal foibles and idiosyncrasies, invariably amusing, and his attributes of a commoner rather than of a King are the high points of the stories. The bazaar gossip especially delighted in puncturing the pretensions of the high and the mighty, including the king.

Two alternative world views seem to be in contest here: the court histories portrayed the emperor, the royal family and high nobles as governed by perfect decorum and correctness, even if at times it was infringed and earned severe punishment. This image created a very long distance between the elites and the subjects, who were thus implicitly characterized as ordinary, even stupid, and unfamiliar with the finesse of high culture. Folk tales and bazaar gossip, on the other hand, inverted the imagery and revelled in the stupidities and scandals of the elites. The chroniclers' superhuman figures thus get humanized in the bazaar and the village *chaupal*,[42] and the distance between the stereotypes of human beings at the court and the village minimized. 'As human beings they are also like us, even though they be the rulers and we the subjects,' the *chaupal* and the bazaar seemed to be saying. Social acceptance, too, was implied in the minimizing of the distance.

Only when the court brought affairs to the brink by foregrounding any one element of the polity, resulting in exclusion rather than inclusion of the others, did the reaction in the bazaar also verge on rejection. Akbar's experimentation with a state informed by the ideology of universal paternalism, rather than the conquering zeal of a religion, cohered well with the social ethos. Aurangzeb's reference point increasingly turned to Islam, which was to destroy that coherence; the resultant tensions rent it apart. The contrast is one of the most significant chapters, not merely in the political history of the Mughal empire, but in social history as well. By its very definition, the foregrounding of Islam could not be the agency of achieving coherence in a multi-religious society, with a multi-religious court, for it implied subjugation, even humiliation, of the non-Muslims. Significantly, there are remarkably few folktales and gossip centred on Aurangzeb. On the other hand, it is during his regime that François Bernier records the growth of a Hindu tradition that envisioned liber-

---

42   A kind of community centre in the village where menfolk gather after the day's work to exchange stories, gossip and information.

ation from Muslim tyranny; and Manucci for once records what he specifically refers to as 'a very well-known tale' that 'after the death of King Aurangzeb the line of Taimur-i-lang's descendants will cease to rule' and narrates 'a fable': Timur as a camel-herd encounters a *faqir*, a Muslim renouncer, who promises him an empire in return for food. Timur obtains food for him and the *faqir* then covers him with his cloak and spanks his posterior with his hand. After eleven strokes, Timur throws off the cloak. The *faqir* remarks that if he had taken more strokes, his dynasty would have lasted longer, but now its rule would cease with the eleventh descendant. Aurangzeb was that eleventh descendant. The 'fable' was clearly concocted near or after Aurangzeb's death and interestingly both the giving and taking away of the empire to Timur and his 11 descendants was done by a Muslim *faqir*, even as the tale was 'commonly said by all the Hindus'.

With the very strong feeling of belonging to India, a sense of 'conquest' still remained in imperial Mughal consciousness. If Babur always had it in his heart 'to possess Hindustan' and had claimed the territory from Ibrahim Lodi as his ancestral property, Jahangir has no hesitation in describing his great-grandfather's descent on India as 'invasion'. The notion of Islam's conquest of India, common enough in much of medieval Indian historiography, does not entirely escape even the careful choice of words by Abul Fazl: 'Since the first appearance of Islam, when great rulers conquered India' is his preamble to the narration of the conquest of Garha Katanga in central India by Akbar. In the entire text of the *Akbar Nama* and the *Ain-i Akbari*, Abul Fazl meticulously avoids virtually any references to Muhammad or to any part of the history or jargon of Islam, and lets a momentous event like the completion of the first millennium of Islam pass without notice; yet, in the draft of Akbar's letter to the ruler of Turan, prepared by him, appeal is made unambiguously to the recipient's Islamic sentiment:

> Places and lands, even the boundaries of which, from the time of the rise of the sun of Islam till the present moment, had not been trod by the horse-hoofs of world-conquering Princes and where the swords of obedience-enforcing emperors had never flashed, have [now] become the dwelling-places and lands of the faithful. And the churches and places of worship of the infidels and heretics (lit. deserters, *khazlan*) have turned into mosques and holy shrines for the possessors of true knowledge. Allah be praised!

The expediency of seeking help from Abdullah and thus speaking to him in the language he would appreciate had priority over the making of a philosophical statement. However, in his letter to Shah Abbas of Iran, felicitating him on his accession to the throne, Akbar allows himself full play on the concept of *sulh kul*.

The sentiment of looking back at central Asia as 'our ancestral lands' never quite receded from the hearts of the Mughal emperors. Babur, as a first-generation migrant from central Asia, was understandably nostalgic about any reminder of 'home'. In the midst of the march for a battle, the sight of 'the wonderfully delicate melon' from Nasukh sends him into raptures, and he finds the mountains of Farghana and Mughulistan 'beyond comparison'. In 1528–9, virtually the last year of his life, he was still hoping to return to 'those parts' and at this emotional juncture a melon was brought to him. 'To cut it and eat it affected me strangely; I was all tears.' Akbar too affirms his intention to conquer 'ancestral territory' and include it in his empire, and wished to appoint Prince Salim to take charge of the campaign. The Prince, however, had other things on his mind. It was only when he became Emperor that he remembered that 'the conquest of Transoxiana was always in the pure mind of my revered father', and, since this did not come about owing to varied circumstances, Jahangir himself was keen to start on the mission to recover 'my hereditary territories'. On the ground, however, nothing happened. A while later we can still hear him having made up 'my exalted mind to the conquest of Mawra an Nahr (Transoxiana) which was the hereditary kingdom of my ancestors' by leaving one of his sons to look after India. Nothing happened this time either. The adjective 'our ancestral lands' for Balkh, Badakhshan, Khurasan, Kabul and Herat continues to recur in later reigns of Shah Jahan and Aurangzeb, and Turkish, along with other languages, continued to be spoken within the family until around the mid-eighteenth century. Mostly, however, nostalgia found expression in attempts to conquer some of those lands, rather than in returning to them or even developing anything more than formal diplomatic contacts with their rulers.

There was a strong sense of identification with India, too, from the second Emperor onwards. Babur had conquered India and established his empire here as a second option, forced out of his own homeland by political adversaries, often his close relatives. When Humayun, exiled from India, was the guest of the Shah of Iran at a dinner in Khurasan, arranged in an enclosure of tents put up in the Indian fashion, the Shah's sister Sultanam asked Hamida Banu, Humayun's young wife, whether India too had colourful umbrellas, *chatr*, and cupolas, *taq*, like the ones on display there. The young lady seems to have been touched to the quick and, even though she was a guest at the dinner, responded with a trace of irritation: 'If Khurasan is equal to two grains, *dang*, India is equal to four. Whatever one can find in two grains is bound to be better in four.' The *Ain-i Akbari* makes several assertions attesting to India's superiority over Iran and sometimes Turan: in the amount of revenues collected in the three realms, the refining of bullion, goldsmithy, in the superiority of

Indian camels to those of Iran, and of the parity and even superiority of Indian horses to the ones from the Arab lands. The romance of Indian monsoons becomes an obsession even with dry-as-dust historians like Abul Fazl, and the Sanskrit word for it, *vrishtikal*, becomes part of the common literary vocabulary, colloqialized as *bishkal*. For Faizi, India was a land of love par excellence, and for Badauni, it was 'a bride'. When the great Persian poet Hafiz Shirazi ran down India in favour of Iran, in a verse, Mushfiqi Bukhari, poet in Akbar's court, responded sharply by praising Indian flora and fauna in his verse. Saib, the Persian poet, having migrated to India, finds everything Indian far higher in calibre than anything of renown in Iraq (at times used as synonym for Iran).[43]

> More than everything that is renowned in the country of Iraq
> The satiated land of Hind has turned Saib into its great admirer

and again

> How do I refrain from praising Hind, for even its dark ash
> Has wrapped the flame of my renown in the garment of grace

Jahangir thought Indian flowers were the best in the world and talks fondly of the beauty of red lotuses, the poetry and music that is centred on them and Indians' attachment to these flowers, including that of the legendary musician Miyan Tan Sen. Nadira Begum, wife of Dara Shu-koh, keeping him company in his darkest days after his defeat and relentless pursuit by Aurangzeb in the War of Succession, died of exhaus-tion on the north-western outskirts of India's borders. Her last plea to her husband was to bury her body in the soil of her native Hindustan. Dara had in his married life ignored several of his wife's pleas, but he could not do so to her dying wish and, in one version, saw to the burial in Lahore, even as he took grave personal risks in doing so.

Viewed from the foot of the imperial throne, the conquest of territories within India was tantamount to the spreading of justice and tranquillity in those lands. There was too a strong sense of the civilizing mission, especially in Akbar. Abul Fazl describes every region subjugated by the Emperor as accomplishment of a civilizing endeavour, although the terms he used for it are varied. 'The lofty genius was perpetually attending to the inhabiting of countries, the cultivation of the hearts and the giving of justice to the oppressed.' 'Those savages of the desert of self-adornment' – officers of the Gujarat army and administration – were left in the care of Hakim Ain al-Mulk, presumably to receive lessons in civilization.

---

43   I am extremely grateful to Dr Yunus Jaffrey for bringing these verses to my notice.

Man Singh was commissioned 'to chastise the Tarikis' (Afghan rebels on the north-west frontier); the commission was carried out and 'Zabulistan was rehabilitated (*abadi paziraft*)', i.e. was civilized. Kashmir too was civilized thus, as was the *suba*, province, of Allahabad. At one stage Akbar felt concerned about civilizing the Europeans too, described by Abul Fazl as 'an assemblage of savages' (*guruh-i wahshi*), and made enquiries about the state of their customs, although he seems to have left it at that. Shah Jahan's chronicler, Inayat Khan, also records the emperor's concern about the poverty of civilized life in Kashmir and the need to bring to the region high levels of 'the fragrance of learning'. Thanks to the Mughal conquest, 'by intercourse with the people in the royal camp . . . they have now for the most part become conversant with the Persian language and can even boast of talented scholars, poets, calligraphers and musicians in abundance'.

Down the line, Emperor Shah Alam II did what his more eminent predecessors would have found abhorrent: wrote raucously ribald poetry about banter between a father and the mother-in-law of his offspring, both taken as stereotypes. *Nadirat-i Shahi* is not great poetry, but it is fun poetry. More importantly, it is poetry of the very Indian earth, very earthy, teeming with sexual innuendoes. And if Bahadur Shah Zafar, the last of the Mughal emperors, had no history of conquest and governance, he is yet an eminent figure as poet of the Urdu language.

Interestingly, even as the metaphor of 'the bride', to be caressed and loved, is on rare occasions used for territories open to conquest and governance,[44] there is no instance of a religious identification of 'the bride' as 'the other' in court literature. Nowhere is the territory referred to as the Hindu bride to be conquered and subjugated by the virile Muslim warrior.

However, more often than territory, the association of honour with women stands on firmer ground. Essentially perceived as a chivalrous attribute – even when a female like Rani Durga Vati of Garha Katanga in the tribal areas of Madhya Pradesh propounded the notion in preferring to die fighting Akbar's forces than surrendering[45] – among its many associations was the chastity of the female body, constructed entirely in

44   Baqir, *Mau'iza-i Jahangiri*, ed. Sajida Alvi, New York, 1989: 151: 'Fortunate rulers bring within the embrace of fulfillment their desire for the virgin of dominion.'
45   *AN*, II: 212. Jaswant Singh, among the most eminent of Shah Jahan's and Aurangzeb's nobles, fought valiantly against the combined forces of Murad and Aurangzeb during the War of Succession among Shah Jahan's four sons and was forced to retreat. On hearing this, his chief Queen closed the gates of the fort and would not let the Raja enter his home. Until the very end, she never forgave him for the loss of honour on the battlefield. Manucci, I (1907), 1981; 249–50; also Bernier, *Travels in the Mogul Empire*, Eng. tr. Archibald Constable, New Delhi, 1972 (first pub. 1891): 40–1, for essentially the same story.

sexual terms. Men would consider it of no consequence to kill their womenfolk with their own hands rather than let them fall in the hands of their foe, whether Hindu or Muslim. Following his second and final defeat at Kannauj at the hands of his arch rival Sher Khan, in 1540, Humayun confessed to his brother Hindal: 'In the earlier disturbance, Aqiqa Bibi [his daughter] had disappeared and I suffered from everlasting regret why I had not killed her myself' [lest she fall into the enemy's hands], a sentiment that his brother entirely endorsed. Raja Puran Mal of Kalinjar, when surrounded by Sher Khan, beheaded his 'beloved' wife Ratnavali, 'who composed beautiful verses in Hindi', and asked his followers to do the same to their women. Adham Khan, Akbar's foster-brother and general, vanquished Baz Bahadur, Muslim ruler of Malwa and 'took possession of all his wealth and property, his dancing girls, concubines and female slaves and sent people to search for Rupmati', his Hindu wife. But Rupmati poisoned herself out of love and fidelity for Baz Bahadur, and 'carried her honour to the hidden chamber of annihilation'. In Shah Jahan's time, one of his highest nobles, Khan-i Jahan Lodi, rebelled and was hotly pursued. 'Due to fierce pride', notes *Shah Jahan Nama*, 'the desperate Afghans put to the sword many of their own women and children and other female relatives and maid servants, although others of them were captured.'

Honour embodied in women's chastity stood above any other identity or value. Rustam was a *mansabdar* of 500 in Shah Jahan's reign. His aunt had been 'taken into Shah Jahan's *harem*', an ambiguous phrase sometimes used for marriage, at others for the status of a concubine or a mere inmate. To vindicate *his* 'honour', Rustam killed the lady. Annoyed at the death of a beautiful woman and the challenge to his own discretion, the Emperor ordered Rustam's execution. A while later, he had second thoughts and pardoned the offender, adding another 200 to his *mansab*.

Even as these desperate acts reflected the chivalrous values of first investing the female body with the notion of honour and then assuming the role of its defenders, they also pointed to the male ego that stood over and above religious and sectarian identities.

In the end, with all the institutional safeguards for stability and durability of the empire, it was patronage on the part of the Emperor and loyalty on that of the nobles that became the cornerstone of the empire's functioning. The 'patronage and loyalty' syndrome was strong and fragile at the same time: strong enough to dispel any challenge to the rule of the Mughal dynasty over two long centuries; fragile enough to be filled with tension and rebellions by the most powerful nobles against their masters, and of course by Princes against their emperor-fathers. From Humayun's time onwards, Mughal history was witness to great turbulence within the ruling class, whether in the form of rebellious brothers, sons or high nobles. Indeed, it is hard to encounter an individual at the higher strata of the class of *amirs*, nobles, immune to insecurities of fortune even under the same monarch and as a near certainty under his successor; it is equally hard to come across one who had not been 'forgiven' by the Emperor and his privileges not restored. 'Accepting excuses and forgiving faults' becomes almost an ideological anchor of the Mughal state, as an aspect of its moderation. In return, the ruler expected loyalty.

Even as the institutional structure of power, authority and governance evolved in the empire, allowing a fair degree of assurance of continuing fortune to old 'servants' in the midst of its somewhat wide swings, and even as it allowed entry to diverse new elements, its reliance on the individual loyalty of each *mansabdar* to the person sitting on the throne as much as to the throne itself introduced grave infirmities. Akbar sought to command personal loyalty through the medium of the Din-i Ilahi; all its regulations reinforced the notion of unqualified loyalty to him, which should override all other identities and solidarities. If loyalty became the cornerstone of the system, patronage and punishment were the only mode of ensuring it. Its durability was at best transient and its fragility all too evident. The highest placed nobles – through whose agency conquest and governance were mediated and the network of loyalty knit – were also the most vulnerable.

Loyalty became exceedingly fluid when Princes or high nobles rebelled against the rulers; a realignment and redefinition of loyalty gained momentum immediately. And, again, when the revolt either succeeded or failed, old loyalties and oaths became problematic. Relations had to be re-established, but with a new element of suspicion on both sides. Neither patronage, nor loyalty, nor of course the structure of authority could eliminate those tense moments, the unforeseen turns that in one fell swoop could bring the high and mighty crashing down, from which some rose again, and others became part of the debris. There were virtually no guarantees in life. Since loyalty was constructed as the binding thread that was entirely personal between the King and his 'servants', the slightest tension in the bond could cast doubt on the person's loyalty itself, demonstrating its fragility. By the same logic, the doubt in turn liberated the 'servant' from the bond and in his eyes at least legitimized his rebellion.

Nothing brought the infirmities of the system to the surface as much as the dramatic events of the War of Succession between 1656 and 1658 among Shah Jahan's four sons. It is hard to excel the tragic denouement of these events even in imagination. In those traumatic months almost everything went topsy-turvy: loyalties changed, memories of past obligations lapsed, treachery enacted without the slightest demur, the solemnly pledged word on the Quran by the most orthodox Muslim, Aurangzeb, violated, imperial commands ignored, confidences betrayed. Not an element of tragic drama of the highest calibre was missing.

Yet, once the trauma was over, and the dramatis personae had changed roles, the structure was re-established, and a semblance of order was restored. So too with the family as a source of stability, as well as its fragility. If the continuing existence of the Mughal family was the surest guarantee of the empire's durability, and was the predominant metaphor for the Mughal court society, it is the imperial family that also chiefly disrupted its smooth functioning. Akbar was content with carving out a magnificent empire and a court order conforming to his grand vision; but it was his sons who brought him the tragic realization of the fragility of filial bonds and the need for the ruler to be on constant vigil. Humayun was forever troubled by his three brothers for as long as he sat on the throne. From Akbar on, each Emperor had to face various kinds of challenges and threats from their sons. Yet, again and again, the Emperors and their sons reverted to filial ties as the theatre of possible solutions. Even as Aurangzeb had reigned for 48 of his 50 years, he still felt threatened by his once favourite but later rebellious son Akbar, who had found shelter in Iran; the Emperor sought to resolve the tension through a demonstrative paternal affection.

It is this intersection between order and chaos, mutually generative, that comprises the totality of Mughal history.

2
Etiquette and Empire

In a social milieu where status rather than wealth was the ruling concern, etiquette reflected and reinforced hierarchies. In reality, wealth and status were perhaps not as neatly counterposed as they are in Norbert Elias' magnificent conceptual structure, where he gives primacy to status in the French court and society in the age of Louis XIV; nor indeed are they as neatly dichotomous today, in an age that is fiercely driven by the urge for accumulation of wealth. Yet the distinction helps us identify the paradigmatic presence – the organizing principle that demarcates two epochs of human civilization, the medieval and the modern.

'Loss of wealth', observed Muhammad Baqir, Jahangir's noble, 'is of little concern.' Indeed, 'the door of wealth never opens without bringing countless suffering in its train.' This attitude of indifference towards wealth demarcates the medieval from the modern.

Generosity and distribution of largesse to all and sundry seems to have been a tradition with the Mughal family. Umar Shaikh, Babur's father, is reported by him to have recovered all the goods of a place with a hundred households, which had been overrun by snow, and, tracing their heirs in Khurasan and Samarqand, returned everything to them, 'though he was himself in great want'. On another occasion, he retrieved a good booty from the Uzbegs, who were returning from a raid near Samarqand, but he gave away the entire booty to its original owners 'without coveting a thing for himself'. Babur himself revelled in the epithet of *qalandar*, renouncer, for himself. He distributed to his soldiers and men, besides princes and queens, whatever treasures he captured after each victory; this indeed became such a routine that his daughter Gulbadan says, matter-of-factly after the landmark battle at Panipat: 'The treasures of five kings fell into his hands and he gave these away.' The culture of giving was not confined to the ruler alone and after Panipat, along with Babur, 'Humayun, Mirzas [generally Princes], Sultans [Princes of the royal blood], and *umra* [grandees] distributed from the treasures.' Humayun too was known to have distributed the presents he received from his grandees and courtiers. Abul Fazl of course never tires of narrating stories of Akbar's largesse, but even Abdul Qadir Badauni, no admirer of the Emperor, records many such instances. On one occasion, Akbar is reported to have given away a gold piece each to 100,000 poor men and women, assembled for the purpose in his polo field. In the mêlée some 80 persons were crushed to death and purses full of gold *ashrafis* and coins fell from the girdles of some of the women. 'This affair caused suspicion to arise as to all the poor. An order was issued that in the future just a few persons should be assembled, but he soon laid aside this rule.' A poet who recited a panegyric for Akbar was rewarded with a massive sum of 200,000 *tankas*, predecessor of the rupee.

The culture of largesse was clearly pervasive and seems to have defined courtly finesse. In a moving turn of phrase, Abul Fazl writes of his brother, the poet Faizi: He looked upon wealth as a means of engendering poverty. Implicit in it is the Sufi philosophical assumption that wealth and spiritual attainments stood in opposition to each other. The great *amir* Abd al-Rahim Khan-i Khanan (the chief khan), of Akbar's and Jahangir's reigns, was renowned for numerous accomplishments, among them contempt of wealth. There are innumerable, almost lyrical stories, about his casual doling out of vast sums of money on the slightest pretext. Once a poet, Naziri Nishapuri, lamented to him that he had never seen a pile of 100,000 rupees and couldn't tell how high it would go. The Khan-i Khanan instructed his treasurer to pile up the amount before him. That done, Naziri thanked God that he had been able to see such a huge amount at one go. The Khan-i Khanan in turn observed that this was too trifling a deed to thank God for and gave away the pile to him, remarking, 'it might now be worth your while to thank God'. Himself one of the abiding poets of medieval India, whose poetry is still read by school and college students, his slight partiality towards the less fortunately placed poets is understandable. One such poet, a Brahmin, read out a very pleasing verse to him. The Brahmin was asked his age, which was 35. The Khan-i Khanan calculated his total life to be 100 years, and gave him money at the rate of Rs 5 a day for the next 65 years.

The medieval Indian texts are replete with anecdotes of this kind at the level of the Mughal Emperors and their courtiers. In the numerous brief biographical accounts of the amirs of a reign attached to court chronicles since the thirteenth century, culminating in the massive *Maasir al-Umra* of Shah Nawaz Khan, compiled towards the end of the eighteenth century, references to their wealth are ever so scarce; the accounts focus largely on the lineage of the nobles, their careers in imperial service and above all signs of proximity to the ruler, like kind words said by him or a visit to their habitat by him.[1]

There are ever so few references to fights over money, but history abounds with stories of tension over symbols of status, especially spatial proximity to the King or the throne. Manucci has the delightful anecdote of a noble of Aurangzeb, Mir Wafa, pitching his tent in the space earmarked for the vizir, Asad Khan. This was a sure sign of getting uppity with the normative structure. The Emperor, however, elected to take a rather lenient view and instructed the Khan to visit the Mir and pacify him. This amounted to driving matters beyond the point of tolerance and even the Emperor could not be allowed to overstep the boundaries. The vizir's son, Zulfiqar Khan, took the campaign into his own hands and brought it to a flash point by dramatically laying down his sword – the very symbol of his legitimate existence – before Aurangzeb, recalling that his ancestors had served the empire since the days of Humayun and had won certain privileges which were now being violated. He could there-fore no longer serve his Majesty. Thrice the Emperor asked him to tie the sword back to his girdle and promised to honour his family's ancient privileges; thrice he declined. Aurangzeb then asked his own son Kam Bakhsh to restore the sword to its proper place on the young Khan's waist; this left the Khan with no space for refusal. To add weight to the assurance, Aurangzeb took a dagger from his own waist-belt, and stuck in the Khan's and gave him a robe of honour.

The story of Shivaji's resentment at being placed in the row of *man-sabdars* of 5,000 in Aurangzeb's court instead of the front row of 7,000, and his stage-managed fainting and subsequent dramatic flight from Agra, is part of India's folklore. It is hard to suggest that the course of history might have substantially altered if only Aurangzeb had been slightly more thoughtful of Shivaji's very medieval sensitivities; but the difference in Shivaji's self-perception and Aurangzeb's perception of him, expressed in the space allotted to him in the court, was one of those transient moments that cast a long shadow on the subcontinent's history.

The court was a site where every activity, exceptional or quotidian, was enacted on a scale that would appear theatrical to an outsider either in space or time. Sir Thomas Roe was quick to note this element. After describing the layout of the court, he observes: 'This sitting out hath soe much affinitiye with a theatre – the manner of the King in his gallery; the great men lifted on a stage as actors; the vulgar below gazing on.' This indeed was the point of its legitimacy: like all good theatre, the Mughal court had a vision of social order in which it was to play the role model by distancing itself from the mass of its subjects. Since the state stood at

1   I am grateful to my pupil Urvashi Dalal for this insight.

the apex of the many layers of society, the order in the court was the text for social order and meticulous observation of etiquette was the key to its preservation.

A whole body of literature, known as *Akhlaq*, etiquette, grew up in medieval Iran and India. Its prototype was *Akhlaq-i Nasiri* of Nasir al-Din Tusi, an Iranian work of the first half of the thirteenth century, although this is one of several works on the subject. This text was among the ones read out to Akbar every day. The Delhi Sultanate does not appear to have produced any text of this genre, at least not one that has survived to us, nor do the chronicles of the period record grave offence at the violation of etiquette in the court. We do have Sultan Ghiyas al-Din Balban (r. 1266–86) enforcing almost draconian norms of conduct in his court, but his was an exceptional order of things, without any written prescript. The Mughal era on the other hand saw the writing of several of such texts from the time of Jahangir onwards, although traces of the formulation of norms of etiquette can be found from the very inception of the empire, and observance or the slightest violation of any such norm in the court was not only minutely recorded by historians but was often the cause of favours or severe punishments.

The body of *Akhlaq* literature demonstrates concern with courtly etiquette in and outside the court. It does not seek to explicitly assert the superiority of the court people from the common, rude mass, for that is assumed as given; it seeks to shape individuals of the elite groups to a format. The class distinction between people of the court and those outside must be consciously internalized at the upper end of the social order for the good of all. The *Akhlaq-i Nasiri* goes into very great detail about every aspect of regulating (*siyasat*, both governance and punishment) the mode of eating, sleeping, talking, etc., that children should be socialized into. 'Children', of course, virtually excludes daughters, for whom the all-too-brief prescription is that they should be given no education and should be married off at the earliest. Sons should produce no sounds while eating or drinking water, could drink liquor in moderation, should sit at a place proper to their station, should not intervene in others' conversation nor speak unless directly addressed, should sleep on hard beds and take rough food; they should be introduced to sexual experience with several women.[2] Clearly, the subjects of this discourse are aristocratic sons with the ideal of rugged, virile masculinity before them, able to take life's troughs with the highs, and trained to follow and later enforce modes of orderly elite behaviour, with the aura of presence in the court always around them. The prescription of consumption of

2 Nasir al-Din Tusi, *Akhlaq-i Nasiri*, Mujataba Minawi and Ali Raza Haidari, eds, Tehran, 1354 H./ AD 1976: 222–40.

liquor, and the general tenor, underline the literature's non-religious character.

The norms of behaviour enunciated in this primary work seem to have been internalized in the Persian-speaking world for the next few centuries. Abul Fazl appears to be echoing them in his brief prescription: 'Much speaking and laughing are to be avoided. Sleep is not to exceed one-third part of the day and night.' A brief and not quite enthralling text, written most probably in the early part of the seventeenth century, the *Mirza Nama* by one Mirza Kamran (nothing in common with Prince Kamran, Humayun's brother) reiterates the same norms of austerity, decorum and guarding of one's honour, although its target audience is the lower ranks of the *mansabdars*.[3] *Akhlaq-i Jahangiri*, the first major work on the theme compiled under the Mughals by Nur al-Din Qazi al-Khaqani, dwells upon the themes of good behaviour, courage, patience, bravery, generosity and so on, besides the efficacy of consultation and keeping one's word. It emphasizes justice as the primary principle of governance and declares that 'a just non-Muslim ruler would be preferable to an unjust Muslim ruler'.[4]

For others concerned with etiquette, differentiation between ranks of privilege was at the very centre. In a long passage in his Preface to the *Ain-i Akbari*, Abul Fazl highlights the necessity of maintaining the sanctity of ranks at the court:

> the wise ones have counselled that visionary princes do not appoint every lowly person to their service; of the ones thus appointed, not everyone is admitted daily into the Presence; among those upon whom this privilege has been conferred, not everyone becomes entitled to proximity in conversation; of the ones arrived at this junction in the palace-garden of privilege, not all are to be permitted familiarity of address; among those so honoured, not everyone is admitted into the august assembly; of those upon whom this ray of fortune falls, everyone is not allowed into the assembly of secret counsel; among the carriers of this blessing, not all obtain place in the exclusive council of advisors.

The chapter 'On Etiquette' (literally, 'Regulations about standing and sitting', *Ain-i istadah wa nishast*) in the *Ain-i Akbari* opens with

---

3 Mirza Kamran, *Mirza Nama*, text and translation by Maulana Hidayat Husain, *Journal of the Asiatic Society of Bengal*, New Series, IX, 1913: 8–13 (text) and 1–8 (tr.). Interestingly, one of the recommendations made here is avoiding disputes, especially those pertaining to religion, 'lest these cause bodily harm' to the Mirza, p.11.

4 Nur al-Din Qazi al-Khaqani, *Akhlaq-i Jahangiri*, Persian MS. OIOC, British Library, London, 2207: ff.274b-75a. See also Muzaffar Alam, '*Shari'a* and Governance in the Indo-Islamic Context' in David Gilmartin and Bruce B. Lawrence, eds., *Beyond Turk and Hindu: Rethinking Religious Identities in Islamic South Asia*, New Delhi, 2002: 235.

the observation: 'Just as spiritual leadership is attained through inner regulation and controlling of lust and anger, temporal leadership grows by regulating the external world [and] protecting gradations [in society].'

In a context where the King was the pivot around which the court, and in its view the society, revolved, graded spatial distance between the throne and the courtiers, measured almost to an inch, defined their social standing. If it was each individual whose relationship vis-à-vis the King was so defined, individuals themselves were more frequently perceived as stereotypes whose site of location in the court was immutable unless they moved up the scale or were shown an exceptional favour by the king, so exceptional indeed as never to escape recording. The King too was so envisaged, for it is not he but the throne that becomes the reference point for measuring the spatial and social distance. Abul Fazl in 'On Etiquette' gives us a general outline of the location of each category of persons in Akbar's court:

> When His Majesty seats himself on the throne, all others of awakened fortune perform the *kurnish*, and then remain standing at their places, according to their rank, with the arms crossed.
>
> The eldest prince does not place himself, when standing, at a distance of nearer than one yard and farther than four yards [from the throne] and when sitting, at a distance from two to eight [yards]. The second Prince [stands] from a yard and a half to six yards from the throne and in sitting from three to twelve. The third maintains similar distance; sometimes he is admitted to a closer position than the second prince, and at most others both stand together at the same distance to do their obeisance. But His Majesty often places the younger princes affectionately nearer.
>
> Then come the devotees of the highest rank, who are worthy of the spiritual guidance of His Majesty [i.e. members of the Din-i Ilahi categorized into four ranks] at a distance of three to fifteen yards, and in sitting from five to twenty. After this follow the senior *amirs* from three and a half yards, and then the other nobles, from ten or twelve and a half yards [from the throne]. All other groups of men stand in the *Yasal*. One or two attendants stand nearer than all.

Abul Fazl's is a somewhat cursory and inconsistent outline, for while it enjoins upon everyone in the Presence to keep standing as the Emperor is seated on the throne, it also refers to the space for the princes and the high grandees to sit almost at their own discretion. The court rules were still evolving and flexible. Indeed, permission for sitting as a mark of imperial favour was part of Humayun's court etiquette and appears to have continued into Akbar's reign. Curiously, Humayun seems to have called the courtiers into his presence by the beat of drums after he had seated himself on the throne; this has been recorded as one of his 'innovations'. By the time Manucci visited Aurangzeb's court, however, etiquette had become more detailed, less plastic. We shall return to a discussion of this evolution below.

The Mughal court etiquette had a long lineage behind it, although the Iranian prototype, especially the Sasanid, seems to have been the primary inspiration. Many of the court rituals and norms of conduct, especially the notion of a visible imperial majesty and grandeur that we shall encounter below, are of Iranian provenance, traceable to the Sasanid court. Among those replicated in the Mughal court were: prostration before the Emperor or his throne; kissing his feet or any other limb, the hand in particular; several forms of salutation by bending from the waist downwards; and the custom of distribution of gifts, titles and offices on special occasions such as royal birthdays, or festivals like the New Year. – all of these have a chequered history but can be traced to the Sasanians.

There were several levels of the observance of etiquette: within the court, where concessions could be granted by the King but infractions of the norm led to severe punishments; within the royal family, where age, relationship and gender were important factors, even as rituals of the court were replicated; and, in the relationship between temporal and spiritual power, between the King and the *darvish*, renouncer, where there was defiance, inversion and emulation of the court's format.

Within the family the mother and elderly aunts are shown the greatest courtesy, although there was no standard form for such greetings. In 1507 Babur went to see his paternal aunts in Herat. 'Having bent the knee with Payanda-sultan Begim first of all, I had an interview with her; next not bending the knee I had an interview with Apaq Begim; next, having bent the knee with Khadija Begim I had an interview with her.'[5] It would appear from Babur's various descriptions that whereas reciprocal bending of knees was indicative of symbolic equality of status, non-reciprocal bending suggested status hierarchy.

Akbar was extremely deferential towards his mother, replicating before her the procedure that was due to him as Emperor in the court. Abul Fazl records that in the twenty-third year of his reign, Akbar's mother arrived near his camp on the bank of the river Bihat (Jhelum), and wished to see her son. The Emperor first sent Prince Salim ahead and then, riding a horse of 'lightening and graceful speed', rushed forth to meet her and, 'treating the making of reverence to the visible God [his mother] as an act of worship of the true Creator, he at once performed all etiquette; this exalted the level of his knowledge of God'. Jahangir too

5   *Babur Nama* (first pub. 1922), New Delhi, 1970: 301. The translator, Mrs Beveridge, in a note reasonably doubts whether Babur's 'not bending the knee' has been correctly recorded.

'embarked in a boat and went to a village named Dahr to meet my mother and had the good fortune to be received by her'. He did obeisance and prostration (*kurnish* and *sajda*) before her, and later on 'obtained leave to return'. Besides the exact replication of court rituals, even the language is a virtual reproduction of any court chronicle describing a noble's approach to and subsequent dismissal by the Emperor. Jahangir takes care to record that the show of respect was due from the young to the old 'according to the custom of Chingiz [and] the rules of Timur' – a standard form of validating any practice under the Mughals – to which he adds 'common usage' as a third source of valorization. We have seen above details of the etiquette for meeting aunts, given by Babur and later replicated by his daughter Gulbadan Begum, who was in her nephew Akbar's estimation perhaps next only to his mother as far as the ceremonies of visiting her or being visited by her went.

However, with other female members of the family, including elder sisters, various mixes of court rituals and considerations of age governed the relationship. When in 1519 Babur went to see his 'honoured elder sister' (his cousin Sultanam Begum), he 'out of respect and courtesy to her... bent the knee. She also bent the knee. We, both advancing, saw each other mid-way. We always observed the same ceremony after-wards.' Bending the knee, Babur had recorded earlier, sufficed as a greeting to one's superior or equal in informal situations as the abbreviated form of an elaborate ceremony. Even so, his qualifications, prior to the actual bending of the knee before his sister and her reciprocation, are suggestive of departure from the norm, more like a convenient personal arrangement between the two. When the female members of Babur's family followed him from Kabul to Agra in 1527, after he had established himself in India, his daughter Gulbadan, still a young lass, did *mulazimat*, 'presented' herself to him. *Mulazimat* is the term for a courtier presenting himself before the throne. Afterwards, her father held her in his arms and showered her with affection that she still remembered decades later. In Humayun's reign, the Emperor's servant Bayazid Biyat reports a reunion of 'his sisters and female relations and everyone among the group related to His Majesty by ties of slavery had the honour of kissing his feet'.[6] A considerable distance had been covered

6   Bayazid Biyat, *Tazkira*, 1941: 59: '*Hamshirha wa beguman wa har kas ki azan jama't ki nisbat-i bandagi-i anhazrat dasht bataslim sarafraz shudand.*' Bandagi, literally slavery, is a term of honour, indicating master-servant relationship vis-à-vis the emperor or his court. Much later, Prince Muhammad Sultan, son of Aurangzeb, who helped him imprison Shah Jahan, wrote him a letter affirming with pride that he was merely carrying out the duties of a slave and a 'house born' (*qawaid-i ghulami wa khanazadgi baja awurdah...*), Munshi Abul Fath Qabil Khan, *Adab-i Alamgiri*, 2 volumes, ed. Abd al-Ghafoor Chaudhuri, Lahore, 1971, I: 242.

from the bending of the knee to *mulazimat* and the kissing of the feet in redefining filial relationship between the Emperor and his female relatives.

Age difference between male relatives could also moderate the demands of courtly etiquette if ties of sovereignty did not intervene. When in 1495 Babur went to a garden at Sharukhiya, near Akhsi in Farghana, to see his uncle Sultan Mahmud Khan, his mother's half-brother, who was like 'my father and elder brother', he walked up to 'a large four-doored tent set up in the middle [of the garden]. I knelt three times, he for his part rising to do me honour. We looked one another in the eye, and he returned to his seat.' Permission to wash one's hands in the same ewer as the king's was a privilege, even for his brothers. Humayun was pleased to sit with his brothers Kamran, Askari and Hindal, and his uncle Mirza Sulaiman, over dinner. The ewer was brought to him to wash his hands and Kamran followed. The other two brothers ordered the ewer to be taken to the Mirza first, in view of his seniority in age, and then washed hands themselves. The Mirza in the meanwhile 'did something awful with his nose'; Askari and Hindal were greatly enraged and said 'what kind of rusticity is this? First, what right did we have to wash our hands in his Majesty's presence? However, since he had graciously permitted us to do so, we could not defy his command. On top of that, what kind of manners are these that you play with your nose?'

Respect for age through demonstrative humility had to precede the symbolic reciprocity of honour due to an equal, which was reinforced by looking each other in the eye – a complex range of meanings inhered in these ceremonials, each side very conscious of them. Once the symbolic meanings had been publicly demonstrated, 'much affection and friendliness' flowed from the elder to the younger relative. In 1506 a meeting took place between Babur and his cousin Badi al-Zaman Mirza. The Mirza demanded that consideration be shown to his 15 years' seniority and Babur bend his knee. On Babur's behalf the claim was advanced that though younger in age, his capture of Samarqand several times by exercise of the sword gave him precedence in terms of *turah*, rules of Chingiz, the perennial court of appeal for the Mughals. In the end a compromise was worked out that Babur should bend his knee once on entering and Badi al-Zaman would honour him by advancing to receive him.

Mirza Sulaiman, ruler of Badakhshan from Babur's time, fled to India to escape his grandson's attempt to do him in. Akbar went all out to receive him with great pomp, himself riding out a long distance. Five hundred elephants, adorned with European velvet and embroidered fabric from Constantinople, were lined up for 10 miles from the gate of Fatehpur. Between every pair of elephants, there was a cart containing a cheetah with a collar of gold around its neck. When the Mirza and Akbar came face to face, the visitor descended from the horse and came forward to do *taslim* to the Emperor. Akbar exempted him from the formality in view of his age and embraced him instead.

However, the factor of age did not always face up to the demands of sovereignty, particularly if the men involved were unrelated. In 1526 Ghazi Khan, an old Afghan who Babur had once addressed as 'father', showed defiant disinclination to kneel before him; Babur ordered his servants to 'pull his leg and make him do so'. Bairam Khan too, whom Akbar as a child had learnt to refer to as father, placed his head at the young Emperor's feet after his rebellion had proved infructuous.

No general concessions were made to male relatives of Emperors, irrespective of age and relationship: Itimad al-Daulah, father-in-law of Jahangir; his son Asaf Khan, father-in-law of Shah Jahan; Shaista Khan, maternal uncle of Aurangzeb, each had to conform to the rules of court etiquette. Medieval societies made no distinction between public and private spaces and the performance of rituals was as much a requisite in private, even familial assemblies, as in court. Shah Jahan went for a feast at his father-in-law Asaf Khan's house, and entered the room walking between his mother-in-law on his right and his daughter Jahan Ara on the left, followed by Dara and the host. The Emperor showed great courtesy to his mother-in-law and addressed her as 'mother' throughout. As the journey from the door to the inner chamber was completed, Asaf Khan's and the Emperor's families 'suddenly knelt down' to perform the *kurnish*. Shah Jahan implored his mother-in-law to sit on his right and asked others too to sit down. He had to urge them thrice before they actually sat down. Manrique, with a clear division of humanity into the polite and civilized Europe and the barbarian others in his mind, was 'astonished and surprised to see so many polite usages and good order in practice among such barbarians'. Indeed, if they were barbarians, they should in Manrique's perception also have been poor; his astonishment at seeing 'the abundance and diversity of dishes' is therefore understandable.

Even as an Emperor's brothers conceded the supremacy of his position, at times tensions arose over the assertion of superiority vis-à-vis the other brothers. In 1540, as Humayun fled to Lahore and thence to Sind and Iran, following two decisive defeats at Sher Shah's hands, he was resting on the other side of the river Ravi in Lahore when a messenger of the Afghan victor arrived. Humayun decided to see him the next morning. At that point Kamran made a petition to be allowed to sit on a corner of Humayun's carpet 'so that I could be distinguished from my brothers; this would be a great honour' for him. Greatly weakened by the defeats as Humayun was, besides being generally kind to his brothers by his nature and his father's dying advice, he still would not accede to Kamran's request, for it had the hint of shared sovereignty. Shorn of this hint, a very favourite noble might yet be given permission to sit on the same carpet and even share food off the same plate with the Emperor, as Shah Abul Ma'ali was once given by Humayun himself; but that must have been an exceptional occasion, unrepeated in the rest of Mughal history. Royalty was too awesome to brook any division.

On a later date Kamran duly performed the court ritual of doing *taslim* thrice when he came to see Humayun at Kabul. Later still, Bairam Khan resorted to subterfuge to have Kamran stand up to receive Humayun's *farman*. Guessing that Kamran would not do so, he first presented him with a copy of the Quran and, as he stood up to receive it, the *farman* was handed down to him. If it was a rather laboured enforcement of protocol, the point was still made.

However, some concessions could still be made as a privilege in recognition of an extraordinary deed. Another of Humayun's brothers, Hindal, was on one occasion allowed to pay his respect to the Emperor while riding his horse; this was for bringing one Sher Ali as prisoner. It was a major concession allowed only to royal brothers or sons in exceptional situations. In the first few days of Akbar's accession to the throne considerable tension arose when Shah Abul Ma'ali insisted on sitting on the Emperor's carpet as he had once done on Humayun's, and performed the *kurnish* on horseback to assert his very special position. Akbar ordered 'the mad man to be put in chains and handed over to Shihab al-Din Ahmad Khan to be sent off to Hijaz', the pilgrimage to Mecca, a veritable exile, standard punishment meted out by kings to offending nobles or relatives.[7] 'The regulations of State and the rules of affection are distinct', Akbar sermonized Abul Ma'ali, 'and you have not the same relationship with me as you had with the late Emperor [Humayun].' Even so Abul Ma'ali does seem to have wrested one mark of privilege from Akbar; he was allowed to sit in the Presence, though at a later date.

Yet the space for exercise of discretion by the Emperor was beginning to contract. When Bairam Khan appeared on horseback before Akbar and held him by the hand, as he would have done many a time before Akbar began to assert his role as king, the violation of etiquette was so grave that Akbar included it amongst the Khan's most serious offences, justifying his dismissal from the post of *vakil*.

---

7   Badauni says Abul Ma'ali once came riding up to Akbar and on another occasion tried to precede Akbar on horseback and was arrested on the emperor's orders. Nizam al-Din Ahmad and Ferishta have slightly different versions.

On his part, Akbar had strictly demarcated spaces in the court for each of the princes, priority following the order of their birth as a norm; their distance from the throne and from each other thus stood clearly defined, eliminating even the notional possibility of divided sovereignty. At what point of time these demarcating lines were actually drawn is not clear, for we learn of them from the *Ain-i Akbari*, written towards the end of the sixteenth century. There yet remained a little allowance for the Emperor's personal affection for the younger princes, which might alter the practice of norm as long as they were young children, suggesting that these rules of etiquette had been formulated several years earlier when the royal sons were still small. Even this space for the public display of differential affection for the princes on the Emperor's part was gradually to diminish with time; henceforth it had to be earned by them, mainly in the battle-field, as brave young princes. Roles were evolving and expectations of conformity to these roles were directly related to proximity to the throne.

Besides the historical texts, Mughal miniatures open a window on the formatting of etiquette over time. In a painting of around 1615 in Jahangir's reign, depicting Babur in his court receiving a visitor, the ambience is one of considerable fluidity: the space occupied by the court itself is very small, as is the throne on which Babur is sitting. Of the nine figures besides the Emperor inside the court's precincts, one is looking out into the horizon, another is standing with an affected limp in his body, the chin resting on his inverted palm placed on the upper end of his stick. The visitor is presenting his gift to the Emperor, who is depicted looking at it approvingly. Babur's imperial status is reinforced by the centrality of his location, the throne and his figure dwarfing those of others, even in his sitting posture. But it could well be the depiction of an informal gathering of friends.

In contrast, the many paintings of Shah Jahan's court are marked by the display of overpowering grandeur, order and immutability: A very large number of courtiers, richly attired, each standing in the exact spot assigned to him according to his rank and all of them in the same erect posture, eyes fixed on the Emperor's face or on the Jewel Throne, on which Shah Jahan is usually depicted sitting as the personification of the centre of the universe, his centrality emphasized by the large solar halo around his head, and the pillars symbolically enclos-ing the world on all sides in their fold. In a painting, even an assembly of theologians and mystics in Shah Jahan's presence follows the same format. The obsession with a very large solar halo seems to have grown with Jahangir onwards down to Aurangzeb, and the names – indeed more like titles, which two of them had adopted on accession to the throne and one had carried from his days of princehood – emphasized their ambition to be the determinants of the world's destiny

Figure 4 *A Ruler Holding Court.* By permission of the British Library (J.26.21).

Figure 5 A leaf from *Padshah Nama*. By permission of the British Library (100611).

by conquering and ruling it. From Jahangir's time several of the Mughal miniatures depicting the King also had the globe, often located in the miniature's centre, in the Emperor's palm, at the base of the throne or under his feet. Being the world's symbolic pivot provided them with more than a personal thrill; it gave meaning to their dream of universality, order and eternity.

On entering the court, shoes had to be left at the main door, much as they were to be left outside the precincts of a holy place like a tomb, temple, mosque or hermitage. For the court was a sacred space, its sanctity emanating from the Emperor's person. The gradations of sanctity rose as one approached the throne, from which a certain distance was always to be maintained, except on rare occasions when commanded by the Emperor to advance. Once Prince Azam, Aurangzeb's son, sought some information from the Emperor and on not receiving a reply moved towards the throne in a state of agitation. Absentmindedly, he touched the throne with his foot, which so angered the generally cool Aurangzeb that he dismissed the court for the day.

Sanctity was also maintained by complete temperance and total silence, again reminiscent of the ambience of a place of worship. Shah Jahan added to the solemnity by instituting the playing of very soft music when the court assembly was on. The observance of total silence was 'fundamental to Fatimid, Sasanian and Byzantine audiences... All speech was to be conducted in subdued voices, with no gesticulation, and to be confined to brief statements made without flourish, in full humility and clarity.'[8] Even as many Umayyad and Abbasid Caliphs had set aside specified days of the week for drinking in public,[9] and even as most Mughal Emperors were rather fond of a daily cup or two of good wine in the company of their families and friends, the precincts of the court were completely out of bounds for the cup. The first incident Badauni records in his account of the reign of Akbar is that Shah Abul Ma'ali swaggered into the court in a tipsy state three days after the new reign had begun. The fact that Badauni opens his account of Akbar's reign with the narration of this incident would underline the seriousness of the infringement of court etiquette, but it was overlooked for once, perhaps because it would mark an inauspicious inauguration of a new reign. But a few years later when Shahbaz Khan, who was the empire's Mir Bakhshi as well as Diwan-i Arz (Paymaster and Chief of the Department of the Army), came to the court in a drunken state, he was relieved

---

8 Aziz al-Azmeh, *Muslim Kingship*, London/New York, 2001: 139. For enforcemnt of silence in the Sasanian court, see Murtaza Rawandi, *Tarikh-i Ajtama'i Iran,* vol. I, 4th print, Tehran, 1354 H./AD 1976: 645
9 Aziz al-Azmeh, *Muslim Kingship*: 69.

of his post and thrown into prison. On the intercession of Akbar's favourite nobles, he was released from prison and Akbar sent him a shawl from his own wardrobe and an arrow from his own quiver, but the posts were not restored to him. He decided to turn into a recluse and gave away all his possessions, including his elephants and horses. Interestingly, Jahangir, with the image of being perpetually drunk that popular lore and history has preserved of him, was particularly strict in enforcing temperance, and Sir Thomas Roe tells us that guards would smell each courtier at the entrance and turn away anyone with the faintest trace of liquor. Indeed, even drinking of water was an exceptional occurrence, and the French traveller and diamond merchant Jean-Baptiste Tavernier was witness to the rarity of Aurangzeb thrice drinking water while sitting on his throne in the court. Even drinking water showed ordinary human needs. There was no space for the ordinary in the court; it was a theatre for extraordinary persons and events only, grimly aware of encapsulating the destiny of a vast territory and its innumerable people.

The privilege of actually speaking in the Emperor's presence was given to a very few and would therefore have been greatly coveted as a mark of high status. References are made again and again to 'those entitled to speak' or 'those who received permission to speak'; nor were courtiers allowed to converse among themselves. If the Emperor was pleased with a courtier, he would raise his brows towards him or look at him at a tangent. Deference in demeanour was expected in the utterance of words.

Sir Thomas Roe and Manucci have given us detailed first-hand accounts of the court's setting and the hidebound etiquette. The court was divided into three levels, each comprising a section with some space separating it from the others. The level nearest to the throne was demarcated with railings of gold; the next, slightly below it, with those of silver; and the third, still lower, with wooden railings. The first section enclosed princes of the royal blood; the second was earmarked for the *umra*, high grandees, standing with their backs to railings of wood painted vermilion. These railings surrounded the whole space. Officers designated Mir Tuzuk and Yasawal were located at the centre of each section to ensure that no one moved from the place assigned to him. Eternal order was not subject to transgression.

Sanctity of whatever symbolized sovereignty was inviolable and no infringement of it was to be overlooked. Several prerogatives of royalty had been earmarked and anyone even appearing to arrogate one of these was subjected to punishment. Among them were the hunting of lions and tigers, parallel to the King in the forest, the use of special types of umbrella, certain colours, especially red, sitting on the throne or anything resembling it, and so on. Prince Muazzam, later to succeed Aurangzeb as Bahadur Shah I, once sat on a raised platform where he held his court in

Kabul. The news travelled to Aurangzeb and he lost no time in dispatching two hefty men carrying maces, with orders to pull the Prince down in full public view and demolish the platform. Even certain forms of greeting were put on the reserved list: no one could raise one's hand to his head to greet anyone other than the Emperor. The beating of drums, an integral part of the Emperor's daily court routine, and some other forms of music, elephant fights, appearing in the *jharoka*, or visiting the *Meena* (fancy) *Bazar* organized by the women of the harem for the Emperor's amusement, were among other royal prerogatives. Akbar had established his exclusive access to some forms of clothing, such as the *Tus* shawl (made from wool pulled off unborn lambs)[10] and a certain garment with *chikan* embroidery on it; Jahangir extended the list and included some other garments, even as he gave them special names such as *nadiri*, unique, worn over other dress on the torso. There were occasional infractions of these, especially by the princes, anxious to assume charge of royalty themselves and impatient with the never-ending life of their fathers. Issuing of coins, having the *khutba* (the Imam's proclamation, which traced the current ruler's political lineage through past Sultans and Caliphs right up to the Prophet) read before the Friday congregation at the mosque, and giving capital punishment were guarded with extreme jealousy by the rulers, for an infringement of any of these was held equivalent to the declaration of rival sovereignty. Princes since the time of Salim (Jahangir) were especially prone to intemperate declarations of it. Aurangzeb's second son Muazzam seems to have set a record of sorts by violating several of his father's prerogatives and earning a reprimand each time;[11] however, none of these included issuing of coins, the *khutba*, or capital punishment. Some of the prerogatives, such as beating of kettledrums, flaunting of parasol, banners, and so on, were given by the Emperors to their sons, wives, or high *amirs* as very special and coveted favours.

The umbrella (*chatr*) and its oval variant the parasol, in particular, have had an interesting history. In ancient monarchies from Babylonia eastwards, parasol and flywhisk were prominent. The parasol became a standard feature on Sasanian royal sculptures. Early Muslim kings do not show evidence of its adoption until the Fatimid caliphs in Egypt, from where it travelled to the Ayubbid and Mamluk Sultans of Egypt and Syria, as well as to the Normans of Sicily.[12] Whether it came to India via the same route is hard to affirm, although it does not seem unlikely.

10   Recently placed under legal ban by the Govt of India.
11   For details, see Mubarak Ali, 'The Court of the Great Mughuls', Ph.D. thesis, Ruhr University, 1976: 26–8, and his *Mughal Darbar* (Urdu), Lahore, 1993: 42–4.
12   Aziz al-Azmeh, *Muslim Kingship*: 13, 136.

However, the Hindu rulers of ancient India also treated the parasol as a symbol of royalty and this route is as feasible as the other for its arrival in the Mughal court. Symbolically, it served two purposes: giving physical form to the sovereign's assumption of being the *axis mundi* and giving protection to the whole earth and therefore its subjects. In a letter written to his father, Prince Aurangzeb, after recounting the usual titles and epithets, cites a verse among others that goes to the heart of the symbolism of the umbrella: 'the earth finds shelter under the shadow of his [the Emperor's] parasol'.[13] The umbrella is thus the symbol of power and protection, its exclusive use by the King encapsulating both authority and paternalism.

However, in the midst of the fixity of order, there was evolution. Several of the court rituals seem to have evolved through an assertion of imperial authority and at times subtle resistance to it. *Kurnish* was one, which expressed subservience to the majesty of the king. The Iranian scholar Syed Haidar Shaharyar Naqvi has rather summarily claimed that when the Mughal Emperor Humayun, in exile from India and guest of Shah Tahmasb of Iran, returned to reclaim his empire with the Shah's help, he also brought with him the rituals of *kurnish* and *taslim*.[14] François Bernier, however, observes that the *kurnish* was not Uzbek, nor Persian, nor Arabic, but specifically Indian. 'It certainly savours of servility,' he concludes.[15] *Kurnish* does not occur among the forms of obeisance to a sovereign or to one's superior in the *Babur Nama*, but Gulbadan mentions it twice, once when Mir Bardi Beg, son of Mir Khurd Beg, 'conveys' his *kurnish* to her royal father, and another time when Humayun had placed a water carrier on the throne for two days as a reward for rescuing him from drowning in the river Chausa and ordered all the grandees, *umrayan*, to do him *kurnish*. This was before Humayun's departure from India. Mir Bardi Beg's 'conveying' of *kurnish* to Babur suggests the beginning of a practice that was to assume a highly institutionalized form when the receipt of a *farman* of the Emperor or even food from his kitchen sent the recipient into performing the ritual. *Kurnish* was always to be performed with the right hand; doing so with the left was a grave insult.

13   D. Streusand, *The Formation of the Mughal Empire*, New Delhi, 1989: 129, and Munshi Shaikh Abul Fath Qabil Khan, *Adab-i Alamgiri*, I 21 (*zamin dar saaya-i chatrash nihan ast*).
14   Naqvi, 'Sasanian wa Hind wa Pakistan' in *Humayish Tarikh wa Farhang-i Iran: Tarikh wa Farhang-i Iran dar Zaman-i Sasanian*, publication of the Dept of Publications, Ministry of Science and Arts, Iran, n.d.: 188.
15   F. Bernier, *Travels in the Mogul Empire, 1656–68*, Eng. tr. Irving Brock, revsd by Archibald Constable (first pub., London, 1891), New Delhi, 1971: 120.

Abul Fazl has an *Ain* (literally 'regulation', but in effect a chapter) on 'Regulations regarding the *Kurnish* and the *Taslim*'. That the show of respect to the king, he says, is a recognition of his being the source of peace and comfort for the subjects is obvious enough; but the embedded meaning is more profound, for it teaches subjects true humility, essential for their spiritual well-being. Whereas some rulers had accepted the bending of the head as a sign of submission, Akbar had commanded the palm of the right hand to be placed upon the forehead and the head to be bent downwards. 'This, in the language of the present age, is called *kurnish*. It signifies that [the saluter], placing his head, which is the source of life's senses and reason, into the hand of humility, has made a gift of it to the sacred assembly; he has thus placed himself in obedience to any [royal] command.' Of *taslim*, 'the regulation is that favoured servants place the back of their right hand on the ground and then raise it gently; as the person stands erect, he puts the palm of his hand upon the crown of his head. In this pleasing manner he makes a submission of himself. This is called *taslim*.'

Taslim was Humayun's creation which followed a playful accident with his son Akbar. Humayun gave his own large cap to the child who had to hold it on his head with the hand as he bent to do *kurnish* to express his gratitude. Humayun was pleased with the gesture and its form and adopted it as the manner of performing *taslim*.

Pabos (also *paibos*), kissing the king's foot, seems to have been first introduced as part of Indian court culture by Sultan Balban, although clearly it did not originate with him. Of Sasanian origin, the ceremony moved into the Caliphal court in the ninth century when kissing the Caliph's foot alternated with kissing his hand or ring, before his person became too elevated to be touched by another human being and kissing the ground began to replace it. We come across references to it again in Mughal literature. It is not clear whether it was confined to the court or was a routine observed in the harem as well, Gulbadan's statement that Humayun's sisters and other ladies of the harem, begums, obtained the honour of kissing his feet notwithstanding. In the court, too, it is unclear if this performance was expected of everyone present; the proximity it allowed to the king's person makes it likely as a reserved privilege, not an open access. Indeed, the mention of *pabos* is usually preceded by the term honour, *sharf*, at least mildly suggesting its rarity. When Jahangir's son Khurram, later Shah Jahan, returned with the imperial nobles after a victorious campaign in the Deccan, the Emperor received them in a more than routine ceremony. The first to be allowed audience with him was the Khan-i Jahan. 'Sending for him above, I selected him for the honour of kissing my feet,' Jahangir records. On such an occasion, the Emperor would normally express his pleasure with the person by placing his hand on the courtier's back. Aurangzeb too 'permitted' his son Muazzam to kiss his feet.

If the King was not sitting on the throne, the courtier's submission to him could be indicated by his kissing the carpet on which the King might be sitting. Abul Fazl tells us of the 'honour' Husain Quli, brother of Ahmad Sultan, governor of Sistan in Persia, obtained by so kissing the carpet on which Humayun was then located.

Outside the court's precincts, if the King were mounted, kissing the horse stirrup and his Majesty's thigh would be adequate. Gulbadan Begum's son, Humayun's nephew Sa'adat Yar Khan, was permitted to perform this ritual when he faced the Emperor on horseback. There are several other instances of this kind.

To these rituals signifying humility, Akbar added another that would elevate him to the status he was not too reluctant to claim, if only covertly: that of God. This was prostration, *sajda*, before him in court, i.e. in public. Once again we are able to trace its history in the Sasanid, Byzantine and some Muslim polities, in all of which prostration was conferred as a special privilege on a select few,[16] and in India to Sultan Balban whose claim to divinity was far more audacious than Akbar's. But since Balban's death in 1286 the performance of *sajda* had lain in disuse. Akbar's revival of it, softening it by calling it *zaminbos*, kissing the ground,[17] went along with his proclamation of Din-i Ilahi which had made him the head and spiritual guide of the members of the sect. 'They count prostration [before His Majesty] as enhancement of blessings and as prostration performed before God,' says Abul Fazl. This ruffled the sensibilities of the hardliners among theologians, already smarting in a losing battle in his court, and protests followed. Human beings owed prostration, total submission, to God alone not to another human being, regardless of his status and stature, they argued. Perhaps the voice of our sources does not match the volume of protest, but Abul Fazl's venom against the protesters and the fact that Akbar made concessions on this point are suggestive:

Even though many among men have become inclined towards performing prostration and count it as a source of blessing upon blessing, since some of the perverse and dark-hearted men look upon prostration as man-worship, His Majesty, from practical wisdom has ordered its discontinuation by the ignorant ones and exempted all ranks from it, forbidding even his private attendants from performing it on days of public court (*dar bar-i 'aam*).

16   Aziz al-Azmeh, *Muslim Kingship*: 30.
17   Badauni, II: 301; Jahangir, *Tuzuk*, I: 203. Shah Jahan kept the distinction and while abolishing *sajda*, retained *zaminbos*, which too was terminated in his tenth regnal year, owing to its semblance to *sajda*. Inayat Khan, *Shah Jahan Nama*: 203.

Indeed, Abul Fazl's elder brother Faizi, the poet whose name the historian never mentions without dipping his pen in adoration, goes a step beyond the facts of the case and records in one of his letters that Akbar's 'auspicious order is against [performing the *sajda*]. Every time when the favoured grandees bow down to perform [it] out of extreme loyalty, His Majesty stops them because *sajda* is performed before God alone.' In the Mughal empire, *sajda* was henceforth allowed in the private assembly alone to those who would perform it of their own will. Jahangir, too, fancied himself the spiritual leader of the sect his father had founded, and therefore continued with the prostration ritual. It was to be banished from the king's public or private assemblies by Shah Jahan almost as the very first act after ascending the throne. The resentment of the *ulema* even against private prostration was at last heeded.

Between *kurnish* and *sajda*, the latter being the ritual of a more definitive surrender, the two stood in a hierarchy vis-à-vis one another. In moments of great delicacy, when claims of two contending sides had to be accommodated, resort could be taken to a sort of negotiation. Akbar received message of the arrival of Mirza Sulaiman, ruler of Badakhshan from the hoary days of Babur, pestered by his grandson who was impatient to become King himself. Akbar travelled a distance of 10 miles to receive him, an extremely rare gesture on his or any Emperor's part, and on approaching each other performed the *kurnish* to him, which was even rarer. The Mirza on his part did *sajda* to Akbar. It is thus that they were placed on a par.

If it were to be assumed that court rituals like *kurnish* were due exclusively to the Emperor, Bayazid Biyat, who had been in the service of Munim Khan Khan-i Khanan for several years, tells us that he performed it before the eminent Khan too. This, however, appears a rare instance and perhaps may not adequately controvert the assumption. Indeed, *kurnish* came to be so identified with the King that it was performed even when his written commands, *farmans*, or any of the Emperor's ensigns were received anywhere within the boundaries of the empire, or when food was sent from his kitchen to the high nobles who stood guarding his palace by turns, or when any present was received from him. The king's presence filled the whole empire and symbolic obeisance was due to him everywhere.

Honour was also differentially apportioned to spaces on the right and the left sides of the Emperor; being allowed to stand or sit on one or the other was acutely observed as indicative of either status or the ruler's (dis)favour. The left side was considered inferior to the right in several medieval civilizations. In early Christianity, Jesus's right hand was 'blessed [and] filled with holiness'[18] and, in later centuries, left was 'in the medieval system of values always judged to be derogatory'.[19] Among devout Hindus the left hand is the dirtier one, and eating with it or even giving a gift with it would send shivers of horror from head to foot. In the Quran, God promises to place the virtuous ones on his right on the Day of Judgement, and vicious ones on the left. The distinction was probably absorbed from pre-Islamic Arab culture. Babur records that in 1500 Shaibani Khan was visited by Sultan Ali Mirza at Samarqand. The Khan 'did not receive him very favourably; when they had seen each other [i.e. looked each other in the eye], he seated him on his less honourable hand'. Babur later on describes the right-hand side as 'the place of honour'. This appears to have been the rule for his successors as well. Badauni tells us that when the poet Niyazi first made his appearance before Humayun, 'he stepped forward towards him at the levèe with his left foot. As his late Majesty was very punctilious in such details of etiquette, he said, "the Mulla is left [handed]" and commanded him to be led out again and brought forward a second time.' The *Akbar Nama* records that sitting on the left or right of the Emperor depended upon one's status. When Jahangir's rebel son Khusrau was brought to him in chains, this was done from the left, for this, says the Emperor, was the Chingizi custom. This would leave no space in the prince's or the courtiers' minds about any suggestion of honour for him. Aurangzeb's second son Muazzam was always allowed to sit on the Emperor's right, but his place was given away to his younger sibling Shah Alijah during a period of 'disgrace' for the elder Prince. Muazzam had to fight for regaining the 'right' from his brother and Aurangzeb too had to devise a manoeuvre to restore it to him.

The number of *taslims* performed also indicated hierarchy. The *Ain* lays down that 'on being presented to the Court or on being dismissed from it, on receiving a *mansab* or a *jagir*, a robe of honour, an elephant or a horse, performance of three *taslims* was called for; on other routine occasions of receiving varied favours, one *taslim* would suffice.' Later, however, the number increased. Careri tells us that princes of the royal blood did two *taslims* to the Emperor; others did three in Aurangzeb's court. When the Emperor bestowed a gift upon anyone, four *taslims* were in order. For receiving a robe of honour, four *taslims* before and four after

18   G. J. Reinkin, 'Pseudo-Methodius: A Concept of History in Response to the Rise of Islam' in A. Cameron and L. Conrad, eds, *The Byzantine & Early Islamic Near East*, vol. I, Princeton, 1992: 172.
19   David Fraesdorff, 'The Power of Imagination: The *Christianitas* and the Pagan North during Conversion to Christianity (800–1200)', *The Medieval History Journal*, Special Issue 'Exploring Alterity in Pre-Modern Societies', vol 5(2), 2002: 310.

were the norm. Shah Jahan seems to have made four *taslims* the rule. In Aurangzeb's reign we also come across princes of the royal blood performing *kurnish* and *taslim* for their sisters and brothers, although this was done in a letter and not on the ground.[20]

Being allowed to sit in the court was an exceptional privilege, never to go unnoticed. Owed again to the Sasanid and Caliphal courts, the privilege underscored the normative subordination of the sovereign/slave relationship existing between the Emperor and everyone else, including his own sons. Of Babur's men, listed by Abul Fazl, only two were allowed 'the honour to sit in his presence'. We have come across above Kamran's desire to sit at the corner of Humayun's carpet as a mark of distinction from his brothers and as an honour. Jahangir had allowed his son Parvaiz to sit in the court after performing *sajda*, prostration, and *zaminbos*, kissing the ground. Jahangir gave Prince Khurram the title of Shah Jahan and a golden chair to sit on in court after a successful campaign in the Deccan. Shah Jahan, the Emperor, on his sixty-fifth lunar birth anniversary repeated the favour to his own eldest son Dara Shukoh, bestowing him with the title of Buland Iqbal, high fortune, and a golden chair near the throne. Dara felt pleased with the honour, but there is conflicting evidence whether he actually sat on it.[21]

Once in a while we hear of instances of favour occurring in court even when the norm had no space for them. Shah Jahan's vizir, Sa'ad Ullah Khan, also husband of Mumtaz Mahal's sister, was once late for the court, usually a grave offence. When asked to explain, the Khan said he was copying some homilies for his Majesty's perusal, which delayed him. He read out the text. Pleased, Shah Jahan kissed him on the forehead.

There was a strict dress code, too, for appearance in the court. Some of the colours, such as red, scarlet or yellow, were reserved for the Emperor's use, although these did not find favour with religious men. The head should be turbaned and the feet bare. Even the length of the beard, four fingers, and that of the leg wear was strictly prescribed. Once Marahmat Khan appeared in Aurangzeb's court with his pyjamas

---

20   Prince Akbar, Aurangzeb's son conveys his *kurnish* and *taslim* to his brothers and sisters; see *Adab-i Alamgiri*, II: 1211, 1212 (brothers) and 1224–27, 1240 (sisters).

21   Manucci at one place observes that everyone in Shah Jahan's court, except Dara, kept standing and at another that Dara was pleased with the honour but out of respect for his father never actually sat on the little throne. Manucci, I (first pub., 1907), New Delhi, 1981: 88, 216. Inayat Khan, *S J Nama*: 505–06, has no doubt though that Dara actually sat on the chair assigned to him. *Qawaid-i Sultanat-i Shah Jahan*, however, states more generally that Princes were permitted to sit near the imperial throne, each one's proximity to it determined by his age (literally 'status', *darja ba darja*), p. 46. There is however one miniature where a prince, presumably Dara, is depicted actually sitting to Shah Jahan's left. Plate 34, *Album of Indian and Persian Miniatures*, Moscow, 1962 (in Russian).

(trousers) covering his feet. This did not go unnoticed and the Emperor ordered him to cut the garment short a few inches from the bottom 'according to court etiquette'. 'Men' he announced, 'should wear simple, white clothes; it is women who should decorate themselves.' Expensive clothes like those made of gold were to be banished, too.

If court etiquette expressed hierarchy and power, the trajectory of its evolution kept close to the contours of state's power empirically, if not in theory. We have observed above the relative flexibility in the observance of rituals of etiquette in the early phase of the empire's evolution. The first three Emperors were also personally very accessible and this fact itself dented a very close adherence to rules of etiquette, the essence of which was a very strict regulation of access to the Emperor's person. Babur fondly held convivial parties with his nobles outside the court and allowed many rules of etiquette to be bent or broken. Humayun's image was one of a forgiving saint rather than a stern king. Akbar's enormous personal energy took him everywhere to places and jobs best left by an Emperor to his subordinates. Fr. Monserrate notices this remarkable quality in him:

> It is hard to exaggerate how accessible he makes himself to all those who wish audience with him. For he creates an opportunity almost every day for any of the common people or of the nobles to see him and converse with him.... He is especially remarkable for his love of keeping great crowds of people around him and in his sight; and thus it comes about that his court is always thronged with multitudes of men of every type, though especially with the nobles.

He would 'sometimes quarry stone himself with other workmen. Nor does he shrink from watching and even practising, for the sake of amusement, the craft of an ordinary artisan', adds Monserrate. An Iranian immigrant, Rafi al-Din Ibrahim Shirazi, who had found a niche for himself in the Deccan state of Bijapur and has left behind a detailed account of his stay in India, once had the chance to see Akbar when he was due to receive the ambassador of Shah Tahmasb of Iran. For the reception, a pavilion had been erected and extensive festivities had been organized amidst a throng of people, Shirazi among them. All of a sudden, clamour of 'badshah salamat' ('long live the king') arose.

> I looked to my left and right but did not find anyone having the appearance of a king. As I turned around, I saw standing there a young man of about twenty years. He was supporting his head on one of his hands that rested on the shoulder of a companion. I could guess he was the king. But the men continued to stand around rubbing shoulders with each other. No one observed the etiquette of showing respect to the king.

Shirazi was understandably curious at the air of informality in a formal assembly of the court and curiosity led him to ask some of those present: 'Is the custom of showing respect not observed at this court? No one has paid respects to the king?' They replied:

> As compared to other realms the tradition of showing respects and observing etiquette is much more elaborate here. But the King is an exceedingly informal person. He often comes out of his private apartment in ordinary dress and mixes with people around him without making any distinction between friends and strangers. In this situation, how could it be possible [for anyone] to all the time observe etiquette?

On another occasion Shirazi saw Akbar flying a kite from the roof of his apartment; he was wearing a *lungi* (a simple, informal unstitched piece of cloth wrapped around the waist and flowing down to the feet, still much in use among the common people) and his head was uncovered, again a rare sight. An aspect of his accessibility was his ability to hear diverse opinions and at times even alter his own as a result. The unseemly fights between priests and theologians of various religions in their search for a seat near the Emperor in the Ibadat Khana, where Akbar engaged in a personal search for the ultimate religious Truth through collective discussion, simultaneously points to the symbolic significance of physical proximity to the king's person and its evolutionary, unsettled state.

The frame of courtly behaviour was normatively strong, but empirically there were many stretch spots in it. Akbar, in his edict dismissing Bairam Khan from the high post of *Vakil* and Khan-i Khanan in 1560, notes that although several courtiers had defied etiquette and had spoken so rudely in the young ruler's presence, as to 'deserve to have [their] tongues cut out or rather to be put to death', the offenders went unpunished because they had enjoyed the Khan's patronage. Muzaffar Khan, one of Akbar's highest and favourite nobles, behaved rudely with the Emperor. Akbar 'cast him off from the pinnacle of confidence and granted him permission to go to Haj so that in his exile from confidence his unsound condition might be amended'.

Proximity to the 'Presence' was clearly not an unmixed blessing; if it was an eminently coveted privilege, it could also fray tempers of the coolest of men and invite severe punishment. Another high noble, Azam

---

Figure 6   Akbar supervising building of Fathpur Sikri. Forever energetic, Akbar was one Emperor who never thought any task too far below his dignity. He was also convinced that every little task needed his personal attention. It was thus that he built a magnificent capital at Fathpur Sikri, a metaphor for his empire. © V & A Picture Lilbrary.

Khan, was rude to Akbar on two occasions. On the first, he passed some truly nasty remarks about Akbar's Din-i Ilahi. He then went away from the court for six years on the pretext of growing a beard. When the Emperor wrote to him enquiring whether his beard had not yet grown long enough, he wrote back a long and rude reply. In yet another incident, also of Akbar's reign, Lashkar Khan, who had held some of the highest posts such as Mir-i Arz, Chief of the Department of the Army, and Mir Bakhshi, the empire's Paymaster General, came drunk to the court and caused some disturbance. He was led round the city tied to a horse's tail and was then imprisoned, though to be pardoned later.

At times, though, even boorish behaviour did not evoke imperial annoyance. Syed Mahmud of Barha had won a victory and was boasting of it in court with repeated references to himself. On being politely cautioned that he owed his victory to the Emperor's good furtune, *Iqbal-i Padshahi*, he misunderstood 'Iqbal'as the proper name of a court- ier and announced in a somewhat loud voice that no Iqbal was with him in the battlefield and therefore the credit for the victory belonged exclu- sively to him and his brothers. Akbar smiled and praised him, even though he may have realized that the 'misunderstanding' was perhaps not unintentional. Manucci and Bernier also tell us stories of audacious defiance of etiquette in Shah Jahan's presence which actually pleased him. In Manucci's account, a *mansabdar*, whom he does not identify, sat down in the Emperor's presence and was therefore dismissed. Upon which the officer sat down again, saying now that he was no longer the king's servant, he could be at ease and sit down. Shah Jahan felt pleased at the man's ready wit and restored his *mansab*. Bernier reports of a trader, always employed in the king's service, leaving behind 200,000 sovereigns upon his death. His son was a spendthrift and the widow was rather wary of handing out the vast amount to him. The son appealed to the Emperor, who decided that the lady must give away half her wealth to the state, a quarter to the son and be content with the second quarter herself. The gutsy lady struggled with the court attendants and succeeded in drawing his attention. She then enquired that while the order to hand over a share to the son was understandable, for he would inherit all the property in the end anyway, what relation did his Majesty bear with her deceased husband to inherit half his possessions? Shah Jahan was might- ily amused by her audacity and let her off. He also appreciated the brusque defence of the ruler of Golconda by its ambassador to his court when asked if his master was the same height as the Emperor's slave whisking flies. The ambassador would not take the implied slight and retorted, 'My King is four fingers taller than Your Majesty!' The reply pleased Shah Jahan and he remitted three years tribute, amounting to a hefty 900,000 rupees, and gave the ambassador a rich robe of honour and a handsome horse. Manucci, who records this episode, was an eyewitness to it.

There are, too, not infrequent occurrences of the King himself losing control of his tongue and letting off undignified language. Akbar himself used a filthy Hindi abuse for his foster-brother Adham Khan, calling him a catamite, when he had killed the Emperor's favourite officer Shams al-Din Ataka. At one time, Akbar sought to proselytize Qutb al-Din Khan and Shahbaz Khan, his nobles, to his Din-i Ilahi, and the two were reluctant. Qutb al-Din in fact became quite rude and asked the Emperor how would foreign rulers such as the King of Constantinople take the suggestion, since they too followed the same faith, i.e. Islam? The question irritated Akbar, who in turn asked whether Qutb al-Din was being rude on behalf of the ruler of Constantinople. Shahbaz too objected to the Emperor's suggestion. Birbal in his turn ridiculed Islam, and Shahbaz in a fit of rage hit back with, 'You accursed infidel! At the moment you are able to talk like this, but someday we shall come up to your level (i.e. shall get even with you)!' This provoked Akbar to say to Shahbaz in particular and to everyone else in general: 'Would that they hit you on your mouth with shoes full of filth!' Aurangzeb's use of epithets wasn't quite up to the imperial mark when he spoke of Qutb Shah, ruler of Bijapur: 'I had at first delayed punishing this vendor of Chinaware, this ape-like buffoon and this drummer. Now that this cock has come forward crowing, how can I wait any longer?' Mercifully, these expletives were not deleted from contemporary records; it feels good to know from them that great Emperors too were human in the end.

The stretch spots get taut with time, and references to disputes over one's placement relative to the king, or testing out one's personal space in the court by violating etiquette and speaking rudely to the king, seem to taper off by Shah Jahan's and Aurangzeb's time.

Akbar's own experiment with the formulation of the Din-i Ilahi attests to the evolutionary stage in the structure of courtly behaviour. Formulated as a sort of universalist religion, literally religion of God rather than of Muhammad, Christ or Krishna, and deriving a good part of its ethos and its format of the spiritual master–disciple, *Pir–Murid*, relationship from the Sufi world, it demanded unquestioning loyalty to the person of Akbar. This one loyalty was to supersede all other loyalties – denominational, sectarian, regional, whatever – and bind the entire ruling elite, the target area of disciples, in a single thread, as John F. Richards has so persuasively argued. Loyalty was to be owed to the person of the Emperor, not to the throne on which he sat. Not yet.

Jahangir seems to have continued the *Pir–Murid* relationship, if somewhat half-heartedly. By the reign of Shah Jahan the transformation had taken shape through its own process of evolution, rather than through determined steps on anyone's part. A formatting of roles of the Emperor and the courtiers had emerged, in which the solidity of structures grew at the expense of personal spaces. When all the numerous courtiers in Shah Jahan's court are depicted in Mughal paintings standing in a nearly uniform posture, or when description of Emperors, princes and high nobles in the court chronicles follows the given pattern of words, persons were being visualized in formats. The eyes of all courtiers were henceforth metaphorically fixed on the throne, or the person occupying it. There was a valorization of the throne and its occupant as long as he sat on it. At one remove, it was an impersonalization of monarchy; loyalty would henceforth be owed to the throne, regardless of who sat on it. Shah Jahan was to pay the highest price for this development: when his third son snatched the throne from him and placed himself upon it, virtually exiling his father to a single room in Agra's Red Fort; it took little time and less embarrassment for the transfer of nobles' loyalties to him. This was an episode whose essence was frequently repeated in what remained of Mughal history.

The giving of gifts as an acknowledgement of status difference seems to have gradually evolved into a norm in the Mughal court. Neither during the Delhi Sultanate nor in the reigns of Babur and Humayun is the giving of presents to the ruler recorded as an obligation, although gifts did change hands. Babur himself had earned the sobriquet of *qalandar*, one possessed of an attitude of detachment to worldly goods, by giving away most precious things to people of various sorts; he leaves the impression of giving away more than he received. There are very few references to his receiving gifts. It was Akbar who made it customary for anyone going to the court with a petition to attach a suitable gift to it. 'He issued a general order that everyone from the highest to the lowest should bring him a present,' writes historian Badauni of Akbar. Gifts were also part of the ceremony of receiving the Emperor in one's own mansion and their competitive lavishness was a step in one's rise in the king's estimation and perhaps of formal status. The chronicles record innumerable occasions when the Emperor accepted invitations to visit the residences of his nobles, some of whom were also his relatives, and received expensive gifts. During the 17 days of New Year festivity in March, it became customary for great nobles of Akbar to invite him to their house and give choice presents of jewels and jewelled things, precious horses and elephants to him. Indeed, 'even food and perfumes and presents fit for entertainers were deposited in the treasury', writes Badauni, tongue firmly in cheek. Of the presents, Akbar would accept whatever caught his fancy and return the rest to the host. Jahangir, ever anxious both to conform and to depart from his father's practices, 'let them off with their gifts with the exception of a few from my immediate retainers which

I accepted in order to gratify them'. Very meticulous recording of the gifts and their values came into vogue as the custom became well established. Interestingly, Akbar's predecessor in Kashmir, Zain al-Abidin, also his precursor in numerous ways, especially in formulating state policy of religious tolerance, had abolished the custom of receiving presents.

Jahangir, however, goes beyond making such general estimates of the value of gifts given and received and never fails to record in his *Tuzuk* the exact price of such gifts. Indeed, even as he admires the beauty or grandeur of a building or a diamond or anything, he seldom fails to weigh his appreciation in terms of its cost. In Gujarat he visited the lofty tomb of Sayyid Mubarak Bukhari, late officer of state, built by his son. 'It is a very lofty cupola', he observes, and 'must have cost more than two lakhs [hundred thousand] of rupees.' In Lahore, on the river bank, he alighted at the 'handsome' palace built for him and records his admiration for its 'great beauty and delicacy' before concluding that its cost was of the order of Rs 700,000. Even the tomb of Shaikh Salim Chishti in the Fatehpur Sikri complex – the one Shaikh who was a sort of patron saint of the Mughal family and to whose intercession with God Jahangir owed his birth and his personal name, Salim – was evaluated in terms of the money Akbar had spent upon it and the adjoining mosque. This trader's mind-set was a little unusual for a Mughal ruler, who was expected to retain a fine distinction between generosity and the business of gifts, even if the dividing lines were easily blurred. His uncle Mirza Hakim, Akbar's half-brother, rival and serious challenger for the throne in 1579–80, was closer to the medieval ethos of giving and receiving gifts without counting exact costs. At Kabul he received warmly the poet Khwaja Husain Marvi on his way back from India. The poet presented his gifts of merchandise, valuables and precious articles from Hindustan. In doing so, he rose and took the list of his presents from the concerned official and started giving details of the quantity and quality, with the name of each article and its price. This breached all decorum of gift giving, historian Badauni tells us, and it so disgusted the Mirza that he dismissed the assembly and ordered all those present to carry off whatever they fancied. 'In the space of a little while everything was plundered,' observes Badauni, never one to miss a chance of being caustic.

The giving and sometimes exchange of gifts implicated several kinds of relationships, with status hierarchy being at the very core. When Babur had conquered India at the battle of Panipat in 1526, he sent gifts for everyone in Kabul where his family awaited the turn in his fortune. This established his personal generosity as well as grandeur as ruler. Giving of gifts to all and sundry on virtually any occasion finds frequent mention in the *Babur Nama*; the Emperor seems to have looked out for pretexts for doing so, in keeping with his image of *qalandar*. Thus 'gifts were made to the stone-cutters and labourers and the whole body of workmen in the way customary for master-workmen and wage-earners of Agra'. Akbar too gave away 'great gifts to everyone' after his victory in Gujarat, though 'everyone' seems suspiciously hyperbolic here. Gifts were received from and given to envoys on their arrival and departure; and of course they were given generously to relatives.

Subtle shades of hierarchy became inscribed in the obligatory giving of gifts. Gulbadan, Babur's daughter, was five years old when his Khalifa and vizir gave her 5,000 *shahrukhis* (coins) and five horses on first encounter; the vizir's wife placed 3,000 of the same coins and three horses before the young princess. Hierarchy gets reflected in two ways here: although the noble had as high a dual position as the Emperor's Khalifa and vizir, he was still inferior to a young female child of royalty; and his wife, though obliged to make a gift, could not equal or exceed her husband's.

Within the family, too, differently valued gifts were given to members in accordance with the seniority of their birth. Jahangir gave rubies of the value of Rs 60,000 to his elder son Parvaiz and of 40,000 to the younger son Khurram, later to become Shah Jahan. Shah Jahan himself exceeded his own legendary generosity as Emperor in giving away to his eldest and favourite son Dara Shukoh 10 million rupees in cash, jewels worth 2.3 million and a pearl necklace off his own neck, worth 1.4 million.

Virtually anything could comprise a gift from or to the Emperor. Babur had received, among other things, two 'Circassian girls' from a Turkman, Sulaiman. Gold, silver, cash, horses, elephants, other rare animals, a shell that sucked out snake poison, shikar (game), books, expensive clothes, jewels and jewelled daggers and swords, fruits, especially melons which remained very dear to imperial hearts, sometimes land, in one case even Arabian dogs – all these and several other commodities are mentioned in our sources in the context of giving of gifts by and to the Emperor. Akbar at one time became rather enamoured of cock fights; an order consequently went out that whoever came to do him *kurnish* should remember to bring a cock along. This gave Shams al-Din Ataka, husband of Akbar's favourite foster-mother Jiji Anaga, the pretext to play a prank and bring a hen to fight with the royal cock, much to the amusement of courtiers. Jahangir records having received 'trustworthy eunuchs' as a gift.

The sources also surprise us by recording the demand of certain items as gifts by the recipients, even at the level of rulers. Muhammad Husain Chelebi had procured a crystal cup in Iraq for Jahangir; the Shah of Iran came to know of it and requested the Mughal Emperor to pass it on to him as a present, which Jahangir did not have the heart to refuse. Jahangir also had to part with the best of his elephants that had endeared himself to Shah Jahan. Jahangir's fondness for it was manifest in the gold chains used to tie it. Shah Jahan asked for it several times and 'seeing no way out it I gave it to him'. Shah Jahan's elder brother Parvaiz had asked his father for a special *nadiri* (unique) robe of honour and a jewelled crown 'so that he might wear them and be distinguished on the day of meeting me and of having the good fortune to pay his respects'. The request was acceded to. On Thomas Roe's testimony, Jahangir seems to have asked him several times what gifts he would like from the Emperor, and each time Roe emphasized that demanding or specifying a gift was contrary to the culture of his own society and that he would receive anything from him with gratitude, even if its value were a mere rupee. On his testimony again, virtually every time he went to see Jahangir, the Emperor would ask him what presents he had brought and at times specified the ones he desired. On one occasion he seems to have asked for some English 'doggs'. Clearly a clash of cultures here, although one needs to be a little wary of Roe's claims, keen as he ever was to establish the superiority of his own and his society's mores. On the other hand, there are also instances of some gifts being declined. Sometimes the gifts received were displayed in public, either for their high value or for reasons of intimacy with the gift giver. Babur received offerings from his favourite wife Mahim and from Humayun, which were set out on display while he sat in the large Hall of Audience. Jahangir descended from the *jharoka* to inspect Shah Jahan's offerings put on display 'to please the prince'.

It was also possible for an Emperor to have very high expectations when receiving gifts and to be pleased or disappointed at the ones received. Jahangir almost greedily enumerates the gifts given him by Shah Jahan and their prices. 'Briefly, the whole of his offerings was of the value of Rs 4,50,000.' His father-in-law Itmad al-Daulah, too, presented him with a throne of gold and silver made by a European when he visited his house 'to raise his standing'; it cost the same as Shah Jahan's gifts. Besides, some other presents amounting to Rs 100,000 accompanied the throne. The Emperor was visibly pleased and wrote: 'What comparison is there between him and others?' On the other hand, he does not refrain from recording his dismay at the presents Muqarrab Khan had given him, for 'there was nothing rare among them, nor anything I took fancy to, and so I felt ashamed' at having received them. Emperors also occasionally passed on gifts they had received to someone else, either because of their low value or because of their rarity. Jahangir had received a rare ruby from the Shah of Iran and gave it away to Shah Jahan.

Gifts were exchanged between husbands and wives, parents and children, and between siblings. The quantum and value of gifts rose manifold if a particular favour or pardon of a grave offence was sought through this medium. Prince Salim, later Jahangir, had waged a serious rebellion against his father and had gone to Allahabad, where he had declared himself the sovereign. When the rebellion did not quite take off, he sought his father's pardon. He presented Akbar with 12,000 gold coins and 977 elephants, of which 350 were accepted.

There are instances of a gift being sought by the Emperor for the grant of a title to a noble. When the fort of Torna (in the Deccan) was captured, Aurangzeb distributed rewards to his warriors. Mir Khan, close to the Emperor's person, became Amir Khan, which was his father's title. The Emperor asked, 'When your father Mir Khan became Amir Khan, he presented to the Emperor Shah Jahan 100,000 rupees for the grant of an *alif* [first letter of the Arabic/Persian alphabet = A, also equivalent to 1]; what will you present me?' The newly promoted but old noble replied: 'May a thousand lives be sacrificed for Your Majesty! My life and property are all propitiatory alms (*tasadduq*) for the sake of Your Majesty!' Next day he presented to the Emperor a copy of the Quran in the handwriting of Yaqut, its legendary scribe. He certainly knew what would gladden Aurangzeb's heart, for the Emperor remarked, 'You have made me a present which exceeds the world and its contents in value,' and gifted him an elephant. Manucci also records Aurangzeb's visit to his dying foster-brother Bahadur Khan, and accepting a magnificent throne costing 5 million rupees, and a plateful of precious stones, horses and elephants from him.

Of all gifts, the most coveted was the robe of honour that the Emperor gave to princes, nobles, ambassadors and so on, owing to the very dense symbolic signification embedded in it. A robe of honour called *khila't* signified extension of part of the glory, prestige and authority attached to the king's person. The Arabic term, *khila't*, has its Persian counterpart, *sar o pa*, 'head-to-foot'. *Khila't* or *sar o pa* comprised apparel from head to foot. The present of *sar o pa*, the entire body wear, carried the impress of completeness, signified in the king's person, now being imparted to the recipient. Since the king's person symbolically expanded into the whole space of the empire, the recipient too was incorporated into the imperial presence and became part and extension of it. Hence the high prestige attached to it. The *khila't* was first touched by His Majesty with his palm; or else it was lightly brushed across his shoulder before handing it over to the recipient. A robe taken from the Emperor's personal wardrobe, and especially off his person, multiplied the glory several fold, and was given as an extraordinary act of favour or in recognition of some exceptional deed of service to the empire. The receipt of the *khila't* necessitated the replication of all court ceremonies, such as *kurnish* and *taslim*. Even as the recipient was publicly proclaimed part of the imperial presence in the empire, *kurnish* was a reminder to him and the empire that he owed his elevation to his subordination. It gave him his *raison d'être*.

There are also episodes on record of gifts either being returned or declined. Akbar refused to accept gifts from Ibrahim Husain Mirza, 'for he was not sincere'. Thomas Roe once presented a European book of maps to Jahangir and the Emperor was apparently pleased with it. A few days later, however, he asked Roe if he would care to take the book back, for none of his learned men could read it, and Roe was glad to accept the offer. John Mildenhall, in India between 1599 and 1606, also mentions that a few of Akbar's nobles refused to accept gifts from him because they had accepted some from his enemies, the Jesuits. Tavernier tells us of an unnamed noble declining one from a Dutch trader 'out of friendship for Europeans'. His own 'tips' (*bakhshish*) to the soldiers of Mir Jumla, among the highest of Aurangzeb's nobles, indeed of all Mughal nobles, were not accepted.

Then there was a bit of haggling over the value of gifts between an Emperor and a poet. Jahangir promised Matrabi, the poet, the gift of a horse with a saddle. He then consulted the poet about the kind of horse and saddle that would meet with his desire. Matrabi was clear about his preference: he wanted the one that was most expensive. Jahangir sought to dissuade him, pleading that if an Iraqi horse was more expensive than a Turkish one, it was also more energetic and faster and therefore difficult to control. Of the saddles, too, the poet went for the more expensive velvety one. Again, Jahangir tried to persuade him to accept the one that cost less, saying it was the more durable, but the poet would have none of it. In the end, he got what he wanted. If the Emperor somewhat belied one stereotype of royal indifference towards lucre, the poet confirmed another, of the combination of genius, penury and a trace of greed.

The Emperor's control over gifts did not end with handing it over to the recipient. Some gifts, like a certain type of bejewelled headgear, *sarpech*, were given only to high nobles of the *mansab* of 4,000 and above, although Aurangzeb gave one to a young son of the great *amir*, Muhammad Amin Khan. This headgear could be worn on Sundays only and the awardee was not permitted to wear another that bore a resemblance to it.

European travellers record their surprise at the prevalence of this custom in a tone of disapproval. Sir Thomas Roe, forever eager to assert the superiority of the evolving subjection of the king's authority to parliamentary control back home and unable to understand an alternative cultural and political milieu, constantly denounces the giving of 'gifts' and 'tributes' to the Mughal Emperor, princes and nobles as 'dayly bribes'. Giving of *nazr* by an inferior to his superior was reflective of the hierarchy of relationship, and estimating the value of a gift given, far from being an index of greed, underlined the status of the giver and the receiver, an all important consideration in medieval societies and polities.[22] Formal presents of symmetrical value are exchanged between equals; unilateral presents or unequal exchanges reaffirm hierarchy of status. If Roe himself presented petty gifts to the Mughal Emperor and nobles, he could hardly expect them to regard his master as a great king, and his country as a major presence in the world scenario. Roe also presented himself as both a representative of King James I and of the English traders, the English East India Company. Perfectly compatible in his world view; totally incompatible in that of his hosts. But Roe could never fathom why.

De Laet observes that giving rich gifts to the King was the best way to obtain favours, and Tavernier talks of 'secret presents' being passed on to Shah Jahan and his daughter Jahan Ara in return for the grant of Governorship of Allahabad, a coveted post. Clearly, there was an enormous cultural distance here.

Etiquette also required the King to engage in lavish gift giving, as we have seen at the beginning of this chapter and elsewhere.

As the microcosm of society, as well as its apex, the court reflected and regulated social order by regulating itself. Understandably then several forms of court etiquette evolved through interaction between social and imperial layers. The notion of the court as a sacred space owed its inspiration to places of worship. The virtual omnipresence of the Emperor in every nook and corner of his empire and obeisance due to any emblem of his being, his *farman*, or the food from his *dastar khwan*, 'table' (actually a white sheet laid out on the floor), or even the slippers he wore, also seem to have been inspired by popular religious vision. Some of the court rituals signifying submission to the king, too, are cast in the general religious idiom of surrender to God; the more specific ones such as *jharoka darshan*, a passing glimpse, and signifiers of master-- disciple relationship are derived from the ground level of the village deity or the Sufi *khanqah*. The covered head and bare feet, as the norm of attendance at court dictated, was perhaps taken up from the ground too, where, as Manucci tells us, it was the mode of appearance before one's superiors amongst the Hindus. Being bare of head and foot on the other hand pointed to an abnormal situation of acceptance of one's defeat, of surrender.

Forms of courtly behaviour travelled downwards as well. In some very interesting ways, the world of the Sufis was the theatre of contest as well as emulation vis-à-vis the court. If the court embodied temporal authority in wielding the sword and exercising administrative control over its subjects, the Sufi saint's power arose from the very fact of his renunciation of it. He contested the state's power by excluding himself from it. If

22   See Colin Paul Mitchell, *Sir Thomas Roe and the Mughal Empire*, Karachi, 2000.

Figure 7 *Jahangir visiting Jogi Jadrup*, imperial Mughal School, *c.*1616–1620. The courtly posture of Jahangir and the casual one of the Jogi are telling; they reinforce the superiority of the power of renunciation to that of worldly possessions, of moral power to state power, a running theme in both Hindu and Islamic cultural streams. Courtesy Musée Guimet, Paris.

he was an outsider to the state, the state's authority also stopped short at his door. Therefore he was bound by neither the laws of state nor the rules of court. Since his own power derived from his moral authority, its superiority to the authority of the state was *ipso facto* established even in the eyes of the rulers themselves. On innumerable occasions Mughal Emperors went to the hermitages of Sufi saints, or for that matter Hindu recluses, and several paintings depict the visits evocatively. The King sits as a deferential courtier in proper decorum before the hermit, legs crossed, arms folded; the hermit on the other hand is postured sitting casually, as if the Emperor is one among the countless and nameless visitors to the recluse seeking solace. If he did go to the court, he still refused to abide by its etiquette, as the ascetic of Agra did when participating in a discussion at the Ibadat Khana. A noble of Akbar's, Shaikh Badr al-Din, turned a recluse, and 'since he was no longer bound to customary etiquette, he infringed it many a time in the mode of sitting, rising and speaking'.

Yet, in the organization of the Sufi *khanqah,* there is much that is modelled on the court. Hierarchy in the *khanqah* follows the spiritual attainments of its inhabitants, with pride of place given to the institution's head. The imagery of titles used for the eminent figures of exceptional attainments among Sufis is derived from the imperial court. Shaikh Nizam al-Din Aulia, the most celebrated of them from the late thirteenth and first quarter of the fourteenth centuries, was reverentially referred to as *Sultan al-Arifin* (Sultan among the mystics) and *Sultan al-Mashaikh* (Sultan among the Shaikhs), although these titles for him seem to be of later origin. Shaikh Ahmad Sirhindi of Akbar's and Jahangir's time warns that it was impolite to speak in a voice louder than one's *Pir*, reminding one of the court ambience. Much like administrative and revenue divisions necessary for governance, the Sufi *silsilah*, order or chain of *khanqahs*, replicated the division of their territorial jurisdictions, too, and operated with an almost rigid, though unwritten, prohibition of transgression of the jurisdiction. Theirs was a sort of parallel government, but modelled after the original.

The Mughal court ceremony was also being replicated in the provinces by governors, often princes of the royal blood and high level *amirs*, to the extent that the Emperor occasionally reminded them of his exclusive privilege to some of them. Among the prohibitions that Jahangir announced for his high nobles was the giving of titles, forcing imperial servants to perform *kurnish* before them, and the beating of drums to announce their arrival. Jahangir indeed records several royal prerogatives being replicated by the high nobility, especially on the empire's peripheries: appearing in the *jharoka*, organizing and witnessing elephant fights, inflicting corporal punishments, and converting people to Islam, among others. The inviolability of the Emperor's harem, with its sanctity and exclusivity, was also reproduced on a much lower key down to the *haveli* in every important street and habitat. It was thus that the imperial presence became culturally expansive and made itself felt in the life of the meanest citizen.

In the end, it was the waning of the empire in the eighteenth century that liberated the Emperor and his nobles from the increasingly inflexible role formats, with their governing rules of etiquette. If the model of austere, rugged and virile masculinity handed down by the *Akhlaq* literature had been lauded, though only intermittently followed in practice,[23] overt sensuality now began to pervade all levels of court life. Nothing evokes this metamorphosis more definitively than a Mughal miniature of the 1740s, depicting Emperor Muhammad Shah in dalliance with a nondescript young woman. Even as Muhammad Shah had impotently watched the soldiers of the Iranian invader Nadir Shah plunder and massacre the inhabitants of Delhi in 1739, the depiction of his masculinity gets centred on an exclusively sexual metaphor: his massive phallus penetrating – conquering – a female body, all visible to the naked eye.[24] Sensuality also brings women as active sexual beings, rather than as revered asexual mothers and elderly aunts, centre-stage at the court. Lal Kunwar, the consort of Emperor Jahandar Shah, epitomizes this sensual moment in eighteenth-century India. She had nothing else to recommend her except her sexuality – no proud genealogy, no history of elite contacts, no inheritance of distinctive culture. Indeed, if anything, her cultural inheritance established her roots in the lowest layers of the soil. When she failed to conceive after prolonged companionship with Jahandar Shah, the two of them bathed naked for 40 days in a tank in Mehrauli (in south Delhi), in search of magic healing of infertility in the genre of folk healing practices. Even as the event evokes a magical commingling of imperial and folk cultures, this was the ambience that shocked later generations of historians in the nineteenth and first half of the twentieth centuries as a manifestation of moral degeneration, steeped as they were in Victorian puritanism. The eighteenth century did not, however, attach any stigma to the denouement, for it did not counterpose sexuality and morality; it did nevertheless draw attention to the change.[25]

---

23   If Akbar and Aurangzeb are always perceived in history as each other's negation, their commitment to austerity is nevertheless a binding thread.
24   Miniature J.66–1 in the Oriental and India Office Collection, British Library, London.
25   The most celebrated bit of evidence of the general ambience of sensuality in the eighteenth century without confounding it with any moral issues comes from Dargah Quli Khan's very evocative account, *Muraqqa-i Dehli*. The Persian language text has been edited and its Urdu tr. undertaken and published by Khaliq Anjum as *Muraqqa-i Dehli*,

The loosening of court etiquette, was, however, the subject of lament among court poets and historians, for whom it had been a way of life. Mir Taqi Mir, the great Urdu poet of the eighteenth century, puts it ever so poignantly:

> Know not this age as the one gone by, Mir
> Times have changed; the very earth and the sky have changed.

For Sauda, another eminent literary figure of the same era,

> The age of the cup of wine has turned into the age of moist eyes
> Look, Sauda, at the havoc played by destiny's vicissitudes.

Indeed, a whole genre of Urdu literature grew in this period; this is known as *Shahr Ashob*, 'Woes of the City', i.e. Delhi. For the court and its dependants the world had indeed come to an end, bringing them close to the 'after me the deluge' syndrome, ever so present in periods of crisis.

Yet nostalgia and pretension to grandeur, and the attempt to remain close to popular expectation, kept the form of court etiquette even as its substance was lost. The form became a site of contest between the declining empire and the rising East India Company during the eighteenth and nineteenth centuries. In a delicious irony, 'Emperor' Akbar II, seeking effective recognition by the British Governor-General for nomination of his third son as heir apparent in preference to his eldest son, took several contorted steps towards this end. At one point, Akbar wrote to the Governor-General, Lord Minto, calling him his 'favoured son and servant', much as his namesake predecessor would have addressed his favourite noble in the sixteenth century. Minto was not inclined to overlook the real state for the ceremonial, and was keen to convey to His Majesty a 'full and explicit declaration' of the 'nature and principles' of their relationship. Slightly later, a meeting between Governor-General Lord Hastings and Akbar II failed to materialize when the Emperor insisted that the Lord conform to the ceremony of a subject approaching the King in his court, with appropriate presents, *nazrs*. When the Governor-General's successor Lord Amherst visited Delhi in 1826, his admission to the Presence was worked out in every nuance. As other courtiers remained standing, Amherst was seated to the throne's right angle and he gave no present. The King gifted a string of pearls to the

New Delhi, 1993. For English tr., Chander Shekhar and Shama Mitra Chenoy, *Muraqqa-e-Dehli*, Delhi,1989. Urvashi Dalal discusses this aspect with elan in her doctoral dissertation, 'Delhi Society in the Eighteenth Century', Jawaharlal Nehru University, New Delhi, 1998.

visitor. Some time later, Akbar returned the visit, following the same procedure, the Governor-General giving the gift this time. This was to become the set pattern of ceremonial relationships between the Mughals and the British at the highest levels.

There was, however, still some space for contest. The British Resident Hawkins was appalled at the implicit servility even in the curtailed ceremonies at the court, especially in the giving of an obligatory present to His Majesty, who was actually a pensioner of the East India Company. He sought permission from his superiors in Calcutta to refrain from doing so; when permission was rather brusquely denied, he subverted the etiquette even as he observed it by giving the present with one rather than two hands joined together. The presents, however, remained a sore point with the British, for they implied the recognition of the Mughal Emperor's sovereign status, when, in fact, in their perception he was dependent upon the Company's charity even for his daily existence. Lord Hastings, on his arrival in India in 1813, had already abolished the ceremony of the Governor-General presenting *nazrs* seven times a year to the King and it was not renewed thereafter. In 1851 the last Mughal Emperor, Bahadur Shah Zafar, was forced to content himself with a monthly monetary equivalent of *nazrs*. The Company had made its point; substance had caught up with the shadow.

Figure 8 A Young Lady Brought to the Harem is a later description of the painting. The ambience for the rendezvous is romantic, with moonshine spread on the palace terrace. The passion of the Prince is hard to cool, what with the moon and the fan. Attendants are an aid, not an embarrassment to the lusting Prince. Courtesy of the National Museum, New Delhi.

3
The World of the Mughal Family

The dominant popular image of the Mughal family is a vast number of women crowding a harem, all for giving pleasure to one man, the Emperor, whose sexual appetite was insatiable. The term harem itself evokes images of an immense fortified playground for carrying out one man's sexual fantasies, with hundreds of women of all shapes and sizes, colours and ethnic groups at his beck and call. In fact, contrary to this image, 'harem' is a sacred word, denoting a place of worship, the sanctum sanctorum, where the committing of any sin is forbidden (*haram*); it was thus at least in concept a site for restraint rather than excesses in sexual among other, filial, relationships.

Estimates of the number of women in the harem vary from one informant to another, often depending upon the dimensions of one's fantasy. With Babur and Humayun the figures were modest, nowhere running into hundreds and thousands; both the Emperors and their chroniclers seem to have been content with less than a dozen wives all told and a couple of concubines. Come Akbar and the number of women in the imperial harem turns mind-boggling. Fr. Monserrate gives Akbar 300 wives in temporary marriages for making political alliances. Abul Fazl, however, arrives at the astounding figure of 5,000 women in Akbar's harem. By zeroing in on this figure, Abul Fazl was making a political statement of the grandeur of his master's imperial presence, not totalling up an exact numerical count. His statement that each of the 5,000 women had a decent apartment of her own, with balconies and gardens, and was looked after by a band of maids is even more of a hyperbole. For to have built apartments on that scale within the rather limited residential complex – first Fatehpur Sikri and then Agra's Red Fort – and yet to have left virtually no trace of them behind, when remains of most other constructions have indeed survived, points to the symbolic nature of the figure: it is clearly a figure of speech rather than a statement of fact[1] and begins to set the trend. Hawkins gives Jahangir 300 wives and Coryat 1,000 'for his own body of which the chiefest is called Normal [Nur Mahal, later Nur Jahan]'. For Beni Prasad, modern biographer of Jahangir, even 300 is a 'monstrous' figure, although the only qualification he introduces is that it would probably comprise all his concubines as well.[2] From Shah Jahan's time, however, the number of wives for His Majesty did not exceed the legally prescribed four, although the harem still had a large space for concubines, but no longer running into hundreds.

Mughal Muslim rulers, however, were not the only ones credited with very large harems. Rai Puran Mal of Kalinjar, whom Sher Shah defeated in his life's last battle in 1545, was reported by Nizam al-Din Ahmad, historian of Akbar's reign, to have 'taken two thousand Hindu and Muslim women into his harem'. The Hindu ruler of the temple city of Thanjavur in present-day Tamil Nadu, too, had the reputation of possessing 700 wives and 15,000 concubines, going by Manucci's count. Akbar's favourite Rajput noble Man Singh was said by Jahangir to have possessed a similarly large harem with 1,500 'wives' and somewhere between 200 and 300 children in his backyard.[3]

If the concept of the nuclear family – the unit of parents and children until they arrive at adulthood – has a touch of modernity to it, the medieval family was not quite susceptible to clear definitions and tended to be expansive. Without a legal or religious prescription of monogamy, except for Christians whose presence in Mughal India was minuscule, polygamy within the ruling class was the predominant practice. Indeed, the number of women in one's harem was perceived as one of the major symbols of the state's power and grandeur. Polygamy, among other factors, ensured the expansive family.

While the King was the only adult male with unhindered access to the harem, it was his mother whose pre-eminence in the harem was universally acknowledged and respected. Paying obeisance to one's mother was a Chingizi custom (*buzurgdasht*, bestowed by ancestors), observes Abul Fazl. Mughal history is full of stories, respectfully told by its chroniclers, of the most powerful rulers standing before their grandmothers and mothers almost like cowering children. Abul Fazl records the early days of Babur, when his grandmother Shah Begum had set up Khan Mirza

---

1   K. S. Lal has discussed this issue in some detail and with conviction in his *The Mughal Harem*, New Delhi, 1988: 38–41.

2   Beni Prasad, *History of Jahangir*, Allahabad, 1930: 26.

3   The Raja's modern biographer, R. N. Prasad, however, stoutly refutes the figure as if it were an uncharitable allegation; *Raja Man Singh of Amber*, Calcutta, 1966: 130. He substitutes the figure with a moderate 'less than two dozen wives and over a dozen children'.

against him. Babur went up to her, knelt before her and said disarmingly: 'If a mother has special affection for one child, why should that cause resentment in another? There is after all no limit to her authority.' He then added: 'I have been up long and have travelled a long distance,' and, laying his head in her lap, went to sleep. When Akbar's mother Hamida Banu, given the title of Mariam Makani (akin to Mary), expressed a wish to visit him almost towards the last years of his reign, it became a major event for him and he showed her the courtesies that were his courtiers' routine towards him. Chronicles record many visits by her to see Akbar, and each time he showed 'reverence to his visible God' and performed court rituals before her. The English traveller Thomas Coryat was struck by Akbar's devotion to her: '[W]hen his mother was carried once in a palankeen betwixt Lahor and Agra, he, travelling with her, tooke the palankeen upon his owne shoulders, commanding his greatest nobles to doe the like, and so carried her over the river from one side to the other. And never denyed her any thing.' When Salim had rebelled against Akbar, primarily for the reason that the father was keeping alive far beyond the son's expectations, on reaching Allahabad, the city Akbar had founded, he declared himself the sovereign of the Mughal empire. His offence was serious enough to be visited by capital punishment; what compounded it further was his commissioning of the murder of one of Akbar's greatest favourites, historian and courtier Abul Fazl, because he suspected that the courtier would stand in the way of reconciliation between the Prince and the Emperor. There could be no forgiveness for all of these offences, even from a generous man like Akbar, and he made no secret of it. Yet, when Mariam Makani interceded for her grandson, there was little Akbar could do except to yield. Still unsure of his father's mind, Salim wanted his grandmother to put his head at Akbar's feet, a request that was acceded to. Akbar embraced his son, although it is hard to imagine that wholehearted forgiveness followed in its wake.[4]

It was understandable then that all the major events like marriages of Princes should take place in Mariam Makani's apartment. When she fell into a coma at the age of over 77, the lamentations of Akbar, the Emperor, himself 62 and nearing the end of his life, were uncontrollable. There were two occasions when Akbar shaved off his head and moustaches in mourning for death in the family: when his favourite

---

4 De Laet mentions several restrictions placed upon Salim – like not being accompanied by more than four persons when he visited his father; or a prohibition on drawing Humayun's sword that Akbar had given him within the precincts of the palace; *The Empire of the Great Mogol*, Eng. tr. J. S. Hoyland and S. N. Banerjee (first pub. 1928), Delhi, 1975: 169–70.

foster-mother Jiji Anaga, mother of Mirza Aziz 'Koka' (also 'Kokaltash', foster-brother), died, and then again when Mariam Makani herself passed away. Jahangir in turn records his obeisance to his mother almost with a sense of pride, demonstrably performing courtesies to her as his 'slaves' would to him, as we have noticed in chapter 2. His reference to his mother was preceded by the epithet 'Hazrat', one that is usually reserved for His Majesty himself.[5] Aurangzeb, too, took recourse to mobilizing the mother of one of his sons to bring him back from the path of rebellion.

If the Emperor had one biological mother, there were nevertheless several 'mothers' in the harem, a phenomenon understandable in the context of polygamy. 'Mothers' was a term often used by Emperors, Princes and Princesses for them, implying an undifferentiated reverence for all. However, there are several indicators of both delicate differentiation and tension among women at the highest levels of hierarchy in the harem. A subtle difference in status was implied in the use of different terms for the ladies. 'Begum' was reserved for royal ladies, sometimes even newborn Princesses of royal blood; *Aghacha*, or *Agha*, on the other hand, indicated a slightly inferior origin and status, regardless of whether she was a rightful Queen married to His Majesty and even if he was very fond of her. Babur's Afghan wife was beautiful, beloved and very popular in his harem, but 'Begum' is never the term for her; she was forever the Afghani *Aghacha*. Talking of his brothers and sisters, Babur mentions Yadgar-sultan Begum, 'whose mother was a mistress called Agha-sultan'. By the time of Aurangzeb, the Hindi word *Bai* had replaced the Turkish *Agha*. Saqi Mustaid Khan, his chronicler, mentions four mothers of his children, one as Begum, two as *Bais*, and the fourth as Aurangabadi *Mahal*.

When our chronicles mention marriages of rulers or Princes, some are described in detail, including the ceremonies and celebrations around them, and become themes of Mughal miniature paintings, while others are casually recorded almost as asides. Clearly then all marriages and all wives were not on a par.

Indeed, marriages would follow a variety of patterns and took place for a variety of reasons. At the level of royalty, marriages as part of political alliances were common. Even as Akbar had fine-tuned marriages with Princesses of Rajput families as a long-term strategy to terminate three centuries of hostility with India's premier ruling groups and transform them into rock-stable bases of support for the Mughal empire, political marriages – especially for achieving immediate

5 *Tuzuk*, I: 401, where he calls his mother 'Hazrat Mariam al-Zaman', Her Majesty, Mary of the Age.

objectives – were a routine phenomenon among his predecessors. There are several instances even in pre-Mughal India when Rajput women were married to Muslim rulers as part of strategy formation. Babur and Gulbadan also give us valuable details of several marriages contracted as part of political network formation. Women had little say in such alliances, although once in a while we do come across some gutsy central Asian women walking out on their husbands, as we note elsewhere in this chapter.

There was more to marriage of course than political strategy. Love and personal choice, too, went a long distance in bringing a King and his Queen together. Babur and Masuma's marriage was a matter of mutual choice. Humayun's sister Gulbadan has lovingly told the story of his pursuit of a nondescript Hamida and her stubborn resistance to his pleas of love for 40 days before she yielded; we shall encounter the story soon again. Being able to persuade Hamida to marry him was one of Humayun's enduring achievements; she was the mother who gave the Mughal empire its greatest ruler, Akbar. Akbar's own love for the wife of a noble of his court left little room for him except to divorce her and let 'the virtuous lady' move into the Emperor's harem. Folklore, if not history, celebrates the tragic and immensely attractive love story binding Prince Salim and a courtesan, Anarkali ('the pomegranate bud'), during the reign of his stern father. Historians have usually ignored the story because 'reliable records', i.e. court chronicles, Jahangir's own *Tuzuk* and other Persian language documents make no mention of it. William Finch and Edward Terry, however, do put it on record in their travelogues.[6] Finch also says that on becoming Emperor, Jahangir did not forget his old love and built 'a sumptuous tombe . . . of stone in the midst of a foure-square garden, richly walled, with a gate and divers roomes over it'. The tomb is located in Jahangir's favourite city, Lahore, and an old-world, sprawling marketplace around it, known as Anarkali Bazar, has done well for traders and tourists for the past nearly 400 years. The date of Anarkali's death, 1008 H./AD 1598, is inscribed in letters and figures on the tomb and its construction is dated 1024 H./ AD 1615. Jahangir himself is said to have composed a verse to give expression to his longing for her and it too is inscribed on the building. It reads:

6 See the travelogues of William Finch in William Foster, ed., *Early Travels in India*, Indian reprint, New Delhi, 1985 (first pub., London, 1921): 166, and Edward Terry, ibid., 330. About Akbar's sternness as father we have Fr Monserrate's testimony: '[T]he king's nature was such that, though he loved his children very dearly, he used to give them orders rather roughly whenever he wanted anything done; and he sometimes punished them with blows as well as harsh words.' *Commentary*: 53.

To the end of the world I shall express gratitude to my Creator
If only I could see the face of my beloved once again.[7]

Both Terry and Finch state that Anarkali was a 'wife' of Akbar's, i.e. a woman in Akbar's harem. Nur Jahan's tomb, also located in the city, is rather a lonely monument on which is inscribed the apt and moving verse, composed by the legendary Queen herself: 'On the resting place of lonely persons like us not a lamp is lit, nor a flower blossoms; no moth burns its wing here, nor the nightingale sing a song' (bar mazar-i ma ghariban ne charaghe ne gule; ne pare parvana sozad, ne sada-i bulbule). A moth burning itself to death in a candle flame is the ultimate metaphor for all-consuming love in Persian poetry.

Shah Jahan's marriage to several women did not stand in the way of his intense love for Mumtaz, immortalized in the Taj Mahal. Aurangzeb too is said to have nurtured a strong inclination for a (probably Hindu) dancing girl, Hira Bai, also known as Zainabadi. The story is told a bit fancifully, rather like a tale from the epics, in Ahkam-i Alamgiri, wherein the Prince, then in his mid-30s and father of several children from more than one wife, swoons at the sight of the young lady and comes to only with great difficulty. The tale is also told more soberly in Maasir al-Umra, and by Manucci, who observes that because of his love for her 'he neglected for some time his prayers and austerities, filling up his days with music and dance; and going even further he enlivened himself with wine which he drank at the instance of the said dancing girl. The dancer died and Aurangzeb made a vow never to drink wine again or listen to music.' Manucci however does not name the girl. Her death at a young age perhaps diminished any moderating prospects of the humane quality of sensual love on the Emperor's chilly puritanism.

Among the later Mughal rulers, Jahandar Shah and his consort Lal Kunwar, a lady from the ranks of courtesans, and Muhammad Shah and his consort Koki Jiu, created new avenues of gender relations, where personal choice was the final arbiter and where sexuality invested women with a powerful resource for redefining their relations with the highest in the land. The preceding generation of historians looked upon this phenomenon with strong distaste; 'malaise', 'tragedy' and 'moral canker' are among the milder terms used for it in their historiography.[8]

7 Ta qayamat shukr goyam kardgar-i khwish ra
    Ah gar man baz binam ru-i yar-i khwish ra

S. M. Latif, Lahore, Its History, Architectural Remains and Antiquities, Lahore, 1892: 186–7.

8 K. K. Datta, Survey of India's Social and Economic History in the Eighteenth Century, 1707–1813, Delhi, 1978: 1–13; Tara Chand, History of the Freedom Movement in India, 4 vols., here vol. I, Delhi, 1961: 170; V. P. S. Raghuvanshi, Indian Society in the Eighteenth Century, Delhi 1969: 1–16.

Even as a marriage proposal from the King or on behalf of a Prince of the royal blood was hard to decline, some self-willed women did demonstrate their mind forcefully. Hamida Banu, of no eminent lineage, rebuffed Humayun's proposal for days and weeks, politely in the beginning, stiffly as he persisted. In the end, though, she succumbed to his persistence and persuasion. Gulbadan tells the delightful story, with a trace of relish, of how Hamida, then merely 14, resisted Humayun's proposal for 40 days before yielding. The day after Humayun had seen Hamida in the apartment of his brother Hindal, where she was a frequent visitor, he sent a proposal of marriage to her. First, Hindal objected, saying she was like a sister and daughter to him and Humayun's marriage to her might be a cause of embarrassment to all of the imperial family. This angered Humayun, who walked away. Later Dildar Begum, Gulbadan's and Hindal's mother, remonstrated with him in a written communication that the girl's mother too had been 'preening herself' (*naz mikunad*) and it was strange that he should be angered by such a small matter. Humayun replied that the admonition from her was very gratifying and that he would honour all the lady's preening. After that, God's will be done. But he would wait!

Dildar Begum then threw a party the next day and invited Humayun to it. Humayun went up to his mother and requested her to send someone to fetch Hamida. The young lady, however, refused to oblige, saying, 'If I was required to pay my respect, I have already done that once; why need I do it again?' For the second time Humayun sent Subhan Quli to Hindal to request him to send her over; for the second time she refused. Hindal sent word that as many times as he had requested her to go and present herself to His Majesty, she had refused every time. Perhaps Subhan Quli could persuade her. To Subhan Quli she said, 'To see His Majesty once is legitimate; to do so the second time is not. I will not go.' Subhan Quli reported the conversation to Humayun. Humayun then remarked that he would render legitimate what was not.

In sum, for 40 days Hamida Banu resisted Humayun. In the end, Dildar Begum said to her, 'Someday you are going to marry someone; who then could be a better choice than the emperor?' The young lass was not through yet. She would indeed marry someone some day, she said, but it would be one whose collar her hand could touch, not one the hem of whose skirt she could not reach. Dildar Begum held forth for a long time to make her change her mind. It was after 40 long and tough days that she ultimately yielded.[9] Among royal mothers of the Mughal age, she stands tall for her grit, sagacity and humanity.

9 Some exceedingly charming details about Humayun's pursuit of Hamida Banu and the consequent tension with his brother Hindal and between Hindal and his mother Dildar Begum are also recorded in Jauhar Aftabchi, *Tazkirat al-Waqiat*: MS. Br. Mus. Add 16711: ff. 39a-b.

Aurangzeb seems to have had a crush on a concubine of Dara Shukoh, Ra'na-i Dil (heart's glory). After Dara had been killed, and Aurangzeb firmly seated on the imperial throne, he sent a proposal of marriage to the young lady. He apparently based his claim upon her on the Mughal custom of levirate, of a younger brother inheriting his elder's widows. 'What part of me makes the most appeal to you?', the lady wanted to know, through the messenger who had brought her the proposal. 'Your hair is the eye's delight,' Aurangzeb responded. Ra'na-i Dil chopped off her hair and sent it all to the Emperor. This defiance only inflamed Aurangzeb's desire for her; he sent word that her face still glowed seductively. She made gashes in her face with a dagger and sent a handkerchief soaked in the blood to him. For once Aurangzeb accepted defeat with grace and did not bother her any further; he looked after her well for the rest of her days.[10]

Besides the regular Queens, some of them reaching the status through political alliances, others through the Emperor's affection, there were mistresses, also part of the household, bearing sons and daughters who faced no overt discrimination on that account, even as a subtle difference of perception persisted. Babur writes of his father that besides several wives, Umar Shaikh 'had many mistresses and concubines'. Of his father's five sons, Babur records matter-of-factly, one was by a concubine named Zuhra Begi Agha. She was his 'most honoured concubine'. She was also the mother of a daughter of Umar Shaikh. Babur uses three separate terms for wives (*khawatinlar*), mistresses (*ghunchachi*) and concubines (*sarari*). Later on the term *parastar* began to be used for concubines. Babur also records the interesting case of a mistress of one ruler having become 'the most influential' wife of another and having borne children to both. 'The Mother of Shah-i Gharib Mirza and of Muzaffar Husain Mirza [sons of Sultan Husain Mirza] was Khadija Begim, a former mistress of Sultan Abu Said Mirza by whom she had a daughter.' Interestingly, while Babur usually mentions the names of wives of eminent men whose deeds he recounts, he mentions others only if they bore their men children or if they had some special reason, like earning their husbands' great affection, to be so recounted; otherwise he dismisses them collectively as 'many concubines and mistresses' of so-and-so. Of Sultan Husain Mirza, he enumerates five wives (two of

---

10   Manucci, I (first pub. 1907), New Delhi, 1981: 342–3. It is interesting that Aurangzeb laid his claim upon both the surviving wives of Dara on grounds of law which laid down that and elder brother's widow(s) was to be married to his younger brother. This was no part of Islamic law but more an inheritance from the Mongol custom named '*yanga-lik*', for which see A. S. Beveridge's note in *The History of Humayun*, Eng. tr. A. S. Beveridge (first pub. 1902), New Delhi, 1996: 245.

these divorced), four mistresses and 'many concubines and mistresses'; those enumerated were his 'respected wives and mistresses'. The subtle gradation originating in the very categories of wives, mistresses and concubines gets a little shaded with respect earned through personal attributes, within the status hierarchy, even as it is never completely erased.

Many of the royal children were born of concubines. Although concubines were ranked a grade lower than the wives, they were no mere pastimes on the sly for the King. They too were often married to the Kings, although we get very few details about the marriage rites in their case. The absence of these details itself places their marriage a rung or two below that of regular wives. However, the fact of marriage itself does not place the wife on a higher pedestal than a concubine. Many marriages of Emperors and Princes are mentioned quite casually in our sources, while some of the concubines are treated with the respect due to a Queen. Beyond the status established by the institution of marriage, or for that matter motherhood, individual relationship counted for a great deal. Gulbadan tells us that when Humayun returned, following his crushing defeat at the hands of Sher Khan at Kannauj, he went to see his mother after a few days. Everyone was asked to leave except Gubadan herself, her mother, Afghani Agacha, Gulnar Agacha, Nargul Agacha, all Babur's concubines, and Gubadan's foster-mother, Anaga. In this company Humayun spoke of forgiving Hindal for his indiscretions, which in the Emperor's perception had led to his defeat. All this points to considerable fluidity in the imperial household.

Within this fluidity, some relationships transcend limits of the norm and others fail to catch up with it. Almost every ruler and Prince seems to have had children from concubines. While some of them earned their father's affection more than those born of the wives, and there are no obvious signs of underrating concubines' offspring, some feeble traces of difference yet filter through. The status of their mother, if a concubine, almost always gets indicated. Talking of his brothers and sisters, Babur mentions Yadgar-sultan, 'whose mother was a mistress called Agha-sultan'; on another occasion he notes with a touch of astonishment that 'of the 14 sons born to a ruler so great as Sultan Husain Mirza, one governing too in such a town as Heri [Herat], three only were born in legal marriage'. Abul Fazl, too, takes notice of the fact that of Umar Shaikh Mirza's sons, the third was Nasir Mirza whose 'chaste mother was from Andijan and was a concubine named Ummed'. Of Akbar's three sons, the younger two, Murad and Danial, had his concubines as their mothers, as indeed had all three of his daughters, though all of this is recorded as a matter of fact. One modern historian has attributed even

Figure 9 Guf Safa. From the Johnson Album. *Portrait of Guf Safa*, 'sweetheart of Dara Shukoh'. Pampered as the sweetheart was, her body carried a lower degree of sanctity than a royal woman's; its contours could be subjected to an outsider's gaze, unthinkable for a royal female. By permission of the British Library (J.13.9).

Salim's birth to a concubine,[11] although popular legend attributes it, without conclusive evidence, to a Rajput Princess who is given the name of Jodha Bai. Princes Jahandar and Shahryar were born to Jahangir's concubines, again put on record matter-of-factly. Aurangzeb was most fond of his son Kam Bakhsh, whose mother was the Caucasian lady Udaipuri Mahal, earlier Dara Shukoh's concubine, one of the two on record. Even as she is referred to as the Emperor's *parastar*, Aurangzeb bestowed upon her all the accoutrements of a Queen. We learn from travellers that each concubine had her own apartment, protected by strong guards, into which entry was permitted only to eunuchs and maids, replicating the ambience of the apartments of royal wives and sisters.

The portrait of Gul Safa in the Johnson Album in the Oriental and India Office Collections at the British Library in London, however, opens up one significant window on the difference between the wife, the concubine and other women involved in a relationship with royalty. Even as Gul Safa is identified as 'the sweetheart of Dara Shukoh' (*m'ashuqa-i Darashukoh*) at the head of the painting, and even as she is portrayed as a very aristocratic figure, wearing the finest of clothes and jewels as becomes the eldest prince's 'sweetheart', the contours of her body are all too visible through the drapery to the naked eye, which, considering that paintings were done for eternity, would surely include a male eye other than her lover's at one or another time. Particularly striking is the visibility of her bosom. Since it is well nigh impossible to get any authentic portrayal of a royal wife, daughter or sister, for their portrayal would have violated the sanctity of their bodies by opening them to male gaze, the display of Gul Safa's body first to the artist's and then to others' gaze underlines the hierarchy embedded in the notion of chastity and honour. For these are virtues exclusive to the women of the uppermost ranks of the imperial household; anyone even a shade below falls short of those highest standards. It is an acknowledgement that her body's chastity is somewhat below par, unthinkable in the case of truly royal women. It is also an acknowledgement that as an individual a woman might be the beloved of a Prince, but as a category she was not up to the mark of a royal female relation: mother, wife, sister or daughter. Some of the boundaries were indeed impermeable even in the midst of fluidity.

What were, however, eminently permeable were the boundaries of personal relationships between husband and wife. Mughal India, much like the Delhi Sultanate, is teeming with moving stories of bonds between

11 Refaqat Ali Khan, *The Kachhwahas under Akbar and Jahangir,* New Delhi, n.d.: Appendix 2, 'Jahangir's Mother', 215–18.

Emperors, Princes and their consorts that went beyond a passing affection. The bond was not conditional upon monogamy, although the conditions, such as they were, were asymmetrical for the male and the female consorts. The tales of Jahangir and Nur Jahan, and of Shah Jahan and Mumtaz Mahal, are the stuff of legends. Jahangir also notes the attachment of Itmad al-Daulla, Nur Jahan's father, to his wife. 'From the day on which his companion attained to the mercy of God, he no longer cared for himself but melted away from day to day.... After 3 months and 20 days he passed away.' Dara Shukoh had a wife, Nadira Begum, two concubines and a 'sweetheart'; but it was his wife who was his 'intimate friend'. In presenting the Album named after himself to Nadira, Dara inscribed upon it the words: 'To Nadira Banu Begum, my special and intimate friend, companion and sharer of secrets, I present this fine album: Muhammad Dara Shukoh, son of Shah Jahan Padshah Ghazi, A.H. 1051 [1641]'.[12]

Age seems to have been of little consideration in forging marriage alliances. Young children from anywhere between five and seven years get betrothed, and nuptial rites are recorded at the age of 12. In most cases, age of the male was no bar to marriage with a young woman; indeed, the age difference is hardly ever noticed, at least on record. In a few cases the reverse is also witnessed. Akbar himself had been married to his father's sister's daughter Salima Sultan Begum, a dozen years his senior, who had earlier been the wife of his Regent Bairam Khan. That might perhaps explain his disapproval of sexual relations between a man and a woman who was more than 12 years his elder. On the other hand, his censure of old women taking young husbands, 'for this goes against all modesty', testifies to a phenomenon of sufficiently wide prevalence to invite attention.

With several women in the harem competing for the King's attention, rivalry among them could not have been kept on the leash for long. Sometimes rivalry for his attention could take absurd forms. Gulbadan tells us the interesting story of the keenness of Humayun's mother Mahim Begum to see the birth of a grandson and hence suggestion of marriage to Mewa Jan, daughter of one of her high-level attendants (this was long before Humayun's marriage to Hamida Banu and the birth of Akbar); by the evening the marriage had taken place without much fuss. Three days later, one of Humayun's earlier wives, Bega Begum, arrived from Kabul and announced her own pregnancy. In time, Mewa Jan too made a similar announcement for herself. While Bega Begum in due course

12 'Ein muraqqa-i nafis ba anis-i khass wa hamdam wa hamraz ba ikhtisas Nadira Banu Begum: Muhammad Dara Shukoh, wald Shah Jahan Padshah Ghazi, 1051H.' See Toby Falk and Mildred Archer, Indian Miniatures in the India Office Library, London, 1981: 72.

gave birth to a daughter to be named Aqiqa Begum, Mahim felt certain that the other baby would be a son. In anticipation, various preparations for its reception were made, but there was no sign of the baby even after 10 months. The eleventh month began to raise eyebrows and, much as the young lady tried to persuade the harem that sometimes babies took as much as a whole year to materialize, soon her fraudulent claim was exposed. She, however, revelled in all the attention that was hers for all those months. Abul Fazl points to the existence of acute hostility between Jiji Anaga, 'that cupola of chastity', and Maham Anaga, 'the veil of chastity', Akbar's two foster-mothers (Anagas), each with a powerful presence. While court chronicles and royal memoirs would in general be expected to keep silent about such unsavoury episodes, with no more than the throwing of hints and insinuations at best, European travellers are less inhibited. We therefore get to hear some whispers as well as some loud noises from them about tensions in the harem, although a little caution in lending them one's ears is well advised. Among travellers, Edward Terry, Pelsaert, John Fryer, Careri and, of course, Manucci and Bernier are most loquacious; they engage in some salacious gossip about goings on in the imperial harem and take note of the concealed rivalry between wives and concubines, and presumably within each group. It was perhaps tension of this sort that led Akbar to make the profound observation that polygamy 'brings ruin to [the man's] health and woes to his home'.

Aunts, father's or mother's sisters, stood next only to the mothers in the ruler's estimate and attention. Babur would never omit seeing his aunts every Friday. Once his wife Mahim Begum tried to dissuade him, owing to the heat of the season, and was rebuked by him for her efforts. He instructed Khwaja Qasim, architect, to accomplish with 'his heart and soul' (ba-jan o dil) whatever commission his aunts assigned him. Babur himself records going to Sikandrabad 'to wait' upon two of his paternal aunts and, later, going 'into the fort of Agra to bid farewell' to them 'who were to start for Kabul in a few days'. Humayun too spent a good amount of time with his aunts and sisters, and Gulbadan records a great deal of conviviality prevailing in such assemblies. When he visited one of his aunts or sisters, or even wives, all other female relatives accompanied him. The assembly might begin with strict decorum, for Gulbadan observes that the ladies followed the proper order of precedence while sitting in Humayun's presence; but soon revelry overshadowed decorum and long hours of the night were spent in indulgence. When sleep overcame them, they sometimes slept helter skelter. Understandably, such a visit came to acquire a mark of much sought after distinction for the host and, not infrequently, invited considerable envy.

For we hear Bega Begum, wife of Humayun's younger days, at the time of the prayer at the crack of dawn complaining to Humayun that while he visited the houses of some of his female relatives – aunts, sisters and others – quite frequently, she was the one denied the honour. 'After all,' she said ruefully, 'the path to my house has not been sown with thorns.' Humayun kept quiet then, but later called in all his sisters and aunts, and observed that he had been visiting his elder relatives to give them company and solace. He could not possibly visit everyone, but this omission should be taken by all in their stride. They should remember he was an opium eater. In an interesting climax to the story, he obtained in writing from those present that if he did not visit anyone for a long time, they would not hold it against him. Besides allaying the complaints of his relatives, the undertaking demonstrated the greater legitimacy of the written word, even of this sort, than the word of mouth.

For Akbar, his father's sister Gulbadan Begum had nearly the same presence as his mother had. If she was one of the exemplary figures of the Mughal family's finesse, Akbar's reverence towards her, too, was unbounded. Fr. Monserrate tells us that when Gulbadan returned from her pilgrimage to Mecca, 'the King had the street pavements covered with silk shawls and conducted her himself to her palace in a gorgeous litter, scattering largess meanwhile to the crowds'.

It appears, however, that the Mughal family tradition of displaying concern and exceeding courtesy to their elderly female relatives grew a little feebler as time passed, for after Jahangir's touching obeisance to his mother, similar examples become rather scarce. This, however, need not lead us to the opposite conclusion of the absence of courtesy.

The family, of course, was a large and somewhat undefined entity. There seems to be no particular term that can be faithfully rendered into English as 'family'. The one that is frequently used is a compound of three words: *ahl o ayal* (relatives and dependents), itself suggestive of the family's expansive nature.[13] When, at the height of his glory, on one occasion Babur got tired of worldly affairs and wished to hand over his kingdom to Humayun, so he could retire into a corner of the 'gold scattering garden' (*bagh-i zar afshan*), he announced to his son: 'Moreover, Humayun, I commit you and your brothers and my kin and my people (*khwishan wa mardum-i khwud*) as well as yours to Him;

13 See for a brief discussion, Ruby Lal, '"The Domestic World" of Peripatetic Kings: Babur and Humayun, c. 1494–1556', *The Medieval History Journal*, 4, 1, 2001: 47–56. The argument that the conventional family in the Mughal cultural ambience down to the eighteenth century was one that was conceptually extended if existentially nuclear has been elaborated by Urvashi Dalal, 'Women's Time in the *Havelis* of North India', *The Medieval History Journal*, 2, 2, 1999: 277–308.

them I also commit to you.' This is when the 'family', the 'household' and the harem were still within manageable proportions; as the size of the harem grew manifold with Akbar, all these entities would have turned even more amorphous.

The concept of the head of the family seems to have been absent, or at the least ambiguous, for even as the Emperor was de facto head of the royal family, age – irrespective of gender – at times received precedence in some of its concerns. Marriages of Princes often, though not always, took place in the house of the Emperor's mother. On the other hand, it was the Emperor who bestowed names upon his children and grandchildren, reinforcing his status as the head. However, when Aurangzeb imprisoned his father and ascended the throne, among other disturbances the event caused was the regard for the status of the two in relation to the family. In the later years of Shah Jahan's life as prisoner, Aurangzeb did consult him and sought his advice on various problems, generally of state; but then he could have consulted any of his nobles as well.

The concept of an expansive family must contain space for playing out of tensions among its members, as well as accommodation for support and sustenance for indirect victims of conflicts. Mughal Emperors who were single sons – or at least single surviving sons – were in some ways more fortunate than others who had brothers to contend with as they traversed the long path to the throne. Babur and Akbar fell in the first category; others, from Humayun downwards, in the second. Jahangir's two brothers had pre-deceased his succession to his father's throne; but it was his son Khusrau who filled in for a brother and challenged his accession, if in vain. Yet the female relations, wives, concubines and, above all, very young children of the brothers were given complete protection by the fractious Princes. Of his three brothers, Humayun had to face the most intense challenge from Kamran. At one stage Kamran even used the infant Akbar as a shield against Humayun's attack on the Kabul fort, where Kamran was then lodged. Yet, as an infant, Akbar grew up under his uncle's care and, decades later, still remembered with gratitude the affection that Kamran's wife Mah Chuchak had bestowed upon him. Among the descendants of Chingiz, when an infant took his first walk, the father would throw his turban at the child and make him fall, perhaps symbolically encapsulating all future failures in that brief fall and ensuring a trouble-free life from then onwards. In Humayun's absence, Kamran performed this task for Akbar, and Akbar had not forgotten it, long after he had sat on the imperial throne. When the dust raised by the watershed War of Succession among the four sons of Shah Jahan had settled, even Jahan Ara, who had made no secret of her love and support for Dara Shukoh, was treated with generosity and respect by Aurangzeb; and those of Dara's daughters, sons and grandsons, who had no role in the war, were settled by their uncle through marriages within his own immediate family. For he was then ensconced as the head of the extended family and knew his responsibilities well.

Given the predominance of patriarchy, it would be legitimate to expect inheritance of family name from the father's line of descent and for women to adopt the husband's family name after marriage, much as happens now. Such, however, was not the case in medieval India. Indeed, the very notion of family name or surname is an implantation in India of modern colonial regime; prior to that, in its absence, a person was often identified as the son of so-and-so (the father's personal name), who in turn was the son of so-and-so; the length of the list depended upon the lustre of the family or, as in nineteenth-century Awadh, the amount of money that passed into the hands of the professional tracers of the family tree (*shajra*). More frequently in Mughal India, for identification of descent, reference was made to the best-known member of the family, male or female. Scattered in most of our sources are references to 'son of . . . ', 'father of . . . ', 'grandson of . . . ', 'great-grandson of . . . ', 'nephew of . . . ', 'uncle of . . . ', 'younger or elder brother of . . . ', 'brother-in-law of . . . ', 'son of the sister or brother of . . . ' 'paternal uncle of . . . ', 'daughter's son of . . . ', 'wife's brother of . . . ' 'brother of [sister] . . . ', 'son-in-law of . . . ', even 'friend of . . . '. The references are not confined to a family, group or religious community; they appear to be universal in nature.

Within the family, the female members seem to have enjoyed a degree of freedom in the early part of Mughal history, but this declined in the later reigns. In Babur's memoirs the epithet 'chaste' is hardly ever used for a woman, young or old, Princess or commoner, and there are several references to convivial parties in open gardens, in which his female relations participated alongside the men and had their share of intoxication and revelry. Rumer Godden, biographer of Gulbadan, notices that during the Princess's childhood the women were not veiled; they rode horses, went on hunt (*shikar*), practised archery and went out on picnics. Even schooling for royal children was common for boys and girls in the court at Kabul, although the girls are always shown in miniatures with their 'mamas' in attendance.[14] It is noticeable too that in Babur's and Humayun's time all the Princesses of all royal households were 'given away', 'sent out', 'taken' or 'married' off, at times twice or even thrice, unlike in later reigns, especially from the reign of Shah Jahan onwards, when daughters of the King mostly remained single – a point to which we return below. Babur also mentions the interesting case of a young lady,

14 Rumer Godden, *Gulbadan: Portrait of a Rose Princess at the Mughal Court*, New York, 1980: 32, 34.

Masuma Sultan, who visited him with her mother and 'at once felt arise in her a great inclination towards me'. Private messengers then carried messages to and fro, and in the end the affair resulted in marriage. Such clear indication of 'inclination' by a woman for a man becomes rare with time. On the other hand, we have some evidence of a mother refusing to 'give' her daughter to a Prince if he did not measure up to her expectations. Thus, Payinda Sultan Begum would not let her second daughter Kichik Begum marry Sultan Masud Mirza, even though he 'had great desire for her'. She married her off to another suitor instead.

The names of females – daughters, wives, sisters – are also freely mentioned in the early sources. Babur almost always gives the names of both parents whenever he refers to a child, son or daughter, in one context or another, but usually in the context of their marriage. Gulbadan too follows this format. From Akbar's time onwards, however, such names – particularly names of royal wives – begin to get omitted. Instead, their identities are established, if at all, with reference to the place of their birth or location, or some other indicator. Mothers henceforth commonly, though not invariably, came to be identified as Fatehpuri Begum or Udaipuri Begum, or the daughter of so and so, etc. The history of the reign of Akbar's grandson Shah Jahan notes that:

> Ever since the reign of Akbar, it had been ordained that the names of the inmates of the seraglio should not be mentioned in public, but that they should be designated by some epithet derived either from the place of their birth or the country or the city in which they might have first been regarded by the monarch with the eye of affection.

This practice was given a start even as Akbar celebrated the 'joyous occasion' of the birth of two daughters to Salim, 'contrary to [the custom of] contemporaries'. Besides referring to one of his own daughters, Aram Banu, in a Hindi phrase as his 'darling' (*ladla*, generally used for a son), Akbar protests against the unequal share prescribed for daughters in Islam (Ahmadi *kaish*) and suggests instead 'the larger share' for them since they were 'the weaker ones', although he did not proceed any further than making a statement. Akbar also pleaded for monogamy and a certain age for marriage – 14 for girls and 16 for boys, for pre-puberty marriages 'brought forth no fruit'. He seems to have considered the proposition seriously enough to seek to establish some form of state control over marriage by disallowing it until the age of the bride and the groom had been certified by the Kotwal, Chief of city police. Inevitably, this became a source of great corruption and was rendered ineffective. Akbar also expressed preference for the marrying couple's consent, with parents' permission as 'indispensable', particularly as 'here in India among the modest, a woman once married cannot go [again] to anyone else'.[15] He felt pained at the prohibition of the marriage of widows in the Hindu religion, for it caused them 'grave hardship' and was horrified at 'the strange determination of the men that they should seek their salvation through the repression of their wives', the reference here being to the committing of sati. Most of Akbar's views remained an expression of intent, but even intent was important and far ahead of the century that he inhabited. Yet Akbar felt so gravely concerned about the chastity of his female relatives that he denied them a personal name, an individual identity that was open to public gaze.

It appears that he had learnt this particular method of protecting women's chastity from the Rajputs. It is rare to find the personal names of Princesses in Rajput sources once they are married; they are then usually identified with reference to the name of their father or, more commonly, that of their clan after their marriage into another clan.[16]

From Akbar's time chastity gets invested in the female body and is perceived entirely in sexual terms, such that even the sight or the thought of anything implicating the female body was considered a dilution of the purity of her self. Bernier was to observe later on that the slightest glimpse of any woman of the royal family was 'almost inaccessible to the sight of man', although he added that the situation was far worse in Persia, or so he had been given to understand. The exceptions were those designated *Mahram*, formally allowed entry into the harem. These would usually be the women's close blood relations, beyond the boundaries of a sexual relationship. If anyone outside the close circle was so allowed, as was done for Itimad al-Daula, father of Nur Jahan, and as a very exceptional favour, or Prince Karan, grandson of Rana Pratap of Mewar, both in the reign of Jahangir, the fact was so extraordinary as to be placed on record.

Prior to the reign of Akbar, there is little evidence of such obsession with female chastity, although one could hardly view it as a time of libertarianism. Indeed, even as 'the chaste princess' or 'the cupola of chastity' and similar epithets came to be attached to the mention of any female in the royal family, whether a newborn child or a venerable grandmother, from Akbar's and Abul Fazl's time onwards, the terms hardly ever make their appearance in pre-Akbar narratives. Khwaja Kalan, Babur's friend, unable to reconcile himself to living in India,

15 I.e. cannot marry again. *Ain*, I: 201 (the Ain or Regulations on Marriage). The rendering of this passage in the standard tr. by H. Blochmann as 'Here in India, where a man cannot see the woman to whom he is betrothed' is very misleading; *The Ain-i Akbari*, I, New Delhi, 1977 (first pub. Calcutta 1873): 287.

16 Nainsi, *Marwar ri Pargana ri Vigat*, vol.2, ed. N S Bhati, Jodhpur, 1969: 443.

took leave after the battle of Panipat to return to Kabul, and brought with him many gifts from the Mughal Emperor for his female relatives. Besides gifts he also had many tales of India, which he narrated to them in merriment. 'It appears probable', observes A. S. Beveridge, translator of Gulbadan Begum's memoirs, 'that there was no such complete seclusion of Turki women from the outside world as came to be the rule in Hindustan. The ladies may have veiled themselves, but I think they received visitors more freely.'[17] The *Babur Nama* also records garden parties, where the free participation of royal women was matched by the free flow of intoxicants and the ambience was marked by a general revelry. Gulbadan mentions that at a party given by the sister of the Shah of Iran at Khurasan, in honour of Hamida Banu Begum, Humayun commissioned the drawing up of a screen around the tent 'in the Hindu fashion' (*misl-i Hinduana*, literally, 'like the Hindus'); it was clearly a departure for the Iranis in consideration of the susceptibilities of their guests from India. The sister of the Shah herself was quite used to riding a horse behind her brother when out hunting. A different culture was beginning to seep in; it acquires a particularly sharp accent during the reign of Akbar.

If the Persian language texts written in the imperial court begin to focus on the chastity of women, for empirical evidence we turn to local language works in Rajasthan, primarily Nainsi, official historian of Raja Jaswant Singh, writing in the mid-seventeenth century. Sometime in 1572, Nainsi tells us, Rao Kalla, son of the famous ruler of Marwar, Maldeo, was said to have exchanged perhaps amorous glances with an unidentified denizen of Akbar's harem, entering it by disguising himself as a woman. Perhaps entry into the harem was still lax enough to allow such an age-old trick to work. When the grapevine brought the story to Akbar's ears, he was unwilling to forgive the man. He posted the Rao to Nadol in Malwa and instructed Shaikh Ibrahim, in charge of the place, to get rid of him on one or another pretext.[18] The Shaikh carried out the commission with vigour; there is however nothing to go by on the woman's fate. Nainsi also tells us the bizarre story of a pilgrimage by Akbar's mother to the Haj, accompanied by Mirza Sharf al-Din, at one time Akbar's favourite and a highly placed noble. At the entrance to the holy Ka'aba, the guards informed her that she could not enter the precincts unless accompanied by her husband. On the spur of the moment she pointed to the Mirza, identifying him as her husband. On their return, when the report reached Akbar's ears, he was livid with rage at the audacity of the noble to have allowed the impression that he could be the revered lady's husband and, by implication, Akbar's own father; he found the offence grave enough to merit beheading. But the Mirza fled for his life and probably survived.[19]

We also learn from Abul Fazl the story of Akbar's pursuit of one of his foster-brothers, Adham Khan, down to Malwa in central India. The Khan had been sent there by Akbar to crush the local ruler Baz Bahadur, remembered in history for his immortal love for Rup Mati, his beloved Hindu wife, and for their love of music. Having defeated Baz Bahadur, Adham Khan passed on much of the plunder to the Emperor, but eyed some valuable part of it for himself and especially lusted for some of the women captives, Rup Mati in particular. While Rup Mati chose to kill herself instead of falling into the hands of her husband's enemy, there were yet some other women to be accounted for. Reports of the Khan's deceit reached the young Emperor, and he arrived at Malwa by forced marches to surprise his foster-brother. Adham Khan arranged for Akbar to sleep on the terrace of his own house, from where he could look into the Khan's harem and see his women. If he did that, the Khan presumed, it would give him a legitimate reason to kill Akbar, even if he were the Emperor himself. Unfortunately for him, Akbar slept through the night like a log, without moving his head. Implicit in the story, however, is the sanctity of the female body, now so fragile and vulnerable that it could get polluted by even the most innocuous and unintended glance from an unsuspecting male.

Significantly, while earlier sources make innumerable references to the harem, and presumably there must have been some sort of an organization around it, it is only with Akbar that we realize that it was reorganized into a fortress-like institution. Abul Fazl gives us details of the guarding of the harem under Akbar and the emerging picture is a formidable one, in which even a bird would have found it difficult to penetrate without proper vigilance. 'Though there are more than five thousand women, he [Akbar] has given each a separate apartment,' the historian records. The apartments were divided into sections, each under the superintendence of a 'chaste woman'. This ensured that everything 'is in proper order'. The most trustworthy female guards were appointed inside the harem, while outside the enclosures a contingent of eunuchs was posted. The outermost circle was guarded by a group of 'faithful Rajputs', beyond whom were the porters of the gates. If that were not enough, nobles and elite single soldiers, *ahadis*, and other troops were placed on all four sides of the harem walls. All visitors to the harem, 'begums, or the wives of amirs or other chaste [women]', must report at

19   Ibid.: 68.

the entrance and express their wish to be received by an inmate who would be so informed, and on obtaining her consent the visitor would be allowed to enter for a specified period of time, which in some special cases of high-ranking ladies could extend to a whole month. On top of it, Akbar exercised his own vigil over the harem. Decades later, Manucci outlines the security arrangement in much the same detail. The *Ahkam-i Alamgiri* of Aurangzeb's time records that the Mahaldar, Superintendent of the harem, Nur al-Nisa, forbade Prince Muhammad Azam himself, second son of the Emperor, from entering the imperial garden at Ahmedabad because he had refused to let her accompany him. The Prince retaliated by throwing her out of his company. On receiving complaint Aurangzeb upheld the lady's authority and meted out punishment to his son.

This is quite in contrast to the image of the reigns of Babur and Humayun drawn from accounts like the *Babur Nama* and *Humayun Nama*, or, for that matter, later accounts such as the *Akbar Nama* of Abul Fazl, *Mutakhab al-Tawarikh* of Mulla Abdul Qadir Badauni or *Tabaqat-i Akbari* of Nizam al-Din Ahmad, all of which narrate the history of the reigns of Babur and Humayun among others.

What explains the change? A tough question to answer! The easy answer would be to attribute it to the growing influence of Rajput cultural ethos on Akbar ever since his marriage in 1562 to the Rajput Princess, daughter of Raja Bhara Mal Kachhwaha of Amber, now a suburb of Jaipur. There are stories galore of Rajput investment of family honour in their women's bodies and their obsession with female sexual chastity. James Tod tells one remarkable story in this genre. Lakha Rana was the ruler of Mewar, advanced in years, blessed with sons and grandsons. He received a proposal from Ranmall, Marwar Prince, to arrange his daughter's marriage with Chonda, heir apparent to the Mewar throne. The proposal came in the form of a traditional ritual: the family of the bride-to-be sent a coconut to that of the groom. It happened that Chonda was away when the coconut arrived in court. Courtesies observed, Lakha assured the messenger that his son would soon return and convey his acceptance of the proposal. Unable to resist a jest, he added that the coconut couldn't possibly have been meant for a greybeard like him anyway, even as he twirled his moustaches upwards. As the story did the rounds and reached Chonda's ears, he declined to accept the proposal, for the very thought of the young woman being envisaged as his father's wife even in sheer jest was enough to have rendered her beyond the touch of another man. On the other hand, returning the messenger empty-handed would have constituted a grave insult to the house of Marwar. In the end, the old Rana accepted the coconut for himself on condition that their son, if any, would be the old father's successor in lieu of Lakha, a condition readily agreed to by him.[20] This is reminiscent of one *Mahabharata* story, where Bhishma foregoes his claim to the throne in similar circumstances.

We have noticed above Akbar's probable adaptation of the model of clan names as the form of identification for royal women, to that of place of origin or location, to render their 'purity' beyond reproach. All this appears to suggest that incidents of adultery or even remarriage of widows would have been perceived as the most stupendous social crimes in the elite Rajput context. Historical evidence, however, has a habit of challenging all easy assumptions. Nainsi, an impeccable source, leads us on to a whole gamut of stories where married and unmarried Rajput women are on record as having transgressed the boundaries of sexual chastity laid down by their menfolk, and having had a fling or two, at times with men far below their caste or social rank. Suhvadai Joiyani was a wife of the legendary Rajput ruler Prithvi Raj Chauhan. Following a little tiff with him, she moved to her father's home and there developed intimacy with Gudalrao Khichi, from a subclan of the Chauhans. When news reached Prithvi Raj, he led a raid upon the Khichi, who took flight to Malwa. We are not told of the fate of the lady.[21] If, however, she maintained at least caste parity in her illicit liaison, Sodhi, favourite wife of another Rajput, Lakha Jadeja, was less mindful of caste restraints for meeting her sexual needs and went for a man of the lowliest of castes, Dom, to cater to her in the absence of her husband. The husband had been gone for six long months, which included the romance-inducing season of rain and thunder. On learning of her dalliance, Jadeja gave her away to the Dom, whom he had earlier engaged to sing from under a tree outside the palace for her entertainment.[22] The presumably young wife of yet another old Jadeja, Phul by name, sought to entice her stepson by an Ahir wife of her husband into her bed. When he refused, citing her maternal status for him, she threatened to charge him before his father with making sexual advances to her. When even the threat failed, she did actually charge him thus and the old father threw him out of his kingdom.[23] There are indeed several other instances of this nature in Nainsi's multi-volume work. Interestingly, death for women does not usually follow in the wake of the discovery of their indiscretions, although some milder forms of punishments do, suggesting a high level of tolerance for infractions of sexual norms by them.

20   James Tod, *Annals and Antiquities of Rajasthan*, vol. I, Delhi reprint, 1990: 323.
21   Nainsi, *Khyat*, vol.1, ed. Badri Prasad Sakriya, Jodhpur, 1984: 240.
22   Nainsi, *Khyat*, vol.2, ed. Badri Prasad Sakriya, Jodhpur 1984: 232–34.
23   Nainsi, *Khyat*, 2: 230.

Nainsi also tells stories of Rajput women going for a second marriage, at times even before they were widowed. In a fight with Songra, Rao Tida Rathore defeated him and then pursued his wife Sisodini with the offer of 'settling down' with her (*ghar wasa*). She accepted the offer on condition that their son would be the legitimate successor to the throne.[24] Sajan Bhawal, says Nainsi, was an eminent Rajput. Dewri was the wife of Chanpa Sindhal. She left her husband and went over to the house of Sajan Bhawal. As her husband followed her to her new abode, the two men fought it out and killed each other.[25] Nainsi even narrates the story of a Rajput widow marrying a Muslim Chief: the widow of the Rao of Jaisalmer married Ghazni Khan, Afghan Chief of Jalor.[26] Significantly, all these instances belong to either the pre-Mughal period or at best the period before Akbar's reign.

It would therefore appear that Akbar's preoccupation with sexual chastity of women cast a long shadow on moulding cultural attitudes within the ruling class, in which the Rajputs occupied such a prominent space. Akbar's attitudes towards sexuality were an ensemble of paradoxes, with a trace of the puritanical and a strand of the liberal. He felt horrified by any expression of male homosexual predilection, although there was plenty of evidence of its prevalence at the highest echelons of his own court. Generally, he was rather severe on sexual crimes of any sort. Fr Monserrate tells us that 'The King has such a hatred of debauchery and adultery that neither influence nor entreaties nor the great ransom which was offered would induce him to pardon his chief trade commissioner, who, although he was married, had violently debauched a well-born Brahman girl. The wretch was by the king's order remorselessly strangled.' There are several other instances of this sort recorded in our sources. On the other hand, we have already seen above some of Akbar's extremely progressive ideas on women's status in the family and in society. Even in the arena of sexual pleasure, he questions the Islamic prescription of a bath after an intercourse and suggests one before it. This was a remarkable inversion, implicating pursuit of pleasure where the religious prescription implied performance of a pious but necessarily filthy duty which must terminate in a ritual cleansing. Yet, in the midst of these conflicting stances on sexual mores, the centrality of female chastity in his world view stands out prominently. It is understandable

24 Nainsi, *Khyat*, 3, ed. Badri Prasad Sakriya, Jodhpur, 1984: 23.
25 Nainsi, *Khyat*, 1: 182.
26 Nainsi, *Khyat*, 2: 97. In the neighbouring Gujarat, the Dutch traveller de Laet tells us, the prevalent custom in 'the large city called Bysantagar' was that a Brahmin widower would remain single, but a widow of the same caste could marry. De Laet: 87. 'Other sects' he observes, 'have the opposite rule.'

then that his anxieties on this score and the Rajputs' normative placement of high value of honour in their women's bodies, manifest in the
performance of *sati* and *jauhar*, should interact with each other cre-
atively. It became almost imperative that the Rajputs should organize
their harem on the imperial model. We rely upon Nainsi again to tell us
that Raja Suraj Singh of Jodhpur (r. 1599–1620) replicated the model in
every detail in his home.[27]

We also hear of tidbits from the bazaar that would have been too infra
dig for court historians to record. Vegetables of a 'virill shape', carrots,
radishes, cucumbers, etc., were carried into the harem only after being
cut up in pieces; even the semblance of the entry of a phallus in the harem
was anathema.

Yet the normative obsession with chastity of the female body was in
real life considerably, though quietly, moderated throughout the Mughal
era. To begin with, the names of the Mughal Princesses from the beginning to the very end were derived from the sensual pre-Islamic Persian
tradition rather than from the Arabic Islamic tradition. Their names,
such as Gulbadan (Rose Body), Gulchihra (Rose Faced), Dildar Begum
(Jolly Hearted), Jahan Ara (Adornment of the World) Raushan Ara
(Adornment of Light), Zeb al-Nisa (Embellishment of the Female
Body), celebrate sensuality rather than religious piety. Indeed, no Mughal
ruler, not even Aurangzeb, thought of giving a religious name like Fatima
or Khadija to their daughters. Royal concubines are given more inviting
names: *Nazuk Badan* (Delicate Body), *Badam Chashm* (Almond Eyed),
Sukh Dain (Giver of Joy), *Piyar* (Love), and so on. The miniature
paintings of the Mughal Princesses, wherever such paintings exist, and
of women at the fringes of royalty invariably depict them in a very
sensual posture: in a garden waiting for the tryst with their lovers,
often holding the very suggestive narcissus flower, looking at themselves
in a mirror with admiration in their eyes, reading a book of poetry,
holding a cup of wine. Except for the extremely rare depiction of a
royal mother or the Queen herself, the contours of young women's bodies
are revealed to the gaze of the viewer through the expensive transparent
clothes. The portrait of Gul Safa, whom we have encountered above, is

---

27   Nainsi, *Pargana ri Vigat*, vol. 2, N. S. Bhati, ed., Jodhpur, 1969: 562–64.

Figure 10   *Dalliance on a Terrace*, Imperial Mughal style, c.1615–1620, attributed to artist Govardhan. A double entendre inheres in the female attendants
looking intently at the imperial couple: on one hand it underlines the absence of
the notion of privacy of the body and on the other the insignificance of female
presence. From the Nasli and Alice Heeramaneck Collection, Museum Associates
Purchase, Photograph © 2004 Museum Associates/LACMA.

one among innumerable paintings in this genre, although the quality and calibre of each painting varies. Sensuality is the hallmark of all these miniatures.

If the harem was envisaged and organized to express a very high degree of concern with sexual chastity in the midst of preoccupation with sex, it would be legitimate to expect the actual pursuit of sex to be enveloped in a comparable degree of solitude. Although Babur quite cheerfully records his 'visits' to a particular wife or his erotic inclination for a young boy early in his youth, from Akbar's time the silence of the texts on this theme is almost conspiratorial. We are thus impelled to turn to European travel accounts and, more importantly, to Mughal paintings for descriptions of the contrary hues. Hawkins informs us that even the frequency and the choice of the Emperor's 'lying with' a woman in the harem is noted down in registers. Pelsaert reports about Jahangir that '[A]s soon as all the men have left, the Queen comes with the female slaves, and they undress him, chafing and fondling him as if he were a little child'. Hearsay, perhaps, but in itself not a good reason for dismissal. Pelsaert and de Laet also speak of three palaces named after Sunday, Tuesday and Saturday, using Hindi names for the three days 'in which the king's concubines are accommodated; for on these days the King is wont to visit the said palaces. There is also a fifth palace for women in which live foreign concubines of the king. This is called Bengaly Mahal.' Mirza Qateel gives graphic details of the ritual surveillance of newly wedded couples' nuptial bed by the bride's married female relatives among Muslim elites at the turn of the nineteenth century; joyful news of consummation was announced with the public display of evidence of performance in the form of a bloodstained white sheet. Failure on this score resulted in equally public ridicule of the groom.

Although the paintings imply inhibition on the motif of sexual encounters of Emperors and their Queens, or Princes and Princesses, the inhibition is somewhat unequally spread out between the men and the women; with the passage of time even this begins to wear thin, culminating in the miniature *Muhammad Shah in Dalliance* that we have encountered in chapter 2. The painting of the female body also gets to do less and less with clothing in the eighteenth century, compared with the sixteenth and the seventeenth – perhaps a sure indicator of 'moral decay' for the historians of the Victorian world. But, even as talking about the Queens' and Princesses' sexuality was unthinkable for the Mughal court historians, as depicting it was for the painters, Emperors' and Princes' bodies were somewhat less forbidding on this score. Significantly, in most depictions of the sexual motif, explicit or strongly suggestive, in the Mughal miniatures the figure(s) occupying centre space is nearly always surrounded by several female attendants. Clearly, even when engaged in

Figure 11 *Marriage Procession of Prince Dara Shukoh.* One of several paintings celebrating Dara Shukoh's marriage to his parallel cousin. The painting was done nearly a century after the event in provincial Mughal style of Awadh by artist Haji Madani *c.*1740–50. The bridegroom's procession, marked by extravagant display of riches and splendour, going to the bride's home for the wedding, is essentially a Hindu cultural practice that had gradually seeped into Muslim ceremonial landscape. Courtesy of the National Museum, New Delhi.

pursuit of sex, strict privacy of the body is not a prerequisite of the social order. The only allowance sometimes given to privacy in the paintings is suggested by the aversion of direct gaze of the attendants from the couples engaged in the rendezvous: a patch of privacy in the midst of social presence. It is also the case that, if other figures transgress the privacy of an amorous couple, no male attendant is ever depicted in any picture. Even the transgression of privacy was highly gendered.

Marriage at the level of the imperial family or the highest echelons of nobility does not seem to have followed any set pattern in the early part of Mughal history, although such a pattern becomes discernible later on, at least in outline. Babur uses terms like 'taking away', 'giving away', 'setting aside' and 'marriage' interchangeably, suggesting considerable latitude, yet a shade of hierarchy. Babur also uses 'fallen to' as a form of liaison, often involuntary. He thus keeps referring to his sisters and half-sisters as having 'fallen to' victors in battles against him, and having raised children for them. His elder sister Khan-zadeh Begum 'fell' to Muhammad Shaibani Khan and bore him a son upon whom the Khan bestowed the country of Balkh, although the child did not live long after his father's death. The lady, too, returned to her brother after 10 years, while Shaibani Khan was still around. Babur's casual reference to Princesses 'falling to' victors as war booty points to the feature being common, and stands in contrast to the later practice of sparing women of the vanquished and restoring them to their families with honour. His reference to the lady's desertion of her husband to return to her brother is equally devoid of any judgement. By the time of Akbar, such terms as 'setting aside' had been replaced by more 'honourable' phrases. Now, a noble or a Rajput ruler gave his daughter as a 'present' or a 'gift' to the Emperor. Implicit in it was, on the one hand, the assumption of the daughter being an inanimate object (as in the earlier terms) and, on the other, the virtual denial to the Emperor of the option of declining the 'gift'. But the giving of a 'gift' to the Emperor also implicated expectation of some returns on it, making the daughter even more of an object than a person.

Babur also mentions the marriage of another of his somewhat disreputable uncles, Sultan Mahmud Mirza, to yet another Khan-zadeh Begum, daughter of the Great Mir of Tirmiz. Upon her death, he took his late wife's niece, 'her brother's daughter, also called Khan-zada Begim', who bore him five daughters and a son. Even as Babur makes no attempt to put a veil over his personal dislike of this uncle, he still married his daughter Zainab Sultan, on his mother's insistence, although he never fancied her and the two did not quite pull on together.

Existing marriage alliances could also be broken up, and other alliances forged, at times at the initiative of women, with the object of making political or territorial gains. Thus Babur speaks of Sultan Ali Mirza's mother Zuhra Begi Agha, who 'in her ignorance and folly, had secretly written to Shaibani Khan that if he would take her [to wife] her son would give him Samarkand and that when Shaibani had taken [her son's] father's country, he should give her son a country.' Shaibani accepted her proposal, of course, but did not keep the latter part of the bargain. Since Babur himself had set his eyes on Samarkand and felt deprived of it by these transactions, he takes out his ire on the lady by alleging that Shaibani Khan did not care one bit for her and indeed 'did not regard her as the equal of [even] a mistress or a concubine'. If subtle distinctions of status between the wife and the mistress or concubine lie dormant in the normal course, situations of stress do bring them into the limelight.

Marriage between first cousins, both parallel and cross, was common and remained in force throughout the period, even though Akbar expressed his disapproval of it and of marriages between other close relations. Akbar himself had been married to both his parallel and his cross-cousins.[28] Babur's own first marriage was to his father's brother's daughter, Ayisha-sultan Begum, whom both brothers had betrothed to him ('set aside for me') when he was five years old, and some six years later he 'took' her in the last year of the fifteenth century AD. Out of bashfulness, he would 'visit' her once every 10, 15 or 20 days; with time, bashfulness grew and the frequency of the 'visits' diminished to a month or every 40 days, and that on his mother's prodding! She bore him a daughter who died in infancy. Soon after, the young lady too left Babur 'at the instigation of her older sister', as Babur records without a trace of rancour. Formal divorce or actual desertion, even by the wife, had yet to acquire an unsavoury odour. Babur's son Kamran is said to have married the daughter of his mother's brother, Sultan Ali Mirza. Our sources yield instances of close marriages, too. We have also noticed above Sultan Mahmud Mirza marrying his brother's daughter. Shaibani Khan, an uncle of Babur, was married to his aunt and niece at the same time. It took him a little time to realize that simultaneous marriage to the two was unlawful; he divorced the aunt! If Gulbadan was married to her second cousin, her husband's uncles had married her sisters Gulrang and Gulchihra. Prince Salim was married off by Akbar to the daughter of Raja Bhagwan Das; on becoming Emperor Jahangir, he also married the daughter of his father-in-law's grandson, Jagat Singh. And if one daughter of the Khan-i Azam Mirza Aziz Koka was married to Prince Murad, Akbar's son, another was the wife of Khusrau, Akbar's grandson.

---

28   His first marriage was to his paternal uncle Hindal's daughter, Ruqaiya Begum; Salima Sultan, his wife, was his father's sister's daughter.

In many arenas of life in the imperial Mughal family, above all in the arena of imperial daughters' marriage, a sort of cultural seepage was quietly, imperceptibly, occurring over a long stretch of time. This was the seepage of Hindu cultural ethos creeping unnoticed into the Mughal family practices.

We have taken incidental notice above of Babur recording his daughters' and sisters' marriages, often twice or thrice over. He makes no value judgement as he records them. His sister Sultan-nigar Khanum married thrice, as did another sister, Khana-zad Begum, whom we have met earlier. As indeed did yet another, a first cousin, Sultanam Begum, about whom he simply notes: 'Sultan Ali Mirza took her; then Timur Sultan took her and after him, Mahdi Sultan'. A sister of hers was married to Babur, too. In the time of Babur, Humayun and Akbar, nearly all Princesses were married at least once.

Humayun's younger (half) sister, Gulchihra, probably aged over 30, was married off by him a second time to an Uzbeg Prince, Abbas Sultan, and his daughter 'the chaste Bakht al-Nisa' was married first to Shah Abul Maali, the extremely handsome and arrogant noble of Humayun's and Akbar's reigns, and, after his assassination, to Khwaja Hasan Naqshbandi of the Sufi order that was the Mughals' favourite. Another daughter of Humayun's, Bakhshi Banu Begum, was also married twice.

By the time of Shah Jahan, however, the Emperor's daughters, like Jahan Ara and Raushan Ara, could not get married. Shah Jahan had six daughters and Jahan Ara was his second born, the eldest being Parhiz Banu; the latter's mother was the daughter of Mirza Muzaffar Husain Safawi. Jahan Ara was her father's favourite child. After the death of her mother Mumtaz, Jahan Ara became the first lady of the empire. She had been given the title of 'Begum Saheb' and there was just one Begum Saheb in all the length and breadth of the vast empire.[29] Jahan Ara was also an extremely accomplished person: a reasonable poet, builder of mosques, inns and gardens, fond of some very good wines, a great patron of the arts and artists, deeply interested in Sufism, genial, beautiful and fiercely loyal. She was 'most lovely, discreet, loving, generous, open minded and charitable. She was loved by all', observes Manucci, reflecting the universal perception of the young Princess. It should have been hard to come across a more eligible female in the empire of Shah Jahan than the Begum Saheb. Yet she was unable to get married. As a step in his preparation for the War of Succession, Dara Shukoh had promised to let her marry in return for support in the ensuing strife; she gave it wholeheartedly,

---

29   Aurangzeb's second daughter Zinat al-Nisa was also given this title by her brother when he succeeded his father to the Mughal throne as Bahadur Shah, but it did not quite add up to the same thing.

although it is unclear if Dara's promise had any significant role in it. For, long before the war between the four brothers had begun, she had put down on paper: 'I love my brother Dara Shukoh extremely, both in form and in spirit. We are in fact like one soul in two bodies and one spirit in two physical forms.'[30]

Bazaar gossip credits her with a few affairs on the sly. One was with a young man, rather sub par, 'a vigorous youth of goodly presence, son of the chief dancer in her employ who was her mistress of music', himself an accomplished singer, though 'of no very exalted rank'. In Manucci's version, she fondly called him *Dulera*, colloquial Hindi for groom or lover. The news of the secret rendezvous did not remain under covers for long from the Emperor. One evening, he decided to pay her a visit at her apartment while the young man was around. The Emperor had clearly timed his sudden arrival to deny her *Dulera* an escape; the best she could manage was to let him hide in the *hamam*, the warm water bath, though not before Shah Jahan's quietly searching eye had noticed it. Shah Jahan kept exchanging pleasantries with his beloved daughter; then as suddenly as he had arrived he announced that she needed a bath and ordered attendants to heat water in the *hamam* to the boiling point. Thus did the young man's audacious venture end with his life. This is essentially Bernier's version.

Manucci however has a different take on it. The young musician became a little uppity with high nobles, perhaps owing to his relationship with Begum Saheb. This was after fortune had slipped away from Shah Jahan's and Begum Saheb's hands. Once he ordered choice wines, which arrived in bottles of gold and enamel, adorned with precious stones such as were beyond the reach of the nobles. During convivial conversation, Dulera pitched himself at the same level as his companions. This was going beyond the unspoken but firmly drawn limits. The nobles had the man bound and, stripping him of his trousers, forced a lighted night lamp up his bottom until he sought pardon for his transgressions. He was let off at that stage, though not without some parting kicks and blows. The humiliation confined Dulera to his house until his death.

Clearly, the two versions are irreconcilable as factual narrations, even as they share scandalous stories of goings on at the top. Our concern here goes beyond factual narrations. It seeks to capture the competing world views of the court and the bazaar: if the court elects silence over embarrassing breaches of decorum, the bazaar more than makes up for it by its volubility. Whether volubility carries a higher degree of culpability than silence in compromising the truth is rendered hard to judge.

---

30   Jahan Ara, *Sahabiya* (biography of her spiritual mentor, Mulla Shah), cited in Bikrama Jit Hasrat, *Dara Shikoh Life and Works*, 2nd rev. edn, New Delhi, 1982: 84.

At any rate, Jahan Ara was not done yet, in the bazaar vision. Not long after, she picked up another lover, a courtier of her father's, a noble of Iranian origins. Leakages of this affair could not remain plugged either. This time around, Shah Jahan presented the young noble with a *pan*, betel, in court; this was the highest honour accorded to any courtier by the Mughal Emperor. Mixed in the betel, however, was deadly poison, and the second breach of the norm also ended in gory death. It is not unlikely that there were some other men in her life, and at her invitation, who escaped undetected in the winding streets of Shahjahanabad.

Raushan Ara was younger, also a patron, has a garden in old Delhi credited to her where she remains buried, was jealous of all the attention her elder sister received, also slightly less generous and less celebrated than her, which would tend to fuel jealousy. We hear Manucci again: 'She was not very good-looking, but very clever, capable of dissimulation, bright, mirthful, fond of jokes and amusement, much more so than her sister Begam Sahib. But she was not of equal rank with the latter. She was generous, and drank wine when she could get it.' With all her flaws, she too was an extremely attractive candidate for marriage. She also had her share of scandals in currency in the bazaar, some juicier than Jahan Ara's; she could not hope to get married either.

Early on, one of her dalliances was noticed, but Aurangzeb had let the stray incident pass. Among the stories of her pursuit of sexual pleasure, several were in circulation in the bazaar. In one such, the Princess had had a 'young and handsome' man with her for 15 or 20 days. When he was exhausted, she wished to be rid of him and, to pre-empt reports reaching Aurangzeb's ears, she made a dramatic appearance before the Emperor as if in terror and complained about the entry of the young man into the harem. The ruse seems to have worked, at least initially, for Aurangzeb reached the harem unsuspectingly only to see the man jump off the wall into the river. His escape perhaps sowed the first seeds of suspicion in the Emperor's mind, himself unbeatable in playing tricks of various kinds and a master of dissimulation. Raushan Ara, however, did not stop at this feat. In a yet more audacious adventure, she was credited with hiding nine young men in the wardrobes of her apartment at one go. Perhaps the cover might have lasted a little longer if her niece, Aurangzeb's third daughter, hadn't sought to borrow one of the nine for a night and if the aunt hadn't responded with a bland refusal. The niece leaked the secret to her father, who kept quiet on the surface, but successfully plotted to get rid of his sister for stretching defiance of the norm beyond the limits of tolerance. Slow poison was his favourite weapon for being rid of close but unwanted persons, especially relatives; he seems to have resorted to it in this case as well.

Aurangzeb's eldest daughter Zeb al-Nisa, composing creditable poetry under the pseudonym of 'Makhafi' ('Concealed'), had a crush on his vizir, Mir Askari Aqil Khan, an Iranian. But there was to be no marriage for her either.

It is possible that the bazaar revelled in scandals about royalty and circulated entirely concocted stories about the most vulnerable of its members, which also made them the most irresistible subjects of scandal mongering – young, beautiful and unmarried Princesses. Equally probably, at least the core of the stories might yet have been true, for the Princesses were after all human, too, and they conceivably gave precedence to their body's urges over repressive cultural regimes. Some of the travellers do indeed note that in the midst of the rulers' strong, almost obsessive, concern for the chastity of their women, they yet quietly allowed considerable latitude to their daughters if they took some stealthy steps to fulfil their physical and emotional needs. The ruler did not mind a bit of 'Connivance at their keeping Gallants' and that 'the Rigours of the Cloister are often dispens'd with in their Favour'.[31] The roving European travellers, ever on the lookout for juicy and exotic stories, picked them up from the bazaar and put them into circulation. The stories also fitted in perfectly with the vision of the world that had brought them to the sensual Orient, as the 'other' of the rational West.[32]

Things had clearly radically altered from Babur's time. Some of the European travellers noticed the phenomenon and commented on it. Their explanation hinged on the unstated but obvious, i.e., the desire of the Emperor, especially from Akbar onwards, to avert the acquisition of sons-in-law, who could be potential rivals to their own sons for the throne.[33] What actually appears to have happened was less obvious, far subtler and therefore more durable.

Islamic marriage systems are based on a formal written contract between the marrying couple, laying down the terms and conditions of living together as well as of separation. By its nature a contract is open to termination on specified terms; or else it gets nullified with the death of either of the two parties. Secondly, in neither the Islamic social

---

31 F. F. Catrou, *The General History of the Mogol Empire, From its Foundation by Tamerlane, to the Late Emperor Orangzeb, Extracted from the Memoirs of M.Manouchi*, London, 1709: 328

32 Kate Teltscher has sensitively explored the vision that informed European accounts of India in her *India Inscribed: European and British Writing on India 1600–1800*, Delhi, 1995.

33 Manucci, I: 143–4, 210. M. Athar Ali more or less reproduces the same explanation and calls it 'political considerations'; see his *Mughal Nobility Under Aurangzeb*, Bombay, 1966: 142–3.

framework nor the central Asian cultural zone does marriage establish a hierarchy of relationship between the marrying families. The matter-of-fact recording of multiple marriages of Babur's sisters and daughters thus becomes understandable.

On the other hand the Hindu, especially the Rajput marriage systems, implicate the establishment of a hierarchy between the two families, with the bride-taking family placed a rung or two higher than the bride-giving family. Marriage is also constituted as a sacral relationship, which, once entered into, cannot be breached midway. Indeed, even after the death of the husband, the wife remains married to him inasmuch as widows are normatively disallowed permission to marry, if they remain alive at all. The men, however, are not so constrained. Both hypergamy and sacral marriage were central to Rajput sensibilities; at the lower end of society, divorce and remarriage of divorced/widowed women was commonplace.

It was this two-toned seepage of the Rajput ethos that seems to have cast its influence on the Mughal family. For, if marriage placed the two families on an unequal footing, clearly there could be no family superior to His Majesty's in his empire, where his daughter could marry. Hypergamy (*pratiloma* in Sanskrit, opposed to *anuloma*, hypogamy) did not preclude merely the Rajputs from receiving brides from the Mughal household; no individual located in the court or outside, irrespective of his religious or ethnic association, could any longer hope to do so. Although some marriages did take place, especially during Aurangzeb's reign, these were between first cousins, where equality of status was given. When the branches of the imperial family ran out of first cousins, or marriages were not considered feasible for some other reason, Princesses had to remain single.

In the Mughal family, even as marriage was performed according to Islamic rites and was treated as a contract, by the time of Shah Jahan, imperial Mughal widows began to refrain from entering into matrimony again. Manucci notes that the widows of even the higher Mughal nobility 'do not marry again though [it is] in no way prohibited'. Indeed, the scarcity of widow marriage among elite Muslim groups became so pronounced over time that the British lady who married into a noble Muslim family of Awadh, and was known as Mrs Meer Hasan Ali, notes in the middle of the nineteenth century that she had 'never heard of one single instance, during my twelve years residence amongst them, of a widow marrying again – they have no law to prohibit it; and I have known some ladies, whose affianced husbands died before the marriage was concluded who preferred a life of solitude and prayer, although many other overtures were made'.[34] Jafar Sharif, the eminent nineteenth-century

---

34   Meer Hasan Ali, *Observations on the Mussulmans of India: Description of their Manners, Customs, Habits and Religious Opinions made during a Twelve Years' Residence in their Immediate Society,* 2 vols, Delhi reprint, 1973, 1: 26.

chronicler of popular Islam in the Deccan also noted that 'A prejudice against widows marriage exists... amongst many classes of Muhammadans, especially those who are descended from local converts.'[35] Of the women left behind by the three brothers of Aurangzeb, whom he disposed of in one way or another following his studiously crafted victory in the War of Succession, only one seems to have agreed to marry Aurangzeb himself. Of Caucasian origin, she was known as Udaipuri Mahal, and had been Dara Shukoh's concubine. Marriages between sons and daughters of the four brothers did however take place on a considerable scale. We thus have marriages between Aurangzeb's daughter Zubdat al-Nisa and Dara Shukoh's son Sipihr Shukoh, after the son had been kept in prison for 14 years; between Shah Shuja's daughter and Aurangzeb's son, 'and they loved each other very much'; between Dara's daughter Jahan Zeb Banu and Aurangzeb's son Azam; Prince Akbar, Aurangzeb's favourite son, who was to rebel against him later on, was married to Dara's granddaughter, Sulaiman Shukoh's daughter Salima Banu; another of Aurangzeb's daughters, Mihr al-Nisa, was married to Izid Baksh, son of Prince Murad; there was a marriage the other way round, too, between Murad's daughter Dostdar Begum and Muhammad Sultan, Aurangzeb's son. But even in the imperial family, the supply of first cousins could not be unlimited; some of its daughters were therefore denied marriage altogether. Their marriage in the *anuloma*, hypogamy, mode was unthinkable.

Cultural seepage took other forms as well. Babur had lived in India for just about the last four or five years of his life, between 1526 and 1530, and during this time he could never relinquish the memories of home in Turan. The story of his death, told by his daughter Gulbadan, yet demonstrates ever so vividly the imbibing of Hindu religious ethos. In 1530 Babur was greatly worried about his son Humayun's illness, which all his *hakims* (physicians) were finding themselves unable to handle. At the end of his tether, Babur asked his pious companions what else he should do to bring relief to his favourite son. One of them suggested he give away something, anything, that was most valuable and precious to him and in return beg for Humayun's well-being. The adviser perhaps had in mind Babur's precious jewels, which could be handed out. But Babur decided instead that his life was the most precious and was the very thing he would give away in exchange for his son's. Having declared his intent, he went round the sick Humayun's bed thrice, announcing the exchange. From that moment onwards, says Gulbadan, her father's health began to decline and her brother began to recover his. Humayun

---

35   Jafar Sharif, *Islam in India or the Qanun-i -Islam*, tr. G. A. Herklots, New Delhi, 1997 (first pub. 1921; the work was completed in 1832): 56. Also Garcin de Tassy, *Muslim Festivals in India and other essays*, tr. and ed. by M. Waseem, New Delhi, 1997: 147. The book includes a summary of Sharif's famous treatise.

recovered quickly, but it took two or three months for Babur to pass away; the two processes did not quite coincide.

Whether or not Babur's action was the cause of his death and the miraculous recovery of his son is subject to dispute, but that is how it was perceived and enacted by the Mughal Emperor. And in this perception and enactment inhered a phenomenon that was the very antithesis of Islam. For, in both Islam and Christianity, with the centrality of the concept of the Day of Judgement, when each individual will be called to account for the life given them, transference of one's life to another is quite clearly, if implicitly, sacrilegious. For this reason their bodies are buried after death, to be resurrected on the fateful day of reckoning. Hinduism, on the other hand, has no concept of the Day of Judgement, and life does not come one's way just once but innumerable times, through a cycle of births, deaths and rebirths. Transference of one's life within this schema is entirely in order. Thus, when Babur transferred his own life to that of his son, he did something that would have been perfectly intelligible in Hindu cultural ambience but should have been abhorrent to a practising Muslim. The inconsistency of the practice with Islam clearly never struck either Babur or his family members. The strikingly unselfconscious manner of enacting the episode, as well as of its recording, is the most eloquent testimony to the quiet cultural seepage, even in such a brief period of unsettled times.

In the Mughal household, the mode of looking beautiful and the sense of colours also began to change. One scholar has noticed the quiet change in the hairstyles of imperial Mughal women. While the dress was still heavily Turkish in style, the dressing of hair began to follow the typical Hindu pattern. Instead of wearing their hair loose and parted, they began to twist it 'into a flat pad at the back from which a few curls rolled on'.[36] Towards the end of Humayun's reign, Turkish ladies started using the ornaments that the Hindu women usually wore.[37] At the other end of the spectrum of life, black and blue were the colours of mourning for the early Mughals. Babur notes the black dress of mourning worn by Haidar Ali Bajauri, ruler of Bajaur in the north-western frontier region, when his mother died. In central Asia, in Badakhshan, Mirza Sulaiman died fighting and his mother fell 'into prolonged sorrow. She put on blue clothes and wore them as long as she lived.' Muhammad Zaman Mirza, a central Asian noble of the sixteenth-century ruler of Gujarat, Bahadur Shah, put on blue clothes for mourning his master upon his death.

36 Kaumudi, 'Studies in Mughal Painting', unpublished Doctoral thesis, Allahabad University, 1946, cited in Rekha Misra, *Women in Mughal India (1526–1748)*, New Delhi, 1967:120.
37 Ibid.

Hindal, in an act of defiance of his brother Humayun, declared himself sovereign of the Mughal empire. Immediately on hearing this his mother put on blue clothes. Astonished, Hindal asked her why blue at the moment of rejoicing; she answered that for her his action called for mourning. Abul Fazl, at the beginning of his narrative of the reign of Akbar and describing the festivities around what for him was history's most momentous event, cites a verse:

> From the awnings of gold threads
> The air appeared like screen painted in gold
> The sky was captured in unadulterated gold
> For a blue veil becomes not a feast

Urfi, an eminent poet of Akbar's age, also mentions in a verse the same colour for mourning; and Terry confirms it for the reign of Jahangir. However, when Mumtaz Mahal died, breaking Shah Jahan's heart, he immediately put on white garments. Kalim Kashani, the most celebrated poet of Shah Jahan's reign, versifies it thus:

> Running tears turned his garments white
> In Hind, white is the colour of mourning.[38]

White is the colour of austerity and mourning among Hindus. Indeed, by the eighteenth century, white had come to be associated so closely with mourning that when Miyan Maqbul Alam Masih Khan, a noble among those closest to the Mughal Emperor Farrukh Siyar (r. 1713–19), came to the court wearing white garments, the Emperor's irritation showed. 'If there was some mourning in his family' said the Emperor, looking in his direction, 'why did he appear in court?' The English playwright John Dryden, too, in his play *Aurang-Zebe: A Tragedy*, makes 'Melesinda', wife of the slain Prince Murad, wear white as she proceeds to commit sati.

Marriage ceremonies underwent mutations, too. Celebrations accompanying weddings included feasts on a grand scale, but no marriage processions. Gulbadan goes into considerable detail of the wedding of her brother Hindal and mentions a feast and other rites, but no procession. If the marriage of Princes and Princesses in the reigns of Babur and Humayun took place in the house of the groom, from Akbar's time when Hindu brides had found an entry into the imperial Mughal family, marriage ceremonies came to be performed in the bride's home in

---

38 I am very grateful to Dr Yunus Jaffrey for drawing my attention to both Urfi's and Kashani's verses.

accordance with the Hindu custom. The Hindu rite of the bridegroom going on horseback in a procession known as *barat* (Sanskrit *varyatra*, the groom's journey) to the bride's home is perhaps first indicated among Mughal chronicles in the *Akbar Nama*, when Salim's marriage to the daughter of Raja Bhagwan Das Kachhwaha took place in 1584. Two years later we have indications of another procession, led by Akbar to the house of Rai Rai Singh for the marriage of Salim with the Rajput daughter. By and by, music also came to be part of marriage processions, initially in marriages contracted with Hindu Princesses, therefore clearly borrowed from their tradition. Prince Murad's wedding to the daughter of Mirza Aziz Koka, however, took place in Akbar's mother's palace. In the reign of Shah Jahan, a magnificent painting depicts the marriage procession to conduct Dara's wedding to Nadira, daughter of his uncle Parvaiz, headed for the Emperor's 40-pillared hall. Prince Aurangzeb's marriage to the daughter of Shah Nawaz Khan witnessed the procession terminating at the bride's home, where the ceremonies took place. The fact that sometimes the ceremonies were conducted in the bride's home and at others in the groom's (usually in the house of the most senior member, whether on the maternal or paternal side) suggests that the amalgamation of diverse customs was still in process.

About marriage gifts, the evidence in our sources is far from uniform. While Babur talks extensively of marriages, he rarely mentions the gifts that accompanied the pair. On one such occasion, however, he does put on record the giving of 1,000 *shahrukhis* and a saddled horse to the groom by the father of the bride, back in Kabul. Gulbadan mentions Khan-zadeh Begum, Babur's sister, giving several items of garments, furniture, horses, slaves, etc., as gifts to Hindal's bride; Hindal himself received some gifts from his father-in-law. Gulbadan also mentions that Humayun paid Rs 200,000 to Mir Abul Baqa for carrying out the rites for his marriage with Hamida; she calls it '*nikahana*', a sort of fee for performing *nikah*, the actual wedding. She mentions no other exchange of gifts or money between the marrying partners. In Akbar's time, while we have Raja Ali Khan sending his daughter with 'choice bridal gifts' to Salim, Akbar sends 'bridal presents' to his prospective daughter-in-law, Danial's bride, Bijapur ruler's daughter. Raja Bhagwan Das's daughter, on her marriage to Salim, brought with her:

> several strings of horses, 100 elephants, Abyssinian, Indian and Caucasian slaves, male and female, various kinds of golden vessels set with jewels, gold and silver utensils and all kinds of other things in quantities that are beyond all estimates as dowry [*jahaz*, also called *jahez* in Persian and *dahej* in Hindi]. To each of the Amirs who were present, he gave Iraqi, Turkish

and Arabian horses with golden saddles and other precious things
according to their station and rank.

Prince Danial too 'received gold, cash and all sorts of rare and precious
things in such quantity that he could equip his army from it', following
his marriage with the daughter of the Khan-i Khanan, Abd al-Rahim. On
the other hand, when Prince Khusrau, Salim's eldest son, married the
daughter of Mirza Aziz Koka, 100,000 rupees were sent to the Mirza's
house by way of *shir baha* (price of milk, Aziz Koka being the son of
Akbar's foster-mother Jiji Anaga). *Sachaq* was a peculiar central Asian
custom, which required the groom's family to hand out cash to the bride's
at the time of betrothal. We come across the phenomenon repeatedly in
Babur Nama, Humayun Nama and other sources. Jahangir also records
having sent Rs 80,000 to Jagat Singh, eldest son of Raja Man Singh,
when he had sought his daughter in marriage. The marriage took place in
the house of Jahangir's mother a couple of weeks later and the bride
brought with her, among other things, 60 elephants. For the betrothal of
his son Khurram to the daughter of Muzaffar Husain, Jahangir passed
on Rs 50,000. When Jahangir arranged the marriage of the daughter of
Nur Jahan's brother Asaf Khan, Arjomand Banu, later Mumtaz Mahal,
to his son Shah Jahan, the Prince gave presents to his father, the Begums,
his 'mothers', female servants of the harem, and robes of honour to
Amirs. Dara Shukoh's marriage to Nadira Begum was a sort of landmark
in extravagance even by Mughal standards. Jahan Ara was placed in
charge of the wedding. Considerations of economy being alien to
both her personality and her environment, she spent 1.6 million rupees
on the festivities and gifts that were widely distributed among Princes,
their sisters, wives and daughters of high nobles, and so on. The
bride's mother, too, spent 0.8 million on her dowry and put it on display
for approval. Here then was a scenario of customs from various
sources getting intertwined, and evolving into a uniquely Indian cultural
milieu.

A signal aspect of seepage was the imbibing of the culture of *jauhar* by
the Muslims. *Jauhar* is committed when the warrior courageously enters
a battle faced with certain defeat and determined to perish; his women
back in the fortress are burnt alive lest they fall into enemy hands and be
'dishonoured'. Clearly this is an elite, chivalrous value, and was specific
to the Rajputs. Innumerable legends abound in the history and folklore of
Rajput ruling families, recording when *jauhar* was committed and
women willingly sacrificed their lives in defence of their own and their
men's honour. Indeed, stories are told of Rajput warriors, even of the
high stature of Jaswant Singh of Jodhpur, in Shah Jahan and Aurangzeb's
time, returning to his fortress after defeat in battle and his chief Queen

refusing to open the gates, disbelieving that her husband could ever return home except as victor or dead.

Even as Babur made fun of the practice of *jauhar* ('Rajputs know how to die in battle, not how to win it'), its attribute of placing honour on the highest pedestal, above life itself, was for the chivalrous class of all hues, including Muslims, too strongly ingrained to set aside. By and by, we begin to encounter admiration for it among the Muslims and then actual instances of them emulating it. Abul Fazl reasons that the Hindus follow the practice of *jauhar* because they hold their honour high. Bayazid Biyat narrates the story of one Daud being besieged in Cuttack in Orissa. Left with little hope, he decided to kill his women and children, and himself fight to the very end. When Munim Khan, Akbar's second Khan-i Kha-nan, heard of this determination, he took pity on the Afghan who bore a Muslim name. He persuaded Daud to surrender Orissa to the imperial forces; in return the Khan would have him appointed in that territory itself. Baz Bahadur, ruler of Malwa and lover of Rup Mati, had also arranged 'in accordance with the Indian custom' to put his wives and concubines to the sword in case of his defeat at the hands of Akbar's soldiers, lest they fall into strangers' hands. Since defeat actually came upon him, his command was carried out, though only in part. Also in central India and in Akbar's reign, the legendary Gondwana Queen Durgavati's son, Birsa, had put Bhoj Kayath and Miyan Bhikari Rumi in charge of *jauhar* of women once he died in battle. 'These two faithful servants [one Hindu, the other Muslim], who were the guardians of honour, executed this service,' observes Abul Fazl.

In the houses of the Sisodia, Rathor and Chauhan clans of Rajputs, too, 300 women died in the fire when *jauhar* was under way; among the Rathors, it was a Muslim head of staff, Sahib Khan, who organized the 'destructive fire', according to Abul Fazl. De Laet takes note of the recalcitrant governor Qasim in the reign of Jahangir having 'barbarously slaughtered several of his women' as he faced defeat, although his con-sideration was actually one of expediency – being able to move away from the scene more swiftly – than chivalry or honour. But Jahangir himself records the commission of *jauhar* by his high official Khan-i Jahan, a Rajput convert to Islam. He was a descendant of Puran Mal of Raisin, whose women too had burnt themselves 'in the fire of fame and modesty so that no unlawful person should touch the skirt of their chastity' when he was treacherously murdered by his adversary, Sher Shah. Mirza Nathan, a general of Jahangir, had no Rajput blood flowing in his veins, however. Yet, having been defeated by the Ahoms in Assam, he prepared for a last-ditch battle. He placed his wife, sister and a companion in charge of a four-generation-old servant of the family 'with orders to kill the women if Nathan died in battle'. He then ordered 'the fifty-odd women remaining in the fort to perform immolation by fire in the Hindu rite of *jauhar*. Several Mughal soldiers who were afraid of losing their honor if captured, joined the women in this rite of collective suicide.'[39] Aurangzeb's famed general Shaista Khan suffered great humiliation at the hands of Shivaji in a night attack upon his camp. 'With the chastity of the womenfolk in mind, he killed with his own hands a number of ladies and maid servants of the harem.'

A singularly Indian characteristic inhered in the composition of the Mughal ruling elite. Iqtidar Alam Khan, way back in 1968, brought up to the surface what lay implicit in Akbar's very deliberate, almost forced mutation in the composition of the higher echelons of the class of *mansabdars* to make it inclusive. Starting with a near equal distribution of *mansabs* among the Turanis (central Asians) and Iranis at the beginning of his reign, with a slight edge for the former, who were after all of Mughal ethnic stock, by about 1579–80, halfway through his reign, Akbar had incorporated several more ethnic groups, such as the Rajputs, Indian Muslims and Afghans, into this class, thereby reducing every single group to a minority. The Turanis still comprised the largest chunk, but just about 24 per cent of the whole. It ensured that no single group would be in a position to dictate terms to the others. This formed the rock-solid foundation of Akbar's policy of *sulh kul*, absolute peace.[40] Besides various groups, the nobility now comprised even individuals of diverse characters and dispositions, from Husain Khan 'Tukriya', with a passion to convert people to Islam and determined to stick discriminatory patches (Hindi *'Tukra'*) on the garments of non-Muslim inhabitants of his *jagir*, to Raja Todar Mal, accused by Abul Fazl of religious bigotry because he insisted on performing every single Hindu ritual in his daily life, even as he served Akbar and his empire as its legendary organizer of finance. The pluralist character of the nobility reflected the pluralist ground reality of Indian society. Indeed, even Husain Khan Tukriya, in some ways the archetypical fanatical Muslim, took resort to abstinence from food – a very Hindu form of oath – until he had fulfilled a certain task assigned him by the Emperor.

The celebration of the Hindu festivals, Holi, Rakhi, Dussehra and Diwali, along with the various Eids became a regular feature at the imperial court. Several paintings of Jahangir's and Shah Jahan's period depict the scattering of colours in the court and the palace in

39   J. F. Richards, 'The Formulation of Imperial Authority Under Akbar and Jahangir' in Richards, ed., *Kingship and Authority in South Asia*, University of Wisconsin-Madison, 1978: 276–7.
40   I. A. Khan, 'The Nobility Under Akbar and the Evolution of His Religious Policy', *Journal of Royal Asiatic Society*, 1968, Parts 1 and 2.

Figure 12 Hindu festival of Holi. The celebration of the Hindu festivals of Holi in spring and Dussehra and Diwali in the autumn at the court had become routine from Akbar's time on and, barring a part of Aurangzeb's reign, continued throughout. © The Trustees of the Chester Beatty Library, Dublin.

His Majesty's presence.[41] In a fascinating reminder of the *Mahabharata*, when Dara Shukoh set out for the decisive battle against his brother Aurangzeb at Samugarh, on his father's suggestion he set out in a chariot from the very steps of the imperial palace, because 'it was considered auspicious in Hindustan'. It was also an implicit public acknowledgement of Dara's deep involvement with Hindu mythology and philosophy. Unfortunately, the gesture did not prove auspicious enough for the Prince.

Yet some subtle distance in cultural sensibilities remained. The day after Akbar's mother died was the day of Dussehra. A devout Hindu would have found celebrations unthinkable until a year after his mother's death; Akbar, however, exceedingly grieved as he was over his revered mother's demise, nevertheless celebrated the festival and invited his courtiers to participate. It is possible to imagine this as separation between the Emperor's private grief and his public function; but this distinction has far too recent origins to be transferred retrospectively to Akbar's century.

41   The celebration of these festivals, Holi in particular, by Indian Muslims, seems to have become widespread in society as a whole. Writing in 1811–12, Diwani Singh Khatri of Batala, Distt. Gurdaspur, Panjab, the only one in his family who had converted to Islam and taken the name of Mirza Muhammad Hasan Qateel, goes into great detail of the celebration of Hindu festivals by the Muslims and is particularly rapturous when he describes Holi. He begins the section, 'Muslims and Holi' with the statement, 'barring Afghans and a few orthodox Muslims, all Muslims play Holi with great zest.' See his *Haft Tamasha*, Urdu tr. by Muhammad Umar, Delhi, 1968: 92–4. The nineteenth-century Urdu poet, Nazir Akbarabadi, wrote some extremely popular poetry on the theme of Holi. Over ten years ago, in 1992, this writer too had been witness to every inhabitant of a small and predominantly Muslim town near Aligarh, some 80 kms east of Delhi, singing Radha and Krishna songs and playing Holi with great zest. This was also the month of Ramzan when during the day the Muslims observed fast.

4
Folklore and the Mughal Court Culture

In any epoch the ruling ideology is the ideology of the ruling class.

Karl Marx

Even as Marx in this epigram enunciated a thesis that was largely shared by social and political thinkers of his time, he would perhaps have had no problem if the epigram were expanded somewhat to substitute culture where ideology stands now. The thesis could thus as easily be restated as 'In any epoch the ruling culture is the culture of the ruling class,' without doing much damage to the Marxian formulation.

The formulation carries within it the strong implication that cultural phenomena and values invariably percolate down from society's higher to lower ranks, and the traffic moves in that one direction alone.

The singular linearity of such a programmatic construction should have been worrisome at any stage; time has added to the intensity of the worries. The meaning of culture here privileges certain overt modes of its expression and therefore its elite location: articulate philosophy, 'classical' forms of music, dance, literature, and architecture, and so forth. The studies of cultural anthropologists around the world have demonstrated its partial nature, and their theoretical inferences derived from fieldwork have modified the linear and particularistic perspective considerably. Clearly, cultural production and diffusion is too complex, inclusive and universal a phenomenon to follow a straight path from the top down to the bottom; a great deal of interactive nuancing becomes integral to the entire process. Anthropological fieldwork methods have also redefined the ways of looking at the process; participant observation and empathy with the subject of study have displaced the distance and self-assumed superiority that inhere in the foot-of-the-pedestal view of the culture of people out there in the huts and fields, 'still' engaged in chasing magic cures for their ailments, and a whole range of superstitious practices.

We shall in this chapter look at this interactive process in the medieval context to see how the basic premises of folklore had a significant presence in the imperial court culture of the Mughals. We have already observed in chapter 1 the continuum running between popular visions of the medieval state's legitimacy, in terms of its assimilative character, and its imperial construction along the same lines at the deft hands of Abul Fazl; the same continuum also understandably characterizes the broader cultural arena.

As we enter this arena, a fascinating paradox stares at us: in some important ways the court and its culture stood in splendid isolation from the rest of society, though supported by it, somewhat like a film of oil on water; and in some very profound ways, the two merged with each other and became inseparable.

By the time of the Mughals' arrival, India had been familiar with the use of the Persian language for anywhere between three and five centuries. Familiarity began with the great patron of Persian letters Sultan Mahmud of Ghazni, at the level of state, and with the great Sufi saint Shaikh Muin al-Din Chishti, at the popular level. As the language of court and administration in India, Persian had had a run of more than three centuries when the Mughal empire was established in 1526. Yet, even at the end of the sixteenth century, after a long duration and close acquaintance with it, to a large extent the Persian language and the court culture it encompassed remained an alien presence. For one, Persian was no one's mother tongue. For the Mughals, Turkish, spoken in and around Uzbekistan, was the mother language. For most nobles, except those of Iranian descent, Persian was at best their second language. The Persian language expertise that developed in India was mainly as the language of administration, much as was the case with English in India under the British rule, until very recently when some Indian writers in English have been accorded due recognition. At the plane of intellectual and literary creativity in Persian, Indians had rather meagre accomplishments to show. Historians, barring Abul Fazl, wrote with a sort of mental translation of their formulations from the native Hindawi (medieval Hindi of north India) into Persian, with some queer phrases that made sense only to one at home with the Hindustani idiom. On one hand this process of adoption, adaptation and appropriation diminished the distance between the alien language and the Indian cultural ambience at the elite planes; on the other, the repetitiveness of the format and the imitation of the Iranian historiographical tradition, with its limited range and scope, still pointed to the alien character of the language and its culture. Its 'alien-ness' was not confined to the Hindus; it extended to the Mughals themselves, to the Indian Muslims and, to a smaller extent, the Afghans. Abul Fazl was one exceptional figure, who made creative experiments with pre-Islamic

Persian language and used the experiment to formulate an alternative, overarching world view.

At the level of literary creativity, there is even less to show. The towering literary figure of India's medieval centuries is Amir Khusrau (1253–1324). With a number of poetic and some prose compositions in Persian, he demonstrates his mastery over the language more as a skilled craftsman who could produce things to order than an artist whose heartfelt emotions find expression and flow.[1] Indeed, it is Amir Khusrau's Hindawi poetry, particularly verses centred on the daughter's loneliness in the family, that is really moving in its simplicity and sincerity compared to his Persian creations. Much of Khusrau's Persian poetry is highly contrived. In *Qiran al-Sadain*, composed under commission to commemorate the meeting of Sultan Kaiqubad (r. 1286–90), grandson of Sultan Balban, and Bughra Khan, the Sultan's father and Governor of Bengal, Amir Khusrau pads the thin plot by contriving a conversation between the bow and the arrow! In Akbar's court, the poetry that earned appreciation and reward was of the kind of a poem composed at the birth of the second Prince, Danial; the first line of each verse gave the date of Salim's birth, the second that of Danial. The poet was rewarded with 100,000 rupees by the Emperor for this stuff! It is hard to find less poesy than in these kinds of composition. There was no Hafiz Shirazi or Shaikh Sa'adi in medieval India. Where Indian poetry did reach seductive finesse was in the native Urdu, born in India of mixed Persian and indigenous parentage, and taking pride in it. But this was in the period of the Mughals state's decline, i.e. the eighteenth and the nineteenth centuries.

Akbar's historians attest to the absence of notable literary creativity in the Persian language in medieval India, if unwittingly. In the *Ain-i Akbari*, following an age-old Iranian and Indian historiographical tradition, Abul Fazl appends a list of the most eminent poets of Akbar's reign. Of the 59 poets listed, and an additional enumeration of another 15, from amongst 'thousands of poets [who] are continually at court', there are just two who could be clearly identified as Indians: at the top of the list is Abul Fazl's elder brother Abul Faiz Faizi Fayyazi, of course, and at number 58 is Sheri, of Panjabi Shaikhs' stock. All the poets writing in Persian who had, in Abul Fazl's perception, distinguished themselves and were included in the list belonged mainly to parts of Iran and some to central Asian and Arab regions. Clearly, a mere single Indian, besides Faizi, had earned barely noticeable recognition as a poet, and that just

---

1   Wahid M Mirza, Amir Khusrau's eminent modern day biographer and critic, remarks: 'Like a wandering minstrel he went from door to door, turned his lyre to a different pitch according to time and convenience, and sang with as much gusto the praises of a murderer as those of his victim.' See his *Life and Works of Amir Khusrau*, Calcutta, 1935: 234–5.

short of hitting the bottom. Interestingly, all the names included in the list are those of Muslims; not a single Hindu had come anywhere near taking to the Persian language for the expression of his literary genius. In Badauni's similar list of poets, comprising a total of 168, there are two or three Indian Muslims and one, possibly a Hindu, known charmingly as Muhammad Manohar. Badauni claims to have compiled the list 'without any discrimination'.[2] This scarcity of Indian presence becomes even more pronounced considering that the language had been learnt by all who operated the vast state machinery and that it had percolated down with its administrative and general vocabulary into all languages, but especially those of the Indo-Aryan family, in the whole of India north of the Vindhyas. In the list of learned men, preceding the poets in the *Ain*, there is a good representation of both Indian Muslims and Hindus.

But Persian had yet not been imbibed in the subconscious sufficiently to enable the expression of intense emotions in the language – emotions like anger or love, or in which one dreams or abuses. Bayazid Biyat is mercifully naïve enough to put on record one such moment of intense anger in Akbar's life. Early in his reign, Adham Khan, son of Maham Anaga, a foster-mother of Akbar, went and sliced off the head of Shamsuddin Ataka, the Vakil, chief among the nobles and courtiers, and husband of another of the Emperor's foster-mothers, Jiji Anaga. With blood still dripping off the sword, and with the clear intention of repeating his feat on Akbar as well, he moved towards the harem where Akbar was resting. The cacophony woke up the young Emperor and, making a quick reconnaissance of the scenario, he advanced towards his foster-brother with determination. Bayazid then records: 'After this, His Majesty said in Hindawi, "You catamite, why did you kill my Ataka?"' Action swiftly followed words, and in one sharp blow of the fist Akbar crushed the ambitious intruder; he then had him thrown off the fort wall twice over, if only to make sure. The word translated here as 'catamite' sounds innocuous, if a bit impolite, in English but is deadly in its original Hindawi, picked up straight from the gutter. Clearly, Akbar's command of Persian did not quite match the intensity of the moment.

If the alien Persian language defined the cultural ambience of the court, a great many of its elements had risen from the ground level, with their roots going into folklore. Folklore here is understood as a phenomenon that pre-dates as well as survives the formation of religious identities. Thus, folklore is not identifiable as Hindu or Muslim or Christian. Its regional and sub-regional identities are slightly more discernible,

---

2   Nizam al-Din Ahmad too appends a list of some 84 poets, but gives such scarce details that ethnic identification becomes less certain. Many of the names are however common to all three lists.

although even here the boundaries are eminently porous. Some elements of folklore are indeed timeless and spaceless; there is a high degree of universality in them.[3] Transference is one such element. Transference is mediated through miracles and magic, central to all forms of folklore.

When sickness strikes one and physicians are unable to heal it, magic healing occurs through the transference of the ailment to another through making a 'gift' of it or through making an effigy and placing it on the village crossroads, where it gets transmitted to anyone touching it or even to one who happens to pass by it. Among many anthropological studies in several cultural zones, the principle of transference surfaces everywhere. Gloria Goodwyn Raheja has, in her fieldwork in a north Indian village, established the transferral of various forms of inauspiciousness, current or anticipated, through gifts to Brahmins, beggars or relatives whom custom or marital ties bind down to being recipients.[4] With this insight, the story narrated by Manucci about Shah Jahan and Jahan Ara falls in place.

Shah Jahan one day complained to his daughter that his men no longer obeyed him with customary promptitude, on the assumption that his reign was nearing its end. Jahan Ara, on hearing this, gave away large sums of money in alms and freed many slaves, both male and female. Before doing that, she made them circumambulate her father three times and then sent them out of the palace 'as if they carried away with them the royal infirmity outside'. Manucci adds to the story the observation that 'This custom is very common in Hindustan, and this superstition being very widespread, everyone distributes, according to his ability, alms of food and other things.' No Indian villager and few city dwellers, then as now, would need explanation of the meaning of Jahan Ara's deed on her father's behalf; the meaning would be understood all around as given.

The story of Jahan Ara's garments catching fire and the body being seared is told in several accounts. The Emperor 'first sought spiritual remedies and sought recovery for her through the blessed prayers of pious saints and by throwing open the doors of charity'. For three days, 5,000 gold coins and another 5,000 rupees were distributed each day in alms. 'He also turned his attention to temporal means and directed all those skilled in the science of medicine and surgery... to devise remedies

---

3 Nothing evokes the universality and timelessness of folkloric belief in magic and miracles more decisively than the sticking of a large portrait of Mao ze Dong on the glass screen of a long distance coach in China in August 1988 as charm against a possible accident. *The Times of India*, 22 August 1988 for the picture and its rationale.
4 Gloria Goodwyn Raheja, *The Poison in the Gift: Ritual, Prestation and the Dominant Caste in a North India Village*, Chicago and London, 1988.

for her cure.' The order in which the search for the Princess's cure was followed is telling. A total of a half-million rupees had been earmarked for distribution in charity to aid the recovery of the Princess back to complete health; of this amount, 150 thousand were dispatched to Mecca and Medina. In the end, thanks to the plaster developed by a mendicant and applied to the lady, Jahan Ara recovered completely and miraculously within three days. The mendicant, always in want of the next meal, was endowed with vast sums of money. Charity clearly brought the ultimate magic cure; medical treatment seemed almost like a placebo.

Akbar also has a similar story of his foster-mother Jiji Anaga, narrated to Abul Fazl. One day the lady came to His Majesty's presence and 'before I knew anything, she revolved a cup of water round my head and drank the water. When I inquired the reason for it, she said, "This night I had a dream that something disagreeable was going to happen to the Shahinshah [Akbar]. I have drawn it upon myself."' This was late in Akbar's career.

Long before, at the outset of his reign, the first major challenge to Akbar was from Himu, the Hindu general of Adil Shah, at the second battle of Panipat. On the general's defeat, Bairam Khan suggested that Akbar decapitate his adversary. Akbar then related a story that long ago, when Himu's name was unknown, he, Akbar, had made an effigy of him and had chopped off its head. He need not therefore repeat the effort. Abul Fazl cautions against taking this story as a simple amusement; 'in reality a malevolent life had been extinguished'. In transferring Himu's 'malevolent life' to the effigy and then symbolically 'extinguishing it' in a manner that its actual extinction should follow in due course, Akbar was resorting to a magic practice of antiquity that had a long tradition behind it and is not unknown in the twenty-first century in India, where effigies of an 'enemy' are pricked with pins and the limbs so pricked are the ones where the 'enemy' suffers pain in his body. Sometimes death is also caused thus. The *Mahabharata* also records an episode in this genre. On his part, Himu, too, had constantly repeated a charm at Panipat, hoping that it would see him through the battle. We have already encountered Babur's transference of his life to his son Humayun. Transference is central to all these stories and to many others besides.

Manucci was right about the widespread nature of these and other practices in India, although 'superstition' in his observation adds a value-judgement to the phenomenon that a modern-day social scientist would rather avoid. Raheja's fieldwork was among the middle Hindu caste of the Gujars; Shah Jahan and Jahan Ara were practising Muslims, each one having erected a mosque, among other things. Babur, too, was a devout Muslim in more than one aspect of his life. Yet the practice of transference through magic operates in both groups, for it pre-dates both religions, as it does Christianity. Indeed, high priests of all religions frown upon miracles and magic, and, having done that, they appropriate them. Our sources are teeming with evidence of the practice and popularity of miracles, omens, charms and magic throughout the period and at all levels of society. Miracles are attributed to living or dead saints and boons are retrieved from them through devotion by performing difficult tasks, such as walking a very long distance on foot or giving out large sums of money to a point that it hurts. Hence, the exhausting pilgrimages to the tombs of saints.

Akbar celebrated many of his triumphs by walking to the tomb of Shaikh Muin al-Din Chishti at Ajmer, a journey from Agra he performed several times for a variety of boons he had received from the saint who had been dead for five centuries. Beginning with Babur, almost all Mughal rulers and their nobles engaged in the circumambulation of the tombs of saints. They had much in common with the huge crowds of people who thronged the tombs in search of wish-fulfilment. Firuz Shah, the Tughlaq ruler in the second half of the fourteenth century, had sought to ban the gathering of crowds around the tombs, for he suspected that anonymity in the crowd gave enough latitude for licentiousness; some 400 years later, the crowds had by no means diminished and tombs were still the site for their gathering. Still later, the Muslim theologian Shah Waliullah was bemoaning the play of licence at the saints' tombs, where large crowds gathered regularly and periodically. Indeed, local legends centred on almost all Sufi saints credit them with the performance of some miracle or the other, and in the whole of south Asia this continues to be the rationale of their popularity to this day, centuries after their burial.

But it was not saints alone who could be the medium of the transference of divine benediction. Sometimes the Emperors themselves could be invested with these virtues and their transference was sought by the subjects. *Jharoka darshan*, beginning one's day with the glimpse of His Majesty's profile in a window, was premised upon the same principle. A whole *dashaniya* sect, which began the day with a glimpse, *darshan* – a term imbued with strong religious overtones – developed from the time of Akbar onwards. In chapter 1 we noted the performance of miracles being attributed to Akbar, and his benediction sought by multitudes. A soldier of Muhammad Ghuri had turned into a saint and his tomb is still the object of worship in Bahraich in modern UP; the soldier-saint is known as Ghazi Mian. Even inanimate objects could acquire such properties and crowds would worship them in exchange for some wish-fulfilment. Fr. Monserrate reports that at Mandu, the old and abandoned capital of Baz Bahadur, ruler of Malwa in modern Madhya Pradesh, he saw 'a fragment of a huge iron gun which for some superstitious reason or [an]other the heathens revere and worship. It is smeared with oil and coloured red'.

Manucci again tells us the story of the transference of the fertility of a tree to the womb of a barren woman. In return the tree was rendered sterile and had never borne a fruit since. To this he adds yet another story of a 'well-born woman' of Bassein, near Mumbai, who gave birth to a tray of sand, following a magic prescription gone awry, for she had asked for a son. We have noted above Emperor Jahandar Shah and his consort Lal Kunwar bathing naked for 40 days in a pond in the Mehrauli area near Delhi's Qutb Minar to seek a cure for the lady's sterility, for folklore attributed fertility to that pond and its transferability to human couples who bathed in it naked.

There are several other forms of transference practised. 'Nisar', a sort of sacrifice when some money is gathered in one's palm, revolved round the head of a sick person, a bride or bridegroom, or anyone affected or liable to being affected, so that the present or potential inauspiciousness is embodied in the money which is then scattered around to be picked up by beggars. The person is thus secured against the recurrence of the affliction. The term 'Nisar' is of Persian origin, although the practice is common to all communities. This in effect was the quintessence of the ceremony of weighing the Emperor on his solar and lunar birthdays against gold, silver and several other materials, and giving these away in charity, usually to those stated to be 'the needy ones'. Tavernier informs us that coins specifically meant for the ceremonies of nisar, with the word struck on them, were minted under the Mughals.

Jahangir tells us a superb story following the birth of his half-sister Shukr al-Nisa. 'The first time when, according to the custom of pressing the breast of a child and a drop of milk is perceptible, they pressed my sister's breast and milk appeared, my revered father said to me, "Baba! drink this milk that in truth this sister may be to thee as a mother".' Motherhood was captured in a trace of milk and transplanted on to sibling relationship; it also implicated pre-emption of the slightest trace of sexual attraction between them, the more so as they were half-brother and sister.

If transference is central to the working of folklore, it has an equal place in the functioning of the imperial court culture. Living as we do in the age of written constitutions and laws codified in minute detail, we have to imagine a medieval scenario which was still a long distance away from the highly institutionalized mechanisms of governance of our time. In that scenario, in the absence of highly perfected institutionalized governance, all power, glory and authority must rest symbolically in one person, the monarch, and it was through the transference of these by the monarch to his nobles and functionaries that the system found its operative modalities. Within the parameters of this loose structure, both the notion of absolute power of the monarch and implicitly shared sovereignty found space.

Khila't, robe of honour, was the epitome of transference. Giving away of robes of honour was a daily routine in court, and Akbar even had a small workshop for manufacturing robes in the outer fringe of his capital, Fatehpur Sikri. Elaborate rituals were enacted while giving and receiving the robes. The most highly prized one was from His Majesty's own cupboard, one that he had actually worn, even if just once. For such a robe imbibed wholesome attributes of His Majesty's person, now being passed on to the receiver. Short of that, a virgin robe was brushed across the monarch's back before being handed over to the recipient; the touch transferred on to the person receiving it a minute particle of His Majesty's glory. The routine was repeated even when the robe was sent to a recipient in a far-off corner of the empire. He in turn was to perform rituals of *kurnish* and *taslim*, as if the robe actually carried His Majesty's presence to him.

While the robe was the most visible form of honouring, there were other forms as well. A headgear (*sarpech*), the more cherished being one off His Majesty's head, sometimes as part of the ensemble of the robe, called *sar o pa* (head-to-foot, though literally it should mean 'head and foot'), and at others by itself, was an equally coveted piece of largesse received from the King. A horse, or a portrait of the King, even a letter signed or unsigned by him, could substitute for the robe. These gifts were subject to some strict regulations. The grant of headgear was confined to the highest amirs alone, those above the *mansab* of 4,000, although on occasion, as a very special favour shown by the Emperor, it could be given to young children of great amirs, such as the one Aurangzeb gave to Amin Khan's son. The headgear so given could be worn only on Sundays and the awardee could not wear another one resembling it. The regulations reinforced the principle that His Majesty's person still inhered in the gift; symbolically these could not be torn apart from him.

While *sar o pa*'s, robes and horses, etc., were given away mainly by the King, there is evidence of other members of the royal family and nobility replicating the ritual at their levels. Bayazid Biyat, always a rich source of evidence for deviations from the norms, gives us entry into a variety of such gifts. Following the second battle of Panipat, in which Himu's head was chopped off, Munim Khan sent his servant Bayazid to the royal Begums to convey the news of the imperial victory. When the Begums were satisfied with the authenticity of the news, they were pleased to 'promise him a horse and *sar o pa*'. Munim Khan, too, gave a horse and a complete robe (*sar o pa*) to Ali Quli Shaibani who had repaired a fort near Varanasi in preparation for battles with eastern Afghans.[5] Munim Khan, in turn, himself received these from Akbar when he set out for Kabul to crush Akbar's ambitious half-brother, Mirza Hakim. A distinguished service of a military or non-military nature was not the only reason for the award of a *khila't*; even a message of condolence could be wrapped in it. Jahangir sends *khila'ts* to the children of his father-in-law Itmad al-Daulah 'to take them out of their mourning garments'. Aurangzeb, too, sent a robe off his own person to Umdat al-Mulk Asad Khan on the death of his maternal uncle Jafar Khan, also the Emperor's uncle. *Khila'ts* were often used to win over political opponents or to make allies out of adversaries.

The robe of honour apart, another almost daily court routine was the grant of *mansabs*, new or higher, to state functionaries. If transfer of His Majesty's personal glory was the central feature of the symbolism of the robe of honour, the grant of *mansab* carried to the grantee an authorized portion of the King's authority and power. Since notionally all power and authority were vested in the King, its actual operation was effected through its daily transmission through a highly ritualized procedure. But the transmission was never terminal; it did not signify the *alienation* of any part of the King's authority from him. While the *mansabdar* imbibed the part of King's authority assigned to him, he was never its autonomous possessor; he was indeed forever subject to dismissal, demotion (or promotion) at the King's will. Even his property, acquired in the process of functioning as *mansabdar*, reverted upon his death to the King; his family and progeny could demand no share of it as a matter of right. Indeed, we have several examples of the escheat of *mansabdars'* property to the King's treasury upon the *mansabdar's* death, not as a measure of punishment but as routine, though it is hard to think of it as an invariable practice. This, and the frequent transfer of *mansabdars* from one part of the empire to another, left many a European visitor to Mughal India aghast, for both these stood in stark contrast to the characteristics of feudal property back home. It was from them, especially from François Bernier, that the observation was passed on to European commentators as the explanation of the fragility of the medieval Indian state structure. It found its way back home in the early 1960s in the very skilful hands of Irfan Habib, who posited the collapse of the mighty Mughal empire on the disastrous consequences of the system of transfers of *mansabdars*,

---

5 Stewart Gordon records several agencies and several objectives for the grant of *khila't* in medieval India; see S Gordon, ed., *Robes of Honour: Khil'at in Pre-Colonial and Colonial India*, New Delhi, 2003:1–30. Gavin R. G. Hambly also gives instances of a varied nature for the grant of robes of honour in the same book: 'The Emperor's Clothes: Robing and 'Robes of Honour' in Mughal India', ibid.: 31–49.

just as Bernier had done around the middle of the seventeenth century and John Fryer slightly later.[6] For us, it symbolizes the centring of all authority, power and glory in the King's person, and the evolution of a mechanism for effecting conquest and governance through transference of power and authority. The two are often mutually inconsistent, yet not incompatible. Indeed, the greater the tension between them, the more the need to reinforce the symbolic centring in the King.

Sociologist M. N. Srinivas, and anthropologists McKim Marriot and Pauline Kolenda, open a seductive cultural perspective on the theme: specifically embedded in the south Asian, especially Hindu, cultural and social stream is the coding of certain attributes, *guna*, in a person, and their partial transferability to another at the person's will. For Srinivas, some individuals, owing to their status at birth, are permanently imbued with certain superior qualities (purity) and others permanently with inferior qualities (impurity). It is possible however to transfer, very transiently, a part of the qualities of one to the other on special occasions, without altering the status of either; nor are the temporarily transferred qualities inheritable by the recipient; indeed, the transfer is forever tentative and subject to resumption.[7] In some ways these cultural codes, guidelines of life at society's ground level, were being enacted at the imperial court.

That was the model, the paradigm, captured in the notion of the monarch's absolute power – a highly dubious notion in actual fact. Power by its very nature is shared, if unequally; it remains a terrain for multipolar contests, sometimes erupting in explosive spasms, at most times finding utterance in silent, almost imperceptible manifestations. The grandiose claims of rulers of exercising unbridled power and an absolute quantum of centralized authority need to be viewed with suspicion, or, at the very least, caution.

However, our chief concern here is transference as the central feature of both folklore and the functioning of the court, and more broadly the

---

6   Bernier, *Travels:* 224–7. John Fryer, *A New Account of East Indies and Persia, 1672–8,* Indian Reprint, New Delhi, 1985 (first pub. 1698): 195. Irfan Habib's major intervention elaborated this thesis, mediated through W. C. Smith's brief exploratory article, 'Lower Class Uprisings in the Mughal Empire', *Islamic Culture,* 1946: 21–40; see Habib, *Agrarian System of the Mughals,* Bombay, 1963, ch. IX, 'The Agrarian Crisis of the Mughal Empire': 317–51 and revised edn. New Delhi, 1999: 364–405.

7   M. N. Srinivas, *Religion and Society among the Coorgs of South India,* Oxford, 1952; McKim Marriott, 'Hindu Transactions: Diversities Without Dualism', in B. Kapferer, ed., *Transactions of Meaning,* Philadelphia, 1976; McKim Marriott and Ronald B. Inden, 'Towards an Ethnosociology of the South Asian Caste System', in Kenneth A. David, ed., *The New Wind: Changing Identities in South Asia,* Chicago, 1977; Pauline Kolenda, 'The Ideology of Purity and Pollution' in *Caste in Contemporary India: Beyond Organic Solidarity,* Prospect Heights (Illinois), 1985.

state system. Is one the source and the other its offshoot? It would appear nearly impossible to resolve this problem satisfactorily. It is important, however, to emphasize the common ground between them, irrespective of the 'chicken-and-egg' dilemma, and to note that a similar 'language' of transference forms the basis of the functioning of both systems, highly complex as these are. It should therefore not be hard to imagine some level of interaction between them, not one that is deliberate, but rather one that is implicit and subterranean.

There were other forms of perhaps more direct borrowing from folklore by the court: the practice of omens and auguries, important elements of magic, and employed as diagnostic indices in folklore. On this, our sources leave us with rich evidence at imperial as well as popular levels. Not being located in the post-Enlightenment context, the Mughal rulers and elite intellectuals did not suspect even a trace of inconsistency between these practices and a rationalist attitude. Abul Fazl, perhaps the greatest 'rationalist' of the sixteenth century in India, sought out omens from the poetry of Hafiz Shirazi to predict victory for imperial soldiers. When Akbar himself drew an omen from the death of two elephants, which had saddened 'superficialists' (*zahir parastan*, worshippers of the apparent), that this in fact foretold the death of two rebellious brothers, Abul Fazl felt overwhelmed. 'What spirit, what intellect, and what vision!', he gushes. Akbar also read shoulder blades to foretell the coming events, and made decisions about dispatching his armies on campaigns after consulting his astrologers and taking omens.

Indeed Akbar, of all the Mughal Emperors, himself became the embodiment of many miraculous powers. Most evidence of such powers comes understandably from Abul Fazl, but not from him alone. He could bring down rain through prayers when there was drought; his breath on a mirror, thrown into fire, stopped rain when there was excess of it. He could very politely tell rain to refrain from spoiling a banquet in his palace; the rain poured all around but skirted the palace. His breath had 'Messiah's qualities', which cured ailments of human beings and animals. His presence could calm even the usually turbulent Wular Lake in Kashmir. Indeed, he could avert calamitous consequences of a solar eclipse by commissioning rain until the hour of the eclipse had passed. A bullet fired at a man touched his clothes and went cold (*sard shuda bud*) because of his physical proximity to His Majesty. Another pierced a soldier's clothes but went cold on touching his sweat; he too was standing close to the King.

Akbar was not alone in embodying occult powers or following the occult; he was in the eminent company of his ancestors and successors, who all went by omens and auguries in a variety of situations that touched upon virtually every aspect of life. Babur claims knowledge of a talisman for stopping rain. Once, when he and his friends were forced to have a drink inside the house instead of out in the orchard, owing to a heavy downpour, he taught one of the companions the talisman. 'He wrote it on four pieces of paper and hung them on four sides; as he did it, the rain stopped and the air began to clear.' The fact that Babur does not treat the event as out of the ordinary testifies to the efficacy of the talisman as routine in his perception. When Sultan Husain Mirza sent word to Babur that he intended to invade the Uzbegs and invited him to join in the venture, Babur 'sought the meaning of the word from God', records his daughter ambiguously, with a faint hint at some omen. Babur himself records looking for an omen before launching his project of the conquest of India. As he prepared to lead an expedition there in 1519, the news of the birth of a son reached him. 'I took it as an omen and gave [the child] the name Hind-al [taking of Hind].' Before his final and decisive assault in 1526, he set up a condition for the launch: if he received a typically Indian product – a mango or a betel nut – he would march forth to battle at Panipat. When Daulat Khan, a disgruntled noble of the Indian ruler Ibrahim Lodi, brought him half-ripe mangoes preserved in honey, his mind was fully made up.[8] On the eve of the battle of Khanuwa, in the following year, the day before battle was joined he sent out some soldiers to bring back the heads of slain men from the enemy, as an omen. And since a whole series of victories had followed his taking of Kabul, he took it as a good omen and turned the city into *khalisa* or crown land, lest any one of his sons covet it, presumably for the same reason. It is fascinating to imagine the tension between the father and his generally obedient sons over the occult meaning embedded in the capture of a territory, rather than in the territory itself.

Humayun in his turn was even more inclined to let events develop under the influence of omens, auguries and astrology. In the conflict with his three brothers, before he set out for Badakhshan in central Asia in pursuit of Kamran, he stood waiting in a room with a white cock for company. 'Suddenly it came upon his holy mind, "If this white bird were to come upon my shoulder and crow, it would be a sign of victory and good fortune for me." ' The bird followed the Emperor's thought and did as expected; gratified, Humayun put a silver ring on its foot by way of thanksgiving. On another occasion, his sister Gulbadan tells us, Humayun's helmet bearer picked up the helmet (*baqcha*) to bring it over to him; at that moment someone sneezed, a bad omen. The servant replaced the helmet on the ground and waited for a while to raise it again.

---

8 *Babur Nama*: 440. Translator Mrs A. S. Beveridge's reconstruction.

Jahangir, too, resorts frequently to omens and auguries for various purposes, often from the book of Hafiz Shirazi's verses. He also records having brought about rain through prayers in parched Mandu. Mirza Nathan, a general of his, fell sick and was cured by the Emperor's appearance in his dream. God-fearing Prince Aurangzeb, on his part, perceived his beheading of a large serpent while on his march towards the decisive battle with his brother Dara Shukoh as a sign that God would give him victory. Clearly, for him the serpent stood in for Dara. Manucci, who passes on this tidbit, observes for good measure that 'Mahomedans are very superstitious'. Manucci also observes that several stories of Emperor Aurangzeb's humility, kindness and saintliness were in circulation, and that a belief had gained currency that he could make himself invisible whenever he chose to and go to Mecca to confer with Muhammad. A woman who was unable to conceive, reports Manucci again, vowed a sacrifice of 5 rupees to Aurangzeb in person, if she succeeded. She did. Aurangzeb accepted the money and gave it away in charity.[9]

Yet another form of folk culture – overt sensuality – rose high up the social ladder. Overt sensuality finds expression and social acceptance on some very special occasions. The celebration of the spring festival of Holi allows, especially in north India, a great deal of licence of body and language if only for a few days, opening a regulated aperture in the rather tight societal norms of deportment and conduct which seek chiefly to suppress sexual exuberance. An aperture also opens up on occasions of marriage.

Holi, which coincides with the onset of spring, has a religious association with Hindu mythology. Historians and anthropologists have traced multifarious connections between tribal, agricultural and Brahmanical lineages of the festival, emphasizing over and over again its origins in pre-religious cultural zones of magic and miracles and their continuance down to modern times, even as several other streams have merged in the celebrations.[10] A carnivalesque ambience is created in which dry or

9   Simon Digby has recently translated several popular stories in this genre about yogis, Sufis and other characters, mostly located in medieval India; see his *Wonder Tales of South Asia*, Jersey, 2000.

10   See for example McKim Marriott, 'The Feast of Love' in Milton Singer, ed., *Krishna: Myths, Rites and Attitudes*, Chicago, 1966 and idem, 'Little Communities in an Indigenous Civilization' in Marriott, ed., *Village India*, Chicago, 1955; Margaret Stutley, *Ancient Indian Magic and Folklore*, Delhi, 1980; Surajit Sinha, 'Vaisnava Influence on a Tribal Culture' in Singer, ed., *Krishna*; Lawrence A. Babb, *The Divine Hierarchy: Popular Hinduism in Central India*, New York, 1975; Jyotirmaya Khatri, 'Evolution and Structure of Holi: Towards an Understanding of the Social Morès of a Festival', unpublished M.Phil. dissertation, Centre for Historical Studies, JNU, 1993, an excellent pioneering work by a young historian.

wet colour is thrown on everyone around – friends, family members and strangers. In the heartland of the celebration of the festival, the Vrinda-van area near Mathura, the area with the closest association with Krishna and Radha, the festival's central figures, women from Radha's village actually beat up men – and rather severely – from Krishna's village with ropes and sticks. Men defend themselves with shields but will not hit back at the aggressive women. Men and women, young and old, participate in the carnival, which allows a lot of touching of bodies, and a great deal of obscene, sexually explicit bantering occurs while similar songs are sung in public in the presence of both sexes with no one batting an eyelid. If taboos are socially regulated to keep the order intact, their breaches too are socially sanctioned and for the same objective.

The lower caste origins of Holi are highlighted by a number of com-mentators. *Ain-i Akbari* observes that the community of Sudras, the lowest among the four-caste structure of the Hindus, count it among its great festivals. Lawrence Babb, anthropologist, observes pithily: 'Indeed, on Holi every participant becomes a Sudra.'[11] By and by the festival had travelled up the social scale and had reached the imperial level, where playing of Holi became part of the festivities at the imperial court, along with Dussehra and Diwali. At large in society too, Holi, Dussehra and Diwali were celebrated by Hindus and Muslims alike by the eighteenth and early nineteenth centuries. Ghulam Ahmad Tabtabai, author of the three-volume *Seir al-Mutakhireen*, written in the 1780s, notes that the Muslims celebrate Holi as much as the Hindus, and Mirza Qateel observes that except for the Afghans and the fanatics among Muslims, everyone plays Holi and celebrates Diwali.

At marriage ceremonies, too, several social taboos are breached and bawdy looks, touch, jokes and lyrics replace the hidebound norms of cross-sexual relationships. The relationship between the cross-parents of the bride and bridegroom – between the bride's mother and the groom's father and the other way around – is opened up to a great deal of sexual innuendo through the cracking of ribald jokes and bantering, and recita-tion of lyrics with double entendre, where subtlety is often conspicuous by its absence. By the eighteenth century the lyrics had arrived at the imperial court, and the later Mughal Emperor Shah Alam II has left behind some choice verses in this genre in the Hindi language, as he has compositions in celebration of Holi.[12]

---

11   Lawrence A. Babb, *The Divine Hierarchy*: 147.
12   The verses were published in 1797 at the command of the Emperor himself. See *Nadirat-i Shahi*, Rampur, 1944.

If the travel of folkloric principles and practices to the imperial court was one facet of the cultural movement, traffic in the opposite direction was equally dense. The percolation of the Persian language and the evolution of Urdu, the concept of *haveli*, a miniature replica of imperial mansion at the level of the locality, the holding of *mushaira*, assembly of poets where each poet recites his verses for public approbation, certain strands of classical music and dance, especially *dhrupad, khayal* and *kathak*, and not least what passes for Mughalai cuisine, are all evidence of cultural diffusion from the court to the street corner. Even the mode of demonstrating respect to one's senior or elder by standing up before him and, if seated at all, occupying a lower seat than the senior's, keeping largely quiet in his presence except for answering his directly addressed questions, etc., all owe their origin to Mughal court culture and have devolved downwards to become part of everyday Indian culture.

Indeed, the eighteenth century in Indian history is witness to a particularly dynamic cultural flux, with the perceived distance between hidebound elite norms and exuberant popular culture crumbling, and a hyperactive common cultural space emerging as the defining feature at both ends. 'Ends' in fact seem to have dissolved their margins. Much of it marks India's daily life today, even as twenty-first century technology is rapidly reshaping life's patterns.

Glossary

amir	Noble of high rank.
anuloma (Sanskrit)	Hypogamy.
ashrafi	Gold coin.
barat (Hindi)	Groom's marriage procession.
chakrvartin (Sanskrit)	A world conquering ruler.
chatr	Literally parasol. Symbolically protector, hence an imperial prerogative in early and medieval India.
chaupal	Informal village assembly of males to exchange information, gossip and stories.
Dar al-Harb	Territory that Muslims seek to snatch from other religions in order to convert it into *Dar al-Islam*.
Dar al-Islam	Territory inhabited exclusively by Muslims.
Darshaniya sect	A sect that grew in Akbar's reign, engaging in the quasi-religious Hindu practice of breaking fast only after having a glimpse (*darshan* in Sanskrit and Hindi) of the Emperor in *jharoka*.
Delhi Sultanate	The period of Indian history from 1206 to 1526 when the pre-Mughal Muslim rulers conquered and ruled over much of the land.
Farman	Written edict or order issued by the Emperor, properly attested by his personal seal.
farzand	In Persian language, son; also affectionately used for son-in-law.
fath nama	Edict issued after a victory; usually follows a format where victory is attributed to Islam's glory.
faujdar	*Pargana* level administrator.
hazrat	A venerated person, usually reserved for the Emperor, though also used for his mother or other senior members of the family.
Ibadat Khana	Literally 'house of worship', established by Akbar for holding discussions among professors of different religions and sects.

Iqta system	Evolved with the Delhi Sultanate as the mechanism for territorial expansion, revenue collection and maintenance of law and order throughout the imperial territories. Holder of *Iqta*, the *muqta*, could be governor of a province, or a mere collector of revenue from a piece of land for his own maintenance. Precursor of the more refined *mansab* system of the Mughals.
jagir	State's alienation of (primarily land-) revenue to *mansabdars* as payment of their salaries. Custom duties could also comprise a *jagir*.
jauhar	Among the highest values of the warrior class, especially treasured by Rajputs: fight unto death, resorted to in desperation. Accompanying *jauhar* was the custom of sati.
jharoka darshan	Akbar adopts this Hindu religious practice of having a glimpse of a god or goddess and carves out a *jharoka*, window, where he appears every morning to give a glimpse of himself, *darshan*, to his admirers among the common people. Stopped by Aurangzeb.
khalisa	Part of the imperial territory, not assigned in *jagir*. The revenue collected from this part went directly into the imperial treasury for meeting expenditure on the imperial family, the army maintained by the emperor, and administration, etc. Usually less than a fifth of the total.
khanazad	'House-born' in Persian language, i.e., sons born in the harem or born to nobles and *mansabdars* in imperial service. Even as *mansab* system was theoretically open, the *khanazad* came to acquire a special status.
khanqah	A Sufi hospice.
khilat (Arabic)	Robe of honour.
khutba	Edict read by the Imam from the mosque's pulpit in congregational prayers every Friday. Considered a source of legitimacy of the King within the Muslim community.
kurnish	A form of court etiquette performed before the Emperor by bending one's torso.
mahram	A male allowed entry into the harem. Considered intimate and yet outside a possible sexual liaison with harem's inmates.
mansab, mansabdar, mansabdari system	Often called the 'steel frame' of the Mughal empire; *mansab* literally means rank. Taking off from the *iqta* system, Akbar organized his entire administration by giving each official a military rank, *mansab*, regardless of their duties. The *mansabdar*, holder of the *mansab*, was paid salary according to his rank, either in cash or

more often in *jagir*. Apart from the lowest ranks who merely derived their income from *jagirs*, the higher *mansabdars* were to maintain law and order as well as maintain soldiers and horses according to their rank, receiving a separate allowance for it. Towards the end of Akbar's reign, a *mansabdar* began to be assigned two different ranks; the first indicated his *zat* or personal status and entitlement to salary, the second, *sawar*, the number of soldiers he was expected to command, the latter usually inferior to the former. Thus a *mansabdar* of, say, 1,000/400 would be one whose personal status and salary in the hierarchy was equal to the commander of 1,000 soldiers, but who actually commanded 400. The number of *mansabdars* was clearly rising faster than the state's resources. By the time of Shah Jahan *zat* and *sawar* ranks usually stood in the ratio of 5:1. The system sought to extend uniform rules of governance throughout the vast empire; it also created enormous tensions within the class that governed.

maryada (Sanskrit and Hindi)	One's moral bounds or obligations.
Mir-i Arz	In-charge (equivalent to minister) of the Army at the Centre.
Mir Bakhshi	Minister in-charge of paying salaries to the Army.
Mulla	Orthodox preacher of Islam.
murid	Disciple, especially of a Sufi saint.
mushaira	Assembly of poets where each recites his poems, earns appreciation and patronage. Originally confined to the imperial residence, the eighteenth century witnessed its proliferation in the streets and bazaars.
nazr	Gift given by a person of inferior status to one of his superiors.
nikah, nikahana	Muslim marriage ceremony, payment for its performance.
nisar	Literally sacrifice. A ritual of transferring one's present or future pitfalls or ailments through 'sacrificing' money or anything precious.
pabos	The ceremony of kissing the Emperor's feet.
pargana	Administrative unit akin to a district.
pratiloma (Sanskrit)	Hypergamy.
Ram rajya	Ancient Hindu utopian concept of ideal state where everyone – above all the ruler, the legendary Ram – will remain true to his/her moral obligations.
sajda	Prostration.
sar o pa	Robe of honour from head to foot. Persian equivalent of *khilat*.

sarpech	Bejewelled headgear, given by Emperor as a special favour.
sati	Self-immolation by the warriors' women, freeing them of anxiety about the loss of 'honour' if the women fell into the enemy's hands. The value pre-dates conflicts with Muslims and was creeping into the Muslim warrior class as well.
Shahinshah	King of kings.
shajra	Family tree; also the tree of spiritual descent among Sufis.
sharf	General Persian language term for honour.
Sharia(t)	Source of Islamic jurisprudence.
Silsilah	A whole Order of Sufi hospices. Thus Chishti, Naqshbandi, Suhrawardi, etc.
Sulh kul	Absolute peace. Theory elaborated by Abul Fazl; was Akbar's state policy.
Surya Namaskar	Salutations to the Sun, a prominent Yogic practice.
taq	Arch or any kind of vaulted work in a building.
taslim	A variation on *kurnish*.
Turah(-i Chingizi)	The edicts of Chingiz, the ultimate court of appeal for the Mughals.
ulama, ulema	Islamic theologians, plural of *alim*, literally scholar.
umra	Nobles, plural of *amir*.
Vakil	High official of state, often next to the Emperor.
yanga-lik	Mongol custom of a man inheriting his brother's widows; levirate.
yasal	Earmarked enclosure for lower *mansadars* at the court.
Yuga	Hindu concept of Time divided into four *yugas*, ages.
zaminbos	Kissing the ground before the Emperor.
zamindar	Indigenous rural potentates with permanent superior rights in land.
Zil Allah	Shadow of God.

Select Bibliography

It is not so much in the unearthing of new sources but in the fresh utilization of existing ones, looking at them with a different set of glasses, with a different set of questions, that the endeavour of this book is manifest. The professional historian of Mughal history should know most sources listed below and many more, though a few are such as to claim special attention.

The extent of sources even in the Persian language is immense; only a fragment of it has been accessed for this book, as it would be for any book. Clearly a different – and perhaps more rounded – picture would emerge if another historian were to access other sources with the same or similar problematique in view. There is besides an almost untouched sea of data in India's regional language literatures, folk literature, folk paintings, popular proverbs and stereotypes, and not least in Sanskrit. The immensity of such data is both inviting and humbling.

I list below a large segment of the sources I could lay my hands upon for writing this book; there is still a very large number that has remained outside the list. The brief comments are a form of introduction to the lay reader. The Persian language sources have been listed in the order in which they are likely to have been listed in that language.

Primary Sources in Persian

Abul Fazl, *Akbar Nama*, originally composed in 2 vols, edited by Maulavi Abd al-Rahim, in 3 vols, Calcutta, 1878–86. A kind of 'world history' from the birth of Adam to the near close of Akbar's reign. Charts out remarkable new historiographical paths. English tr. by H. Beveridge in 3 vols, Calcutta, 1902–39.

Abul Fazl, *Ain-i Akbari*, originally 3rd vol. of *Akbar Nama*, edited by H. Blochmann in 2 vols, Calcutta, 1872–7. English tr. in 3 vols; tr. of vol. 1 by H. Blochmann, revised by D. C. Phillott, Calcutta, 1927; tr. of vols 2 and 3 by H. S. Jarrett, revised and further annotated by J. N. Sarkar, Calcutta, 1949 (vol. 2) and 1948 (vol. 3). An enormously painstaking compilation of a sort of gazetteer of information about the Mughal empire in the reign of Akbar.

Abul Fazl, *Makatibat-i Abul Fazl*, 3 vols, Lucknow, 1846. Letters drafted by Abul Fazl on behalf of the Emperor, addressed to rulers in the neighbourhood and others, some *farmans* or rescripts of imperial commands, a few to princes and nobles, etc. The 3rd vol. comprises Abul Fazl's miscellaneous writings.

Abul Fazl, *Munajat-i Abul Fazl*, ed. S. A. A. Rizvi, *Medieval India Quarterly*, vol, 1, 1950. Author's invocations of God.

Abul Fazl, Preface to the *Razm Nama*, Persian tr. of the *Mahabharat* done at Akbar's behest, Bibiliothèque Nationale, MSS. Persans Supplément 1038, Paris, no. 218 in Blochet's catalogue. The copy belonged to Naqib Khan, who helped in the translation. Gives the rationale for the tr.: reducing knowledge deficit between the learned men of the Hindu and Muslim communities about each other, who were otherwise at loggerheads.

Jauhar Aftabchi, *Tazkirat al-Waqiat*, MS, BM. Add 16711. Jauhar was the ewer bearer for Humayun. Commisioned by Akbar to write memoirs for helping Abul Fazl in the *Akbar Nama* project.

Nizam al-Din Ahmad, *Tabaqat-i Akbari*, ed. B. De, vol. III partly re-edited by M. Hidayat Hussain, Calcutta, 1913–35. A straight and non-controversial narrative of events.

Ali Muhammad Khan, *Mirat-i Ahmadi*, ed. Syed Nawab Ali, Baroda, 1927–8. Authoritative history of Mughal Gujarat with a few *firmans* and a lot of statistical data.

Anonymous, *Tarikh-i Khandan-i Timuriyya*, a general history of the Tmurides in Iran and India, written under the aegis of Akbar up to his 22nd regnal year; the title was attached to it sometime in the eighteenth century. Profusely illustrated with Mughal miniatures. Khuda Bakhsh Oriental Public Library, Patna.

Aurangzeb Alamgir, *Ruqaat-i Alamgir*, ed. Syed Najib Ashraf Nadvi, Azamgarh, 1930. Urdu tr. by Abd al-Wahid Khan as *Aurangzeb ke Khutoot*, Patna, 1996. Letters of Aurangzeb.

Zahir al-Din Muhammad Babur, *Babur Nama*, memoirs of Babur, originally written in his mother tongue Turki, translated into Persian by Akbar's great noble Abd-al Rahim Khan-i Khanan, into English by A. S. Beveridge as *Babur Nama (Memoirs of Babur)*, in 2 vols, first published 1922; New Delhi repr. 1970. Recently W. M. Thackston has done another tr. as *The Baburnama: Memoirs of Babur, Prince and Emperor*, Washington, DC, 1996.

Abd al-Qadir Badauni, *Muntakhab al-Tawarikh*, 3 vols, eds Maulavi Ahmad Ali and W. N. Lees, Calcutta, 1865–9. Written in secret as a counterweight to Abul Fazl's adulatory *Akbar Nama*.

Muhammad Baqir Najm-i Sani, *Mau'za-i Jahangiri*, ed. Sajida Sultana Alvi, New York, 1989. The volume also has a somewhat below par Eng. tr. by the ed. 'Advice on Governance', in the genre of Mirror of Princes.

Bakhtawar Khan, *Mirat al-Alam*, ed. Sajida S Alvi, 2 vols, Lahore, 1979. History of the first decade of Aurangzeb's reign.

Shaikh Farid Bakkari, *Zakhirat al-Khawanin*, ed. Syed Moin al-Haq, 3 vols, Karachi, 1961–74. Biographical accounts of Mughal nobles compiled in the seventeenth century.

Zia al-Din Barani, *Fatawa-i Jahandari*, 'Advices on Governance', Eng. tr. by Mohammad Habib and Ms Afsar Khan, as *Political Theory of the Delhi Sultanate*, Allahabad, n.d. A major theoretical text by a practising historian and courtier, written in the mid-fourteenth century. Along with the author's *Tarikh-i Firuzshahi*, it is the subject of several studies.

Bayazid Biyat, *Tazkira-i Humayun wa Akbar*, ed. M. Hidayat Hussain, Calcutta, 1941. An 'informal' account of events of the reign of Humayun and early part of the reign of Akbar. Written at Akbar's commission to feed information to Abul Fazl for *Akbar Nama*.

Sujan Rai Bhandari, *Khulasat al-Tawarikh*, ed. Zafar Hasan, Delhi, 1918. A general history from early times down to the 1660s, though written at the century's end.

Bhim Sen, *Nuskha-i Dilkusha*, MS, BM, Or. 23. A personal account of a scribe and soldier located in the Deccan towards the end of Aurangzeb's reign and the beginning of his successor's. Some observations are very perceptive.

Chander Bhan Brahman, *Qawaid-i Sultanat-i Shah Jahan*, Calcutta, 1795. A very interesting brief text, describing rules and regulations of Shah Jahan's court. The text has been little used by Indian historians. It is part of the author's *Chahar Chaman*.

Dara Shukoh, *Majmua al-Bahrain*, ed. Syed Muhammad Raza Jalali Naiyini, Tehran, second impression, 1380 H.Solar/2002. The Prince's writings, more like notes, on some of the religious and philosophical notions of Islam and Hinduism converging on monotheism, entitled by him poetically as 'The Confluence of [two] Oceans'.

Dargah Quli Khan, *Muraqqa-i Dehli*, ed. Khaliq Anjum, New Delhi, 1993. The author arrived in Delhi from Hyderabad just after the invasion of Nadir Shah. Makes a casual reference to it. Describes the prevalent atmosphere of gaiety and revelry with relish and without sitting in moral judgements.

Mirza Muhammad Haidar Dughlat, *Tarikh-i Rashidi*, Eng. tr. by E. Denison Ross, ed. with commentary and notes by N. Elias, Patna, 1973. First pub. not mentioned, but after 1895.

Muhsin Fani, *Dabistan-i Mazahib*, ed. Nazar Ashraf, Calcutta, 1809. Famous mid-seventeenth-century description of world's religions. The attribution of authorship is problematic.

Abul Qasim Farishta, *Tarikh-i Farishta*, also known as *Gulshan-i Ibrahimi*, Bombay, 1832. A general history of India from the spread of Islam to Iran and its arrival in India to the early years of Jahangir's reign. Begins with a cursory description of the Hindu society.

Shaikh Abd al-Quddus Ganguhi, *Lataif–i Quddusi*, Delhi, 1311 H/1894. Episodes in the life of the eminent Sufi of the sixteenth century.

Gulbadan Begum, *Humayun Nama*, ed. A. S. Beveridge, London, 1902, New Delhi repr. 1996. A sensitive view of the imperial family from the harem.

English tr. by A. S. Beveridge, as *The History of Humayun*, first pub. 1902; 3rd New Delhi repr. 1996.

Hamid al-Din Khan, *Ahkam-i Alamgiri*, ed. Jadu Nath Sarkar, Calcutta, 1912. Sarkar has translated the work as *Anecdotes of Aurangzeb*. Irfan Habib is doubtful of the reliability of the 'anecdotes'.

Hasan Ali Khan, *Tawarikh-i Daulat-i Shershahi*, part of the text and Eng. tr. of another part by R. P. Tripathi in *Medieval India Quarterly*, 1, 1, 1950. History of the reign of Sher Shah, Afghan ruler who had defeated Humayun.

Ilahadad Faizi Sirhindi, *Akbar Nama*, MS, BM, Or. 169. Written on his own towards the end of Akbar's reign. No remarkable feature.

Inayat Khan, *Shah Jahan Nama*, Eng. tr. by A. R. Fuller, ed. and completed by W. E. Begley and Z. A. Desai, Delhi, 1990. A simpler rendering of Lahauri and Waris's works.

Nur al-Din Jahangir, *Tuzuk-i Jahangiri*, Saiyad Ahmad Khan, ed. Ghazipur and Aligarh, 1863–4; Eng. tr. in 2 vols by Alexander Rogers, ed. by H. Beveridge, as *The Tuzuk-i-Jahangiri or Memoirs of Jahangir*, London, 1909–14, repr. New Delhi, 1989. W. M. Thackston too has recently done another tr. as *The Jahangirnama: Memoirs of Jahangir, Emperor of India*, Washington DC, 1999, though a trifle less accurately than Rogers.

Muhammad Salih Kambu, *Amal-i Salih* or *Shah Jahan Nama*, ed. Ghulam Yazdani, revised by Wahid Quraishi, Lahore, 1967–72. Episodes from the lives of Shah Jahan's ancestors going up to Amir Timur, but essentially the history of Shah Jahan's reign. Completed in 1659, some two years into Aurangzeb's reign, when Shah Jahan was in prison.

Kamgar Husaini, *Maasir-i Jahangiri*, ed. Azra Alavi, Bombay, 1978. Written just after the end of Jahangir's reign, valuable for his life as Prince Salim.

Mirza Kamran, 'Mirza Nama', *Journal of the Asiatic Society of Bengal*, New Series, vol. 9, 1913: 8–13. Kamran was a petty noble whose concerns too are confined to his stratum.

Kamwar Khan, *Tazkirat al-Salatin-i Chaghta*, MS No. 591, Khuda Bakhsh Oriental Public Library, Patna. A general history of the Mughals up to 1724. Muzaffar Alam has edited the part covering 1707–24, published in New Delhi, 1980.

Waiz Husain Kashifi, *Akhlaq-i Muhsini*, Bombay, 1308 H, 1890. Written towards the end of the fifteenth century in the genre of *Akhlaq* literature, popular in the Persianate world.

Munshi Muhammad Kazim, *Alamgir Nama*, eds M. Khadim Husain and M. Abd al-Hai, Calcutta, 1865–73. Official history of the first decade of Aurangzeb's reign. Aurangzeb is said to have terminated the long tradition of official history-writing after this, though histories did continue to be written.

Kewal Ram, *Tazkira al-Umra*, MS, BM, Add. 16,703. Compiled towards the end of the eighteenth century, at the same time as the massive *Maasir al-Umra*, the *Tazkira* enumerates with bare biographical notes separately on the Muslim and the Hindu nobles of the Mughal empire, from the reign of Akbar to that of Aurangzeb.

Muhammad Hashim Khafi Khan, *Muntakhab al-Lubab*, eds Kabir al-Din Ahmad and W. Haig, Calcutta, 1860–74. Useful for the reign of Aurangzeb and a couple of decades after; before it, the book copies earlier works.

Hasan Ali Khaqani, *Akhlaq-i Hakimi*, MS, BL, OIOC, 2203. Written in 1579–80 in Kabul at the height of conflict between Akbar and his half-brother Mirza Hakim and Hakim's tensions with Badakhshan. Dedicated to the latter.

Nur al-Din Qazi al-Khaqani, *Akhlaq-i Jahangiri*, MS, BL, OIOC 2207. First major work on *Akhlaq*, etiquette, composed in India. Completed in 1622 and dedicated to the reigning Emperor.

Shaikh Zain Wafai Khawafi, *Tabaqat-i Baburi*, MS, BM, Or. 1999. The MS is incomplete. It gives details of the battle of Panipat in 1526 where Babur defeated the Afghan ruler of India Ibrahim Lodi, first step towards the establishment of the Indian empire of the Mughals.

Khwund Mir, *Qanun-i Humayuni*, ed. M. Hidayat Hussain, Calcutta, 1940. A courtier writes of the rules and regulations of Humayun's court.

Abd al-Hamid Lahauri, *Padshah Nama*, eds Kabir al-Din and Abd al-Rahim, Calcutta, 1866–72. Covers the first 30 years of Shah Jahan's reign. Completed after the author's death by Muhammad Waris.

Shivadas Lakhnawi, *Shahnama-i Munawwar Kalam*, MS, BM, Or. 26. Covers the reign of Farrukhsiyar and the first four years of Muhammad Shah, i.e. 1713–22. Contains enumeration of 'episodes' (*waqai*), rescripts of imperial commands (*farmans*) and official letters. A fair account of festivity at the court.

Muatamad Khan, *Iqbal Nama-i Jahangiri*, Lucknow, 1281 H./1864. General narrative of political events of Humayun's, Akbar's and Jahangir's reigns.

Shaikh Rizqullah Mushtaqi, *Waqiat-i Mushtaqi*, MS, BM, Or. 1929. Anecdotes, some more like folk tales, from the time of the Lodi rulers preceding the Mughal dynasty to that of Akbar. The author was a poet and Sufi. A view from the streets of Delhi.

Saqi Mustaid Khan, *Maasir-i Alamgiri*, ed. Agha Ahmad Ali, Calcutta, 1871. Summarizes and supplements the *Alamgir Nama* down to the death of Aurangzeb, though it begins with the War of Succession, from the day Shah Jahan fell ill. Dry as dust, exact in dates; a good deal of useful information.

Matribi Samarqandi, *Khatirat-i Matribi*, ed. Abd al-Ghani Mirzoyef, Karachi, 1977. The boisterous Maulana Matribi ('Epicurean Theologian') recounts his 24 encounters with Jahangir.

Isar Das Nagar, *Futuhat-i Alamgiri*, MS, BM, Add. 23884. Nagar was a Gujarati Brahmin, eyewitness to several critical events up to 34th regnal year of Aurangzeb. Begins account with the illness of Shah Jahan, which marked the start of the War of Succession. If anything, a partisan of Aurangzeb.

Mirza Nathan, *Baharistan-i Ghaybi*, MS, Bibiliothèque Nationale, Paris, Sup. Pers. MS 252. A Mughal general's account of Emperors' efforts to subdue Assam, Cooch Bihar and Orissa, in the north-east and east, in Jahangirs's and Shah Jahan's reigns.

Abd al-Baqi Nihavandi, *Maasir-i Rahimi*, ed. Hidayat Hussain, Calcutta, 1910–31. Composed in 1616, this work is about Abd al-Rahim Khan-i

Khanan, Akbar's great noble and poet. The Khan survived into part of the reign of Jahangir but at a lower level of cordiality and favour.

Munshi Shaikh Abul Fath Qabil Khan, *Adab-i Alamgiri*, 2 vols, ed. Abd al-Ghaffur Chaudhury, Lahore, 1971. Letters written by and on behalf of Aurangzeb to his father Shah Jahan and others, though complied after Aurangzeb's accession to the throne with the title Alamgir.

Arif Qandhari, *Tarikh-i Akbari*, eds Haji Syed Muin al-Din Nadwi, Syed Azhar Ali and Imtiaz Ali Arshi, Rampur, 1962. Beginning with the birth of Akbar, goes up to his 23rd regnal year. Looks at Akbar as a devout Muslim.

Ala al-Daula Qazwini, *Nafais al-Maasir*, MS, Subhan Allah Collection, Farsi 920/45, Maulan Azad Library, Aligarh Muslim University, Aligarh. Biographical notices on 224 Persian poets of Akbar's reign, compiled early in his reign. Abul Fazl drew considerably upon it for his sketches of poets in the *Ain*.

Asad Beg Qazwini, *Tarikh-i Risala-i Asad Beg*, MS, BM Or.1996. Memoir recounting events of Akbar's last years. Gives details of the assassination of Abul Fazl.

Rashid al-Din Fazl Allah, *Jami al-Tawarikh*, portions relating to India in Karl Jahn, ed., *Rashid al-Din's History of India*, The Hague, 1965.

Amin Ahmad Razi, *Haft Iqlim* ('Seven Climes'), written in the last decade of Akbar's reign. Five volumes of different sizes, ed. by different editors, published so far, Calcutta, 1918–72. Described by the publishers as 'The geographical and biographical Encyclopaedia'.

Rustam Ali Khan, *Tarikh-i Hindi,* MS, BM, Or. 1628. A mid-eighteenth-century general account; somewhat more useful for the eighteenth century.

Muhammad Sadiq Khan, *Shahjahan Nama*, MS, BM, Or. 174, Or 1671. History of Shah Jahan's reign by a news reporter (*waqai nawis*), who participated in the decisive battle of Samugarh between Dara Shukoh and Aurangzeb

Abbas Sarwani, *Tuhfa-i Akbarshahi*, also known as *Tarikh-i Sher Shahi*, MS, BL, Persian MSS, I.O. 218. Written under Akbar's commission for Abul Fazl. A lot of meanings embedded between the lines for the Afghans, who had defeated the Mughals and were in turn defeated by them.

Shah Nawaz Khan, *Maasir al-Umra*, eds Maulavi Abd al-Rahim and Ashraf Ali, Calcutta, 1888–91. Great compilation of biographical sketches of the amirs, nobles, of the Mughal empire down to 1747, brought up to date by his son, to 1780, in 3 vols.

Mulla Kami Shirazi, *Waqiat-i Zaman* or *Fathnama-i Nurjahan Begum*, Bib. Nationale, Paris, Pers. Catalogue, 507, Blochet, iii, 1874: *masnavi*, or long poem that tells a story. The proclamation of victory on behalf of Nur Jahan, who joined her husband in captivity and ultimately organized the noble Mahabat Khan's surrender to His Majesty.

Ghulam Ahmad Tabtabai, *Seir al-Mutakhereen*, Lucknow, 1866. History of the later Mughals, written around the 1780s at the behest of the East India Company.

Ahmad Tattavi, et al., *Tarikh-i Alfi*, MS, BM, Or. 465. A brief history of the first millennium of Islam, compiled at Akbar's behest. Begun by Tattavi; others continued, after Tattavi was assassinated. Follows chronology meticulously.

Nasir al-Din Tusi, *Akhlaq-i Nasiri*, eds Mujtaba Minawi and Ali Raza Haidari, Tehran, 1354 H. (Solar), 1976. The prototype of all texts of the Mirror of Princes genre in the Persianate world.

Waqai Ajmer wa Ranthambhor, 21st and 22nd regnal years of Aurangzeb (1678–80), transcript in the State Archives, Hyderabad. Confidential official news reports.

Muhammad Waris, *Badshah Nama*, MS, BM, Add. *6556*, Or. 174. Begins where Lahauri had left off.

European Travellers' Accounts

François Bernier, *Travels in the Mogul Empire, 1656–68*, Eng. tr. Irving Brock, revised by Archibald Constable, New Delhi, 1971, first pub. London, 1891. The most learned of travellers. Lends a theoretical perspective to observations.

Thomas Bowrey, *A Geographical Account of Countries Round the Bay of Bengal, 1669 to 1679*, ed. R. C. Temple, New Delhi, 1997 (first pub. 1905). More than a geographical account.

F. F. Catrou, *The General History of the Mogol Empire, From its Foundation by Tamerlane, to the Late Emperor Orangzeb, Extracted from the Memoirs of M.Manouchi*, London, 1709.

William Foster, ed., *Early Travels in India 1583–1619*, New Delhi repr. 1999; first pub., London, 1921. Comprises accounts of Ralph Fitch, John Mildenhall, William Hawkins, William Finch, Nicholas Withington, Thomas Coryat and Edward Terry.

John Fryer, *A New Account of East India and Persia being Nine Years Travels, 1672–81*, 3 vols, ed. W. Crooke, London, 1909–15. Indian repr. 1985.

Fr Fernão Guerreiro, S. J., *Jahangir and the Jesuits*, Eng. tr. C. H. Payne, New Delhi repr., 1997; first pub., London, 1930. Jesuit, on mission to convert the Emperor.

Alexander Hamilton, *A New Account of the East Indies (1688–1723)* ed. William Foster, 2 vols, London, 1930.

Pierre Du Jarric, *Akbar and the Jesuits: An Account of the Jesuit Mission to the Court of Akbar*, tr. C. H. Payne, London, 1926. Du Jarric, inhabitant of Bordeaux, never visited India. Bases account on letters and reports of Jesuits who were in Akbar's court.

John Jourdain, *The Journal of John Jourdain, 1608–17*, ed. W. Foster, repr., London, 1967.

Johannes De Laet, *The Empire of the Great Mogol*, Eng. tr. J. S. Hoyland and S. N. Banerjee, first pub. 1928, Delhi repr. 1975. Brief but perceptive account by the Flemish geographer, in 'crabbed Latin'.

Niccolao Manucci, *Storia do Mogor or Mogul India*, Eng. tr. William Irvine, 4 vols, first pub. 1907; New Delhi repr. 1981. Full of gossip passed on as historical facts. The Italian came to India in his teens and died here over a half century later. Most extensive coverage both over space and time.

Fray Sebastian Manrique, *Travels of Fray Sebastian Manrique (1629–43)*, Eng. tr. C. E. Luard and H. Hosten, 2 vols, London, 1927.

Fr Monserrate, *The Commentary of Father Monserrate*, tr. J. S. Hoyland and annotated by S. N. Banerjee, Cuttack, 1922. The Fr was at Akbar's court and is an invaluable source.

Peter Mundy, *The Travels of Peter Mundy*, vol. 2, 'Travels in Asia', ed. Richard C. Temple, London, 1914.

Francisco Pelsaert, *Jahangir's India: The Remonstratie of Francisco Pelsaert*, Eng. tr. W. H. Moreland and P. Geyl, Delhi, 1972; first pub. 1925. Dutch traveller; brief but perceptive account.

Sir Thomas Roe, *The Embassy of Sir Thomas Roe to India, 1615–19, As Narrated in His Journal and Correspondence*, ed. William Foster, London 1926, New Delhi repr., 1990. Roe was the first ambassador of England accredited to India in Jahangir's reign. Extensive coverage of court proceedings.

Jean-Baptiste Tavernier, *Travels in India* (1640–67), Eng. tr. V. Ball, 2nd edn, ed. William Crooke, first Indian edn, 2 vols, New Delhi, 1977, first pub. London, 1889. French diamond merchant; extensive travels between 1640 and 1667.

Jean de Thevenot and John Francis Careri, *Indian Travels of Thevenot and Careri*, ed. Surendranath Sen, New Delhi, 1949. In a life of 34 years, the Frenchman Thevenot visited India in 1665–7. The Italian Careri was a Dr of Law and a practising lawyer, before he set out to travel 'around the world'.

Pietro della Valle, *The Travels of Pietro della Valle in India*, ed. E. Grey, 2 vols, first pub. London, 1892. Della Valle left Milan a frustrated lover to forget his misery, and travelled to Near East and India in 1623–4.

Modern Works

Aziz Ahmad, *Studies in Islamic Culture in the Indian Environment*, New Delhi, 1999 (first pub. 1964). A classic exploration of several aspects of India's medieval history.

Muzaffar Alam, Françoise 'Nalini' Delvoye and Marc Gaborieau, eds, *The Making of Indo-Persian Culture, Indian and French Studies*, New Delhi, 2000. Proceedings of Indo-French Seminar on the theme held in New Delhi.

Muzaffar Alam and Sanjay Subrahmanyam, eds, *The Mughal State, 1526–1750*, New Delhi, 2002. A mixed collection of mostly old and a few recent writings on the theme.

M. Athar Ali, *The Mughal Nobility Under Aurangzeb*, Bombay, 1966. Marked a sharp methodological break with existing historiography. 2nd edn, New Delhi, 1997, with a new Introduction.

M. Athar Ali, *The Apparatus of Empire, Awards of Ranks, Offices and Titles to the Mughal Nobility, 1574–1658*, New Delhi, 1985. Painstaking collection of data, useful for reference.

Meer Hasan Ali, *Observations on the Mussulmans of India: Description of their Manners, Customs, Habits and Religious Opinions made during a Twelve Years' Residence in their Immediate Society*, 2 vols, Delhi repr., 1973. A British lady, married into an aristocratic Muslim family of Awadh in the nineteenth century, gives an account both as an insider and an outsider.

M. A. Ansari, *Social Life of the Mughal Emperors*, New Delhi, 1974. An early exploration of social aspects of court life.

Rama Shankar Avasthy, *The Mughal Emperor Humayun*, Allahabad, 1967. Primarily a political account.

Abdul Aziz, *The Mansabdari System and the Mughal Army*, Delhi, 1972. A competent early work on the *mansab* system.

Aziz Al-Azmeh, *Muslim Kingship: Power and the Sacred in Muslim, Christian and Pagan Polities*, London/New York, 2001. A work of outstanding scholarship which traces the historical evolution of Islam through the prism of kingship.

Aziz Al-Azmeh, *Ibn Khaldun: An Essay in Reinterepretation*, Budapest, 2003. First pub. 1982. Primarily historicizing Ibn Khaldun's great works of the fourteenth century, challenging attempts to perceive the oeuvre in very modern, sociological terms

Lawrence A. Babb, *The Divine Hierarchy: Popular Hinduism in Central India*, New York, 1975. Studying Hinduism at the margins.

M. Baqir, *Lahore Past and Present*, New Delhi, 1996. First pub. Lahore, 1952. A fair historical account of the city from about A D 990 to the time of writing. Thins out as it comes to the present.

Karim Najafi Barzegar, *Mughal Iran Realtions During the Sixteenth Century*, New Delhi, 2000. Based upon a doctoral thesis, is a competent survey.

C. A. Bayly, *Rulers, Townsmen and Bazaars, North Indian Society in the Age of British Expansion 1770–1870*, New Delhi, 1992. First pub. Cambridge, UK, 1983. A book that made a difference to the study of the eighteenth century in India. It effectively questioned the dominant historiography, across various divides, that the century was marked by encompassing stasis and gloom.

Rafat Bilgrami, *Religious and Quasi-Religious Departments of the Mughal Period, 1556–1707 AD*, New Delhi, 1994. Mainly a description; good source for information at one place.

Centre of Advanced Study, Dept of History, Aligarh Muslim University, eds, *Medieval India – a Miscellany*, 2 vols, New Delhi, 1969 and 1972. Miscellaneous articles, mainly by inhouse faculty.

Tara Chand, *History of Freedom Movement in India*, vol. 1, 1961. First two chapters give an archetypal nationalist version of India's eighteenth century.

Neera Chandoke, ed., *Mapping Histories: Essays Presented to Ravinder Kumar*, New Delhi, 2000. Kum Kum Sangari's essay, on popular images of Akbar, is sheer delight.

Satish Chandra, *Parties and Politics at the Mughal Court, 1707–1740*, Aligarh, 1959. Innovative Introduction and rather modest text, as if written by two different authors. Reprint, New Delhi, 2001.

B. D. Chattopadhyaya, *Representing the Other? Sanskrit Sources and the Muslims*, New Delhi, 1998. Although the period dealt with in the book precedes the Mughals, the scholarly treatment of the important subject makes it very pertinent. Muslims were far from the demon figure of a much later age.

Kingsley Davis, *The Population of India and Pakistan*, New York, 1951, repr. 1968.

Harihar Das, *The Norris Embassy to Aurangzeb, 1699–1702*, Calcutta, 1959. Useful excerpts from the English ambassador's journal.

K. K. Datta, *Survey of India's Social Life and Economic Condition in the Eighteenth Century (1707–1813)*, Calcutta, 1961. Characteristic example of 'nationalist' historiography.

K. K. Datta, *Some Firmans, Sanads and Parwanas (1578–1802)*, Patna, 1962. Contains valuable documents which testify the grants of land and money by Mughal rulers to Hindu temples and other religious institutions.

Simon Digby, *Sufis and Soldiers in Awrangzeb's Deccan: Malfuzat-i Naqshbandiyya*, New Delhi, 2001. Eng. tr. of 'conversations' of Sufi saints of the Naqshbandi Order, located in the Deccan.

Abbe J. A. Dubois, *Hindu Manners, Customs and Ceremonies*, Eng. tr. Henry K. Beauchamp, New Delhi repr. 1985. First pub. 1906. Good description of the subject. However, the Abbé felt disgusted at the 'depravity and debauchery', i.e. celebration of sensual pleasures of the Hindus.

R. M. Eaton, *The Rise of Islam and the Bengal Frontier, 1204–1760*, New Delhi, 1997. Offers a scintillating new explanation of the coming of Islam to medieval Bengal.

R. M. Eaton, *Essays on Islam and Indian History*, New Delhi, 2000. See especially 'Temple Desecration and Indo-Muslim States'.

R. M. Eaton, ed., *India's Islamic Traditions, 711–1750*, New Delhi, 2003. Anthology of old articles of some 17 historians, covering a wide range of themes.

Norbert Elias, *The Court Society*, Eng. tr. Edmund Jephcott, Oxford, 1983. Challenges history-writing to go beyond the obvious and reconstruct the hidden but powerful structures which condition the functioning of monarchy. Invites historians to look at the driving spirit of medieval polities in status hierarchy, not in acquisition of wealth, which is a phenomenon of the modern capitalist world. The term 'court society' itself draws attention away from the grandiose claims of absolutist monarchy, and points to the court as an ensemble where power equilibrium is a constant dynamic.

Norbert Elias, *The Civilizing Process: Sociogenetic and Psychogenetic Investigations*, 2 vols, vol. I: *The History of Manners*; vol. II: *State Formation and Civilization*, Eng. tr. Edmund Jephcott, Oxford, 1978, 1982. Vol. I in particular seeks to draw a contrast between a relatively more 'natural' medieval society and the modern, where the ironically phrased 'civilizing process' has established standard norms of comportment, increasingly encompassing the whole society. For a critique, see Hans Peter Duerr, *Nudité & Pudeur, Le mythe du processus de civilisation*, French tr. from the German by Véronique Bodin with Jacqueline Princemin, Paris, 1998.

Abraham Eraly, *The Last Spring: The Lives and Times of the Great Mughals*, New Delhi, 1997. Also a good introductory and comprehensive work by a non-professional writer.

Ellison B Findly, *Nur Jahan, Empress of Mughal India*, New York, 1993. A sympathetic, though short of breathtaking biography of one of the most distinguished female figures of the Mughal era.

Y. Friedmann, *Shaykh Ahmad Sirhindi: An Outline of His Thought and a Study of His Image in the Eyes of Posterity*, Montreal/London, 1971. A major work questioning the image of the Shaikh as the progenitor of orthodox Islam in India.

Marc Gaborieau, ed. *Islam et Société en Asie du Sud*, Paris, 1986. As usual in an anthology, some of the contributions are very inviting.

Bamber Gascoigne, *The Great Moghuls*, London, 1971. Reproduces every known stereotype about the Mughal rulers.

David Gilmartin and Bruce B. Lawrence, eds, *Beyond Turk and Hindu: Rethinking Religious Ideas in Islamic South Asia*, New Delhi, 2002. Thirteen essays and Introduction cover a range of themes from the arts to Sufism to the state.

Rumer Godden, *Gulbadan: Portrait of a Rose Princess at the Mughal Court*, New York, 1980. Authentic biography of the Princess.

Stewart Gordon, *Robes of Honour:* Khil'at *in Pre-Colonial and Colonial India*, New Delhi, 2003. Collection of six essays, including the Introduction, itself a research piece with good theoretical concerns. Some other essays are a trifle less inclined to theory.

Peter Gottschalk, *Beyond Hindu and Muslim: Multiple Identity in Narratives from Village India*, New Delhi, 2001. An anthropologist's exploration of a theme whose threads go back to medieval India.

Aron Gurevich, *Medieval Popular Culture: Problems of Belief and Perception*, tr. János M. Bak and Paul A. Hollingsworth, Cambridge, UK, 1988. Extremely perceptive studies.

Aron Gurevich, *Categories of Medieval Culture*, Eng. tr. G. L. Campbell, London, 1985. Some major formulations on categories of analysis, such as time, space, etc., in the medieval context.

T. G. J. ter Haar, *Follower and Heir of the Prophet, Shaykh Ahmad Sirhindi (1564–1624) as Mystic*, Leiden, 1992. Following Y. Friedmann's work on the Shaikh, ter Haar seeks to rectify his image as a rabidly orthodox preacher of Islam.

Irfan Habib, *Agrarian System of Mughal India*, Bombay, 1963. The landmark book that redefined the writing of medieval Indian history. Second slightly revised edn, New Delhi, 1999.

Irfan Habib, ed., *Akbar and His India*, New Delhi, 1997. Proceedings of a Seminar organized by the Dept of History, Aligarh Muslim University, in celebration of the 450th anniversary of Akbar's birth, and some documents and book reviews.

R. L. Hangloo, *The State in Medieval Kashmir*, New Delhi, 2000. Explores three major themes: antique roots of the Mughal state in the region, the question of conversions to Islam and the search for legitimacy.

Ishrat Haque, *Glimpses of Mughal Society and Culture*, New Delhi, 1992. Largely based upon Urdu literature of the eighteenth century.

Bikram Jit Hasrat, *Dara Shikoh: Life and Works*, 2nd revsd edn, New Delhi, 1982. A standard and sympathetic account of the unfortunate Prince. Shukoh ('Glory') is often confused by authors with Shikoh ('Terror').

A. Hintze, *The Mughal Empire and Its Decline*, Aldershot, 1997. Problematizes the notion of 'decline'.

Afzal Husain, *The Nobility under Akbar and Jahangir: A Study of Family Groups*, New Delhi, 1999. Traces the families of nine nobles, including that of Shaikh Salim Chishti, Akbar's patron-saint.

Yusuf Husain, *Glimpses of Medieval Indian Culture*, New Delhi, 1957. Five essays on medieval Indian society and culture.

Abbas Iqbal, *Tarikh-i Mughul az Hamla-i Chingiz ta Tashkeel-i Daulat-i Timur* (in Persian), Tehran, 6th impression, 1365 H. solar/AD 1987. Comprehensive history of the Mughal invasion of Iran by Chingiz, down to the formation of Timur's state.

E. Burke Inlow, *Shahinshah: A Study of the Monarchy of Iran*, Delhi, 1979. Looks at the antique structures supporting monarchy in Iran, written just as Iran was transiting to a new Islamic regime.

William Irvine, *The Later Mughals*, ed. Jadunath Sarkar, 2 vols, New Delhi repr., 1995. Date of first pub. not mentioned. Mainly political narrative down to invasion of India by Nadir Shah in 1739, in the reign of Muhammad Shah, abstracted from primary sources in the Persian language.

S. M. Jaffar, *Some Cultural Aspects of Muslim Rule in India*, Delhi, 1972. First pub. sometime in 1930s. General account of state, religion, economy, culture, etc.

Zinat Kausar, *Muslim Women in Medieval India*, Patna, 1992. A rather conventional account.

Iqtidar Alam Khan, *Mirza Kamran A Biographical Study*, New Delhi, 1964. This slim volume draws attention away from mutual enmity between Humayun and his brother Kamran to explain the crashing of the Mughal empire before the assault of the Afghan Sher Shah, and seeks to locate it in the structure of the nobility – a genre of history that became significant at the Aligarh Muslim University in the 1960s and 1970s.

Iqtidar Alam Khan, *The Political Biography of a Mughal Noble: Mun'im Khan Khan-i Khanan 1497–1575*, New Delhi, 1973. Traces the career of the second Khan-i Khanan (Chief Khan) in Akbar's service.

Iqtidar Alam Khan, ed., *Akbar and His Age*, New Delhi, 1999. Set of papers from the Seminar, celebrating 450th birth anniversary of Akbar, organized by the Indian Council of Historical Research, New Delhi, in 1992.

M. Ishaq Khan, *Kashmir's Transition to Islam: The Role of Muslim Rishis (Fifteenth to Eighteenth Centuries)*, New Delhi, 1994. Very skilful and sensitive retrieval of Kashmir-specific processes of transition to Islam.

Refaqat Ali Khan, *The Kachhwahas Under Akbar and Jahangir*, New Delhi, n.d., but after 1976. Examines the relationship between the premier Rajput house of Jaipur and the two Mughal Emperors.

D. D. Kosambi, *An Introduction to the Study of Indian History*, Bombay, 1956. Written by a Professor of Mathematics, an assertive Marxist, this is the one book that effected a paradigm shift in the writing of Indian history, even though its primary focus was on India's ancient past.

Hermann Kulke, ed., *The State in India, 1000–1700*, New Delhi, 1995. Collection of old essays of eight historians and one anthropologist, with a learned introduction.

K. S. Lal, *The Mughal Harem*, New Delhi, 1988. A descriptive account, reiterating stereotypes.

K. S. Lal, *Indian Muslims: Who Are They?* New Delhi, 1990. Marked by strong anti-Muslim passion.

Stanley Lane-Poole, *Medieval India Under Mohammedan Rule (A.D. 712–1764)*, Delhi repr. 1994. First pub. 1903. Employs the tripartite division of historical periodization in India into 'Ancient, Medieval and Modern' for the first time.

S. M. Latif, *Lahore, Its History, Architectural Remains and Antiquities*, Lahore, 1892. The first well-researched account of the city.

Wahid M Mirza, *Life and Works of Amir Khusrau*, Calcutta, 1935. Authoritative work on the great poet.

Rekha Misra, *Women in Mughal India (1526–1748)*, New Delhi, 1967. Early exploration of medieval women's history, focusing on imperial figures.

Colin Paul Mitchell, *Sir Thomas Roe and the Mughal Empire*, Karachi, 2000. Looks at Roe's *Journal* as reflection of his English political and cultural moorings.

David Morgan, *The Mongols*, Oxford/Cambridge, MA, 1990. Brief but wide-ranging account of the rise of the Mongols and their dispersal and dissipation.

Harbans Mukhia, *Historians and Historiography During the Reign of Akbar*, New Delhi, 1976.

Harbans Mukhia, *Perspectives on Medieval History*, New Delhi, 1993.

K. A. Nizami, *Akbar and Religion*, New Delhi, 1989. Seeks a psychological interepretation with moderate success.

M. N. Pearson, ed., *Legitimacy and Symbols: The South Asian Writings of F. W. Buckler*, Michigan Papers on South and South-east Asia, no. 26, *c.*1985. Buckler's writings between 1922 and 1942 on various themes of Near East and India; especially perceptive is his interepretation of 'The Oriental Despot' as corporate rather than absolute kingship, in which symbols like the robe of honour become central motifs.

Antoine Louis Henri Polier, *Shah Alam II and His Court*, ed. Pratul C. Gupta, Calcutta, 1989. First pub. 1947. A brief first-hand French account of the goings on in Shah Alam II's court.

R. N. Prasad, *Raja Man Singh of Amber*, Calcutta, 1966. Written in the hero-worship mode.

A. J. Qaisar, *The Indian Response to European Art and Culture (A.D. 1498–1707)*, New Delhi, 1982. An early exploration of the impact of contact with Europe on Indian technology and social mores.

A. Jan Qaisar and S. P. Verma, eds, *Art and Culture: Felicitation Volume in Honour of Professor S. Nurul Hasan*, Jaipur, 1993. A collection of varied, and some extremely stimulating, articles.

I. H. Qureshi, *Ulema in Politics*, Karachi, 2nd edn, 1974. Strictly for the faithful; all critical enquiry shunned.

V. P. S. Raghuvanshi, *Indian Society in the Eighteenth Century*, Delhi, 1969. Comprehensive study of the eighteenth century, though slightly short on analytical quality.

Gloria Goodwyn Raheja, *The Poison in the Gift: Ritual, Prestation and the Dominant Caste in a North India Village*, Chicago and London, 1988. Examines the meaning of the popular practice of ritual gift giving. Displaces the dominant paradigm of ritual caste hierarchy by the concept of ritual centrality of the dominant caste.

Manohar Singh Ranawat, ed., *Princely Historian*, Commemoration volume of Maharajkumar Dr Raghubir Sinh, Jaipur, 1994.

Paul Ratchnevsky, *Genghis Khan: His Life and Legacy*, Oxford/Cambridge, MA, 1992. Authoritative account of one of the Indian Mughals' ancestors.

Murtaza Rawandi, *Tarikh-i Ajtama'i Iran*, vol. I, 4th print, Tehran, 1354 H./ 1976. General history of Iran.

J. F. Richards, ed., *Kingship and Authority in South Asia*, South Asian Studies, University of Wisconsin-Madison Publications Series, Publication no. 3, 1978. Contains some very imaginative and interepretative essays. New Delhi, repr., 2001.

John F. Richards, *The Mughal Empire*, Cambridge, UK, 1993. A good summary of the existing body of knowledge as a general introduction.

S. A. A. Rizvi, *Muslim Revivalist Movements in Northern India in the Sixteenth and Seventeenth Centuries*, Agra, 1965. Excellent panoramic survey of the theme.

S. A. A. Rizvi, *Religious and Intellectual History of the Muslims in Akbar's Reign*, New Delhi, 1975. Despite the title, the book centres on Abul Fazl with some significant new insights.

S. P. Sangar, *Crime and Punishment in Mughal India*, Delhi, 1967. Contains some useful information.

Jadu Nath Sarkar, *Fall of the Mughal Empire*, 4 vols, Calcutta, 1932–50, repr. Bombay, 1971. Classic work of the doyen of Indian historians in the first half of the twentieth century. Assigns central role to Aurangzeb's 'religious' (i.e. anti-Hindu) policy in the fall.

Jadu Nath Sarkar, *History of Aurangzeb Based Upon Original Sources*, 5 vols, Calcutta, 1912–30, repr. Bombay, 1971–5. Extensive account of the state and its functioning under the last great Mughal Emperor, with religion and law-and-order as the analytical categories.

Jafar Sharif, *Islam in India or the Qanun-i Islam*, Eng. tr. from Urdu by G. A. Herklots, first pub. 1832, new edn revised and rearranged by William Crooke, New Delhi, 1997. Good introduction to popular Islamic customs, ceremonies and practices, a lot in common with the Hindus, in the Deccan.

R. S. Sharma, *Indian Feudalism c.300–1200*, Calcutta, 1965. A major and influential work in the Marxist mode. Inspired several debates.

S. R. Sharma, *Religious Policy of the Mughal Emperors*, New Delhi, 3rd revised and enlarged edn, 1972; first pub. 1940. A standard work of the old-style historiography.

Ashok Kumar Shrivastava, *Hindu Society in the Sixteenth Centruy*, New Delhi, 1981. Some useful information on the subject.

Iqtidar Husain Siddiqui, ed., *Medieval India: Essays in Intellectual Thought and Culture*, vol. I, New Delhi, 2003. Collection of 11 essays, 5 by the editor.

Percival Spear, *Twilight of the Mughuls, Studies in Late Mughul Delhi*, New Delhi repr., 1969. First pub. 1951. Sensitive evocation of the waning grandeur of the Mughal empire, terminating in its formal abolition in 1858, and the long-drawn transition to a new regime. Also published as *A History of India under the Later Mughuls*.

M. N. Srinivas, *Religion and Society among the Coorgs of South India*, Oxford, 1952. First modern ethnographic analysis of traditional Indian social structure.

Burton Stein, *A History of India*, Oxford/Cambridge, MA, 1998. Posthumously published work of the eminent historian of India, always questioning received notions and always brimming with new ideas.

Margaret Stutley, *Ancient Indian Magic and Folklore*, Delhi, 1980. A pioneering anthropological work on the theme.

Douglas E. Streusand, *The Formation of the Mughal Empire*, New Delhi, 1989. A bit elementary, but with some bold and interesting hypotheses.

Garcin de Tassy, *Muslim Festivals in India and Other Essays*, ed. and tr. M. Waseem, New Delhi, 1997. A good nineteenth-century description of popular Islam in India, very distinct from what the theologians idealized. Also reviews of two books on similar themes.

Romila Thapar, et al., *Communalism and the Writing of Indian History*, New Delhi, 12th impression, 2003, first pub. 1969.

Kate Teltscher, *India Inscribed: European and British Writings on India, 1600–1800*, New Delhi, 1997. Very nuanced and empathetic exploration.

Edward Thornton, *Gazetteer of the Territories under the Government of the East India Company and the Native States on the Continent of India*, 2 vols, London, 1854.

James Tod, *Annals and Antiquities of Rajasthan*, 3 vols, ed. with an Introduction by William Crooke, Delhi repr., 1990; first pub. 1835. A masterly collection of legends, history and lore of medieval Rajasthan; the book itself subject of several studies.

R. P. Tripathi, *Some Aspects of Muslim Administration*, Allahabad, 1972. Some theoretical explorations are still significant. First pub. 1936.

R. P. Tripathi, *Rise and Fall of the Mughal Empire*, Allahabad, 1976. First pub. 1956. Illustrative of the nationalist writing of 'composite culture' school.

Muhammad Umar, *Muslim Society in Northern India During the Eighteenth Century*, New Delhi, 1998. 'Society' here means the royalty and the nobility. Rich in information.

Charlotte Vaudeville, *Myths and Legends in Medieval India*, Essays of the author compiled in one vol. by Vasudha Dalmia, New Delhi, 1996. Vaudeville is a leading scholar of medieval India's religious and cultural landscape.

Articles

Jnan Chandra, 'Autangzeb and Hindu Temples', *Journal of Pakistan Historical Society,* vol. 5, part 4, 1957; 'Aurangzeb's Patronage of Hindu Temples', ibid., vol. 6, part 3, 1958; 'Alamgir's Grants to a Brahman', ibid., vol. 7, part 2, 1959.

Urvashi Dalal, 'Women's Time in the *Havelis* of North India', *The Medieval History Journal,* 2, 2, 1999. Treats women as active beings, creating and enlarging space for themselves in the overall Mughal patriarchy.

Urvashi Dalal, 'Shahjahanabad: An Expression of Mughal State's Legitimacy', *Islamic Culture,* Vol. 74, 4, October 2000. Examines the organizing principle of Shahajahanbad as embodiment of the state's legitimacy.

J. N. Datta, 'Proportion of Muhammadans in India Through Centuries', *Modern Review,* vol. 78, Jan. 1948.

David Fraesdorff, 'The Power of Imagination: The *Christianitas* and the Pagan North during Conversion to Christianity (800–1200)', *The Medieval History Journal,* Special Issue 'Exploring Alterity in Pre-Modern Societies', vol 5(2), 2002.

Afzal Husain, 'Marriages Among Mughal Nobles as an Index of Status and Aristocratic Integration', *Proceedings of Indian History Congress,* 1972.

Iqbal Husain, 'Hindu Shrines and Practices as Described by a Central Asian Traveller in the first half of the 17th Century', in Irfan Habib, ed., *Medieval India,* I, New Delhi, 1992. Contains excereprs from Mahmud bin Amir Wali Balkhi, *Bahr al-Asrar,* account of his travel to India in 1624–31, published by the University of Karachi.

Ansar Zahid Khan, 'The Mughal Marriages: A Politico-Religious and Legal Study', *Journal of the Pakistan Historical Society,* 1985. Hell-bent upon proving that Akbar converted his Rajput wives to Islam before marrying them.

I. A. Khan, 'The *Tazkirat ul-Muluk* by Rafiuddin Ibrahim Shirazi: As a source on the History of Akbar's Reign', *Studies in History,* 2, 1, 1980: 41–55.

Pauline Kolenda, 'The Ideology of Purity and Pollution', in *Caste in Contemporary India: Beyond Organic Solidarity,* Prospect Heights (Illinois), 1985. In the Marriott-Inden company. Empathy for the local systems of meanings.

Ruby Lal, '"The Domestic World" of Peripatetic Kings: Babur and Humayun, *c.*1494–1556', *The Medieval History Journal,* 4, 1, 2001. Argument for a strong presence of the 'domestic world' in giving shape to Mughal family and indirectly polity.

McKim Marriott, 'Hindu Transactions: Diversities Without Dualism', in B. Kapferer, ed., *Transactions of Meaning,* Philadelphia, 1976. Marriott leads the search for the finer semantics of local world views and social relationships.

McKim Marriott and Ronald B. Inden, 'Towards an Ethnosociology of the South Asian Caste System', in Kenneth A. David, ed., *The New Wind: Changing Identities in South Asia*, Chicago, 1977. Inden is part of the same search team.

McKim Marriott, 'The Feast of Love', in Milton Singer, ed., *Krishna: Myths, Rites and Attitudes*, Chicago, 1966.

McKim Marriott, 'Little Communities in an Indigenous Civilization', in Marriott, ed., *Village India*, Chicago, 1955.

C. M. Naim, 'Popular Jokes and Political History: The Case of Akbar, Birbal and Mulla Do-Piyaza', *The Economic and Political Weekly*, 17 June 1995. The only scholarly exploration of Akbar-Birbal stories.

Syed Haidar Shaharyar Naqvi, 'Sasanian wa Hind wa Pakistan', in *Humayish Tarikh wa Farhang-i Iran: Tarikh wa Farhang-i Iran dar Zaman-i Sasanian*, publication of the Dept of Publications, Ministry of Science and Arts, Iran, n.d. Seeks to trace Sasanian influences on India.

G. J. Reinkin, 'Pseudo-Methodius: A Concept of History in Response to the Rise of Islam', in A. Cameron and L. Conrad, eds, *The Byzantine & Early Islamic Near East*, vol. I, Princeton, 1992.

John F. Richards, 'Norms of Comportment among Imperial Mughal Officers', in Barbara D. Metcalfe, ed., *Moral Conduct and Authority: The Place of Adab in South Asian Islam*, Los Angeles, 1984. Very innovative piece, especially the theme of the *khanazad*, the 'house born'.

Surajit Sinha, 'Vaisnava Influence on a Tribal Culture' in Singer, ed., *Krishna: Myths, Rites and Attitudes*, Honolulu, 1966. Figuring out the mainstream Hindu cultural mores' arrival at the margins, i.e. the tribes.

W. C. Smith, 'Lower Class Uprisings in the Mughal Empire', *Islamic Culture*, 1946. Also reproduced in M. Alam and S. Subrahmaniam, eds, *The Mughal State*. An early Marxist essay reinterepreting 'religious' uprisings in the latter part of the Mughal era.

Frances H. Taft, 'Honor and Alliance: Reconsidering Mughal-Rajput Marriages', in Karne Schomer, et al., eds, *The Idea of Rajasthan*, vol. II, New Delhi, 1994.

I. A. Zaidi, 'The Pattern of Matrimonial Ties Between the Kachhwaha Clan and the Mughal Ruling Family', *Proceedings of the Indian History* Congress, 35th Session, Jadavpur, 1974.

Indian Languages

Nazir Akbarabadi's poems on Holi, in Syed Muhammad Mahmud Rizvi, ed. *Ruh-i Nazir*, Lucknow, 1978.

Mubarak Ali, *Mughal Darbar*, revsd edn of author's Ph.D. thesis, Lahore, 1993.

S. H. Askari, *Hindustan ke Ahd-i Wusta par Maqalat*, Patna, 1995. Essays on India's Middle Ages by a senior historian, since deceased.

Muhammad Hussain Azad, *Darbar-i Akbari* (Urdu), New Delhi, 2000. First pub. Lahore, 1898. Delightful sketches of Akbar's court.

Krishna Das Kaviraj, *Madhya Lila: Chaitnaya-charitamrita*, Eng. tr. J. N. Sarkar, New Delhi, 1988, as *Chaitanya's Life and Teachings*; the tr. was first published in Calcutta in 1913, as *Chaitanya: His Pilgrimages and Teachings*.

Muhta Nainsi, *Nainsi ri Khyat*, 3 vols, ed. Badri Prasad Sakaria, Jodhpur, 1960–7. Authentic and unselfconscious narrative of Rajput affairs from the inside.

Muhta Nainsi, *Marwar ri Pargana ri Vigat*, ed. Narayan Singh Bhati, 4 vols, Jodhpur, 1968–74. Contains gazetteer-like description of villages of Rajasthan around mid-seventeenth century, emulating Abul Fazl's *Ain-i Akbari*.

Mirza Muhammad Hasan Qateel, *Haft Tamasha*, Urdu tr. by Muhammad Umar, Delhi, 1968. Very valuable document of popular culture in late medieval India.

Kamal Dhari Singh, *Musalmanon ki Hindi Seva*, Prayag, 1935. Good old work in the cause of nationalism.

Savitri Sinha, *Madhya Kalin Hindi Kaviyatriyan*, Delhi, 1953. Female Hindi poets of Medieval India.

Emperor Shah Alam II, *Nadirat-i Shahi*, ed., Imtiaz Ali Arshi, Rampur, 1944. Some enjoyable ribald poetry in Urdu. Also some lyrics set to various Ragas.

Qazi Abdul Wadud, ed., *Mughal Sant Kavi Dildar ke Dohé*, Patna, 1990. Hindi couplets of the Mughal Saint-poet Dildar.

Art History

Lalit Kala Akademi, *Early Mughal Paintings (Ca. 1556–1657)*, Lalit Kala Series Portfolio no. 40, 1995. Contains reproductions of six superb miniatures and a brief comment by art historian Anand Krishna.

Catherine B. Asher, *Architecture of Mughal India*, Cambridge, UK, 1995. an old theme subjected to new perspectives, supported by new evidence. Covers the entire Mughal era.

Milo C Beach, *Mughal and Rajput Painting*, Cambridge, UK, 1992. A fresh exploration of 'influences' on the evolution of Mughal art.

Milo C. Beach and Ebba Koch, eds, *King of the World*, London, 1997. Contains reproductions of 46 most exquisite Mughal miniatures of Shah Jahan's period, located in the Windsor Castle Library.

Asok Kumar Das, *Mughal Painting During Jahangir's Time*, Calcutta, 1978. Focuses on the mingling of traditions of painting in the time of its greatest Mughal connoisseur and patron.

Toby Falk and Mildred Archer, *Indian Miniatures in the India Office Library*, London, 1981. Mainly descriptive.

Monica Juneja, ed., *Architecture in Medieval India: Forms, Contexts, Histories*, New Delhi, 2001. A large collection of contributions, old and new, with an excellent introduction focusing on looking at art as social history.

Ebba Koch, *Mughal Art and Imperial Ideology: Collected Essays*, New Delhi, 2001. Looks at art forms as ideological expressions.

Bibliothèque Nationale, *A la Cour du Grand Moghol*, Paris, 1986 with an introduction by Francis Richard. Valuable for some 150 reproductions in colour and monochrome, comments and bibliographical references. Brought out on the occasion of the Year of India (l'Année de l'Inde) in Paris.

Amina Okada, *Imperial Mughal Painters: Indian Miniatures from the Sixteenth and Seventeenth Centuries*, tr. D. Dusinberre, Paris, 1992. Explores the expression of the state's legitimacy in Mughal paintings.

M. S. Randhawa, ed., *Paintings of the Babur Nama*, New Delhi, 1983. Mostly done in Akbar's reign, the miniatures are now located in several museums across the globe; 20 Colour and 144 monochrome reproductions.

Nihar Ranjan Ray, *Mughal Court Painting: A Study in Social and Formal Analysis*, Calcutta, 1975. An early attempt at looking at Mughal painting in social context.

Geeti Sen, *Paintings from the Akbar Nama: A Visual Chronicle of Mughal India*, Varanasi, 1984. Looks at the paintings as historical text.

Ashok Kumar Srivastava, *Mughal Painting, An Interplay of Indigenous and Foreign Traditions*, New Delhi, 2000. Explores not only Persian and European, but also Chinese influences on Mughal art.

I. Stchoukine, *La Peinture Indienne à l'èpoque des Grands Moghols*, Paris, 1928. An early classic.

Som Prajash Verma, *Art and Material Culture in the Paintings of Akbar's Court*, New Delhi, 1978. Looks at Mughal painting as database for material culture.

Som Prakash Verma, *Mughal Painters and Their Work*, New Delhi, 1994. An encyclopaedia of the life and work of Mughal painters.

Unpublished Dissertations

Urvashi Dalal, 'Delhi Society in the Eighteenth Century', Ph.D., Centre for Historical Studies, Jawaharlal Nehru University, New Delhi, 1998.

Mubarak Ali Khan, 'The Court of the Great Mughuls', Ph.D., Ruhr University, 1976.

Jyotirmaya Khatri, 'Evolution and Structure of Holi: Towards an Understanding of the Social Morès of a Festival', unpublished M.Phil. dissertation, Centre for Historical Studies, JNU, 1993.

Soma Mukherjee, 'Royal Mughal Ladies and Their Contributions', Ph.D., Dept of History, Banaras Hindu University, Varanasi, 1997.

Index